DOUBLEDAY
CELEBRATES
100 YEARS OF
EXCELLENCE

Also by Brooke Stephens

Talking Dollars and Making Sense: A Wealth-Building
Guide for African-Americans

Men We Cherish

Anchor Books

NEW YORK   LONDON   TORONTO   SYDNEY   AUCKLAND

African-American
Women Praise the Men
in Their Lives

Men We Cherish

EDITED BY Brooke M. Stephens

AN ANCHOR BOOK

PUBLISHED BY DOUBLEDAY

a division of Bantam Doubleday Dell Publishing Group, Inc.

1540 Broadway, New York, New York 10036

ANCHOR BOOKS, DOUBLEDAY, and the portrayal of an anchor are
trademarks of Doubleday, a division of Bantam Doubleday Dell
Publishing Group, Inc.

Book design by F. J. Levine

Library of Congress Cataloging-in-Publication Data
Men we cherish: African-American women praise the men in their
lives / edited by Brooke M. Stephens. — 1st Anchor Books ed.
p.   cm.
"An Anchor paperback original"—T.p. verso.
1. Afro-American men.   I. Stephens, Brooke M.
E185.86.M47   1997
305.32′8896073—dc21   97-2830
                                                        CIP

ISBN: 0-385-48532-8

Printed in the United States of America

First Edition: November 1997

1   3   5   7   9   10   8   6   4   2

To the men who have shaped and shared my life:

Charles Garrette Stephens, Sr. (1885–1991)
Charles Walter Stephens, Jr. (1913–1945)
James Henry Solomon, Sr. (1910–1975)
Harold (Dino-Ganesh) Thomas Washington, Jr.
(1942–1994)

Acknowledgments

*M*y heartfelt thanks go out to the many friends and supporters who helped me to create and complete this collection:

Lorena Craighead, a tireless little trouper of an editorial assistant who showed up at the right time and offered many useful insights during the evenings and weekends when we plowed through the reading and evaluation of many of the manuscripts submitted;

Neeti Madan, my agent at the Charlotte Sheedy Agency, for her faith in this project;

Arabella Meyer, my editor at Anchor Books, for her enthusiasm for this book;

Arthur Flowers, Ethelbert Miller, Tony Grooms—writers/poets/friends who helped me to find the writers;

Lynne Scott, Fern Gillespie, Keith Hudson and Sapphire for the skill of listening and caring enough to cheer me on;

To my dear departed friend, mentor, and writer/role model, DorisJean Austin, who insisted that I do this project on my own;

To the many women writers who submitted material and

shared their special experiences of the men in their lives, I grate-fully appreciate the gift of your effort; and the Ragdale Founda-tion for providing their space, solace, and support.

Thanks to the many women supporters who encouraged me to develop and continue the project even though they were unable to participate in this project because of other commit-ments.

Om Shanti,
Brooke M. Stephens

Contents

Contents

Contents

Contents

Introduction
A Tough Love Letter to My
Battle-Scarred Brothers
Donna Britt

I love Black men.

Okay, so I like men, period. But brothers?

Oh, man.

The slide-y walk, the mighty talk. The power and glory, their survival story. I'm so far gone that I love the smell of a brother, even after he's spent hours taking it to the hoop—or the tennis court or the jogging track. Or the library, if attacking a book gets him in the flow.

I love them so much that though I prayed to have a daughter, God read my traitor's heart and stamped my womb, "For boys only."

I love each and every one of you so much that I'm going to do what everybody who has ever utterly loved someone has had to do:

I'm saying "No."

No. Stop. *This second.* Cease and desist from:

Being so angry—righteously or otherwise—*all* of the time.

Hitting, dissing, lying to, seducing, and abandoning your sisters.

Killing each other.

My reasons for saying this are purely selfish.

I need you. Not just the Black men who, by birth or fate, belong to me. I mean all of you. I don't want to lose another one of you.

Not to drugs. Not to the police. Not to immobilization or despair, to the courts or to blind fury or certainly, for God's sake, to another bullet.

I'm asking a lot. But if you weren't bigger and stronger and more marvelous than any man has a right to be, you'd never have survived. But here you are.

Let's say right off that most brothers are not hitters, thieves, abusers, or shooters. Anyone who doesn't know that, who doesn't realize that most want, very much, to Do The Right Thing, is a fool.

So you millions of African-American men who are none of those things: I applaud and congratulate and offer you my deepest, amazed gratitude. For you are miraculous.

The rest of you: Just stop.

I am not letting white men off the hook. They are just as liable to hurt women, white and Black. To knowingly and unknowingly stick it to brothers, on jobs, in courtrooms, on the streets of every city in this nation. As a rule, they have more money, resources, institutions, external power and even guns than you. The reasons are historic, ongoing and must be confronted.

But right now, in this letter, white men are not my concern.

They aren't dying like you. They haven't learned to hate themselves enough to devalue everyone who looks like them. It's you that I want around tomorrow. And next year. It's you I want to grow old with.

I know what you're thinking.

"What about *you?*" What about Black women doing the right thing?

Fine. Tell me and my sisters to be less grasping, snappish, materialistic, and vengeful. To give you a break. Swallowing hard, I'll listen to every valid criticism you hurl. I want to be worthy of the very-best you. Like I want you to be deserving of the wonderful-est me.

It's hard, being a Black man in America. Tough, being a Black woman. Dealing with so much toughness makes us hard. But it is only by uncovering our softness, our love, that we will survive.

And surviving means rising above some serious crap. Harry Belafonte once told me that during the height of the sixties he saw Martin Luther King, Jr., a guest at his home, looking unspeakably sad.

"I was wondering," King told his concerned host, "if we are integrating into a burning house."

Thirty years later, we live in a world ablaze with greed, lust, grandiosity, and lies. With their resources, white folks may survive in it longer. But for us, holding on to what's left of our sanity, our community, will take all our strength.

That means we need you. Because there is so much to do.

So many kids to teach how to be men and women—not bitter, hate-filled boys or grasping, heartsick girls.

There are books to be read, discussions to be had—on organizing, on making and keeping money, on pooling our resources.

Too many of you are behind bars. A brother in riot-rocked L.A. told me that since more Black men are in jails than universities, we will have to turn jails into universities. Malcolm learned to be a man in prison—you can, too. My friend Nate found God there—an empowering, ennobling Savior worth going the distance for. You can, too.

Perhaps I sound foolish. Love can do that, make you say stupid things.

But how can I stop? I'm sick of my newspaper listing last night's casualties, of the statistics on babies with no daddies. Sick of watching some of you smirking on the evening news, trying vainly to hide your fear and shame after some heinous crime—usually against another Black person. Tired of worrying about what will happen to my sons, once I raise them right and release them into the flames.

So stop it. Despite all you don't have, you still have the keys to the kingdom. Use them to save us all.

I've already seen Michael Jordan's transcendental levitation, doubled over as Richard Pryor and Martin Lawrence and Eddie Murphy made me laugh at stuff no sane woman should. Watched Bryant Gumbel beat the white boys at their own game—then tell the world that *The Autobiography of Malcolm X* was his life's most influential book.

Show me your genius. If you're smart enough to run a drug operation, you can run a corporation—and employ your people without killing them. If your anger can terrify a nation, your love can turn the world around.

You've made it thus far for a reason. What if it's to create a new blueprint for Black maleness? To disarm racism? To learn to love, really love, your sweet Black self?

Maybe it's to raise each baby you make, beautifully. To make me your lady, your mama, or your great-granddaddy proud.

Whatever it is, start today. Please, baby, please, please, please, please, baby *please*. I ain't too proud to beg.

You're worth it.

Preface

Brooke M. Stephens

*N*ews-headlines scream out the grim, chilling message every day: "The Urban League reports that young Black men are becoming an endangered species." "One out of three African-American men are in prison, on probation, or awaiting trial." "Black men in Harlem have a shorter life expectancy than a peasant in Pakistan."

It doesn't take a Ph.D. in cultural awareness to realize that the public image and private character of African-American men are under serious attack in the media. O. J. Simpson's murder trial and Johnny Cochran's rumored spousal abuse; Mike Tyson's rape conviction and Don King's accusation of mail-fraud charges; Mumia Abu-Jamal's pending execution and Rodney King's beating; Tupac Shakur's violent death and Snoop Doggy Dog's "gangsta rap" obscenities; Minister Louis Farrakhan's confrontational rhetoric against white America and Congressman Mel Reynolds' sentence for sexually molesting a minor . . . the list goes on.

Television news, once the highly respected domain of Murrow and Cronkite, originally designed to educate and entertain, is now locked in breathless competition with the most lurid brands of tabloid journalism, which weave fact and fiction and frequently distort, contrive, and create stories in order to excite and titillate. In the process, African-American men seem to attract more than their share of negative press coverage. In our media-driven society where the medium is the message, negative images sell. The fact that these portraits are often extreme and reinforce ugly and offensive stereotypes does not seem to disturb anyone except the most ethical of journalists.

The African-American version of the traditional war between the sexes has reached legendary proportions. The recent proliferation of popular novels, films, and dramas by some African-American women writers seems to have developed "Black male bashing" into a fashionable writing exercise as well as a profitable art form, giving us another bitter indictment of African-American men. Beginning in the seventies, this literary assault represented a cry of pain and anger from sisters who had some bruising life experiences with men and needed to be heard.

Men and women of every ethnic group and cultural background have a love–hate relationship that is older than time. Like most women of any color, I have my own private library of "he-done-me-wrong" stories, but these have been counterbalanced by supportive, inspiring Black men whose influence has helped to shape my life. Beginning with my grandfather, the roster includes my father, who died suddenly while I was still in diapers, my stepfather who stepped in to fill his shoes and treated me as if I were his own daughter, my three half-brothers who shared the typical sibling rivalry with me, and the friends, lovers, and confidants who have come through my life in various stages of my development as a woman and a person.

As I have watched the growing parade of degrading visions of Black men that blight our newspapers and television screens, I have become increasingly disturbed. They have little to do with my own personal reality. I don't know any men who fit the description of what the media would have us believe represents the majority of Black men: the dangerous criminals, scheming politicians, drug dealers, con artists, murderers, and pimps that are the typical lead stories on the nightly news.

Combine this message with the problem of "Black on Black" crime, mix in the frequently quoted statistics about African-American men being an endangered species and the fact that one in four Black men are in jail, and it becomes easy to believe the stereotypes and forget that many news stories are contrived to confirm the fears of whites and some Blacks as well.

A few biographies and autobiographies of high-achieving African-American men have been reviewed in the major media and received shelf space from major booksellers. These men have been held up as praiseworthy individuals and admirable role models: Colin Powell, Reginald Lewis, Henry Louis Gates, Nathan McCall, Brent Staples, and Earl Graves. While these life stories are not to be discounted, such works do little to stem the tidal wave of extreme negativity that pervades our information outlets, since these are men who are generally categorized as "exceptional" or "different." Too often these men and their histories fall into the "jail to Yale" version of the coming-of-age story for a Black man in America. He is presented as having grown up in some urban ghetto, had trouble with the law and, ultimately, lived the proverbial American "up by the bootstraps" story in blackface.

If one were to use most of these books as a guideline to understanding who and what Black men are all about, one would come away believing that the typical rite of passage for most young Black men is to go out into the streets, become a criminal, get arrested, go to jail, find enlightenment in the prison library, get an education as a guest of the state while awaiting parole, and only later, after being released and declared rehabilitated, to become a model citizen in the broader community.

In the mid-1980s, I began to spend time with my grandfather in my desire to record the family stories and personal history that I had started researching in 1974. As I listened to him, I found something that had been missing in my life: someone who could tell me more than I could have ever imagined about how I came to be who I am. He gave me a deeper sense of myself than I was prepared for. The stories he shared were touching, funny, and downright ridiculous, but they encapsulated a part of my history, and, in turn, a universal sense of my history that connected me to experiences that I had only read about. I began to know men who had sacrificed their own ambitions and opportunities to make the path a smoother road for the ones who came behind them, namely, their children. Getting to know my grandfather over the last years of his life and the middle years of mine brought me in touch with a point of view and attitude about men that I had never encountered before — how precious they were to my development.

Just before his death in 1991, I realized how important my grandfather's stories and his life experiences were and began to record our conversations whenever possible. In 1993, for a Stephens family reunion, I began writing the piece "Granddaddy" as a tribute to him. That was the same year that the media and the Urban League inundated us with news reports about Black men becoming an endangered species.

I looked back on the life of my grandfather and saw that good Black men are not a fantasy, a wishful dream, an unfulfilled hope, an unanswered prayer. I also knew I wasn't the only woman to have someone special like him in my life.

I kept wondering when someone was going to write something that presented a different view, a perspective that would focus on the other three Black men ignored by the statistics — the ones who have never been to jail, who have lived up to and exceeded everyone's expectations, yet never make the headlines. I spent years trying to pressure many of my writer friends to create such a collection of positive images, true-life examples that weren't demeaning. They were quick to point out that I was quite capable of doing it myself, since I was so passionately devoted to the topic.

Finally, my righteous rage drove me to develop this collection. I soon discovered that many other African-American women share my exasperation and my sentiments. This anthology, then, is our testament, our statement of support on behalf of African-American men. The women who have written for this collection range in age from twenty-six to one hundred and three. There are some that you will recognize as successful professionals and published writers whose names are familiar to you: Bebe Moore Campbell, Marita Golden, Charlayne Hunter-Gault, the Delany sisters, and Rosemary Bray. Others are newly emerging writers, such as Evelyn Coleman, Patrice Wagner, Pam Ward, and Leslie Woodard. There are several first-time writers who never made the effort to be published until they were presented with this challenging, yet heartfelt subject: Lillian Allen, Kai Jackson-Issa, Donna Wise, and Orian Hyde Weekes.

Decent Black men don't make the headlines, but they are out there. You see them everywhere: driving busses and taxis, sweeping streets and stocking store shelves, teaching algebra and coaching baseball teams, organizing political rallies and trade unions, creating new businesses, healing the sick and injured, and volunteering to tutor our young. They quietly go about the daily business of supporting their women, raising their children, and caring for their elderly parents. They shop with their wives on weekends, take their kids to school, and worry about paying the bills on time. They are committed to making whatever lifelong sacrifices are necessary to sustain their families and their communities. They leave indelible impressions on the women who share their lives. They consistently create quiet images of strength and dignity, wend their way into our hearts, and shape our concepts of ourselves without knowing it. They make their daily struggle for respectability and decency look easy.

There are no famous men here. These are the everyday Black heroes, the men that the TV camera crews never record, the ones that the perfectly groomed broadcaster doesn't moralize over, the brothers that the jaded news reporter seldom writes about. They have gone largely undocumented and have been invisible to everyone but us, the women who know them well, until now.

I, and the other women writers in this collection, wish to offer a different point of view. From Donna Britt's opening salvo, "A Tough Love Letter to My Battle-Scarred Brothers," which is a no-nonsense valentine to Black men of every description, offering chastisement and encouragement to live up to our expectations, to Leslie Woodard's final reflections in "Ready," on the character lesson learned from a ballet teacher, the depictions move beyond the macho manifestations of MTV and offer intimate portraits that assure us that there are some Black men who are not afraid to care about and support the women around them.

The book is divided up according to the many ways in which we relate to these everyday heroes. The list begins with fathers and grandfathers, our first encounter with the nurturing male energy that creates the initial impression in our psyche of what we expect men are supposed to be. Not only do they provide a link to our heritage, but they are the role models that influence our expectations for the rest of our lives. jonetta rose barras' "Same Coin, Different Sides" is an honest appraisal of the contrast in relationships and generational differences between her brother and grandfather and her own role in the level of respect and treatment accorded to her as a woman.

The uncles, brothers, and extended male family give us a healthy balance of images and relationships on many levels. Each of us knows some Black man who has been faithful to the same woman for forty years like Kai Jackson-Issa's adopted uncle "Esco," who, despite the discord between him and his wife, found a way to be there for her, and she for him, until the end of his unusual but quietly artistic life. Or a man like Doc, who took on the burden of another man's children and raised them as his own, in Marcia Dyson's piece, "I'll Call Him Daddy," about her stepfather. Or like Gloria Wade-Gayles's Uncle Prince in "Homecoming," who, despite his deceptive outward appearance as the neighborhood drunkard, inspired her to be a writer, thinker, and an artist, although he never had the opportunity to be so himself. Carolyn Hart-Solomon explores the built-in "bad-news-best-friend" relationship between brothers and sisters, a relationship fraught with competitiveness and rivalry that culminates in the blood bond of friendship.

The furtive prayers of Black women who constantly seek guidance and blessings in the process of bringing up Black sons is addressed in the "Sons and Grandsons" section of the book by Marita Golden. Patrice Wagner's confessional commentary, "My Foghorn," speaks eloquently of the pain of being a mother in this era, when media images of our sons do not fit the reality of the young Black men that we see each day on the subway. Lillian Allen's terse yet amusing anecdote of a grandmother's admiration for her grandson strikes a familiar note of affection.

Donna Wise's fascinating tale of how she met her husband in the most unlikely of places, an AA meeting, and how she managed to surrender her closed-minded standards and expectations is a page-turner in the "Husbands and Lovers" section of the book. Rosemary Bray voices a controversial but painful reality faced by many women in "It's Ten O'Clock and I Worry About Where My Husband Is."

For the brothers who want to know what the sisters are looking for, Pam Ward tells you in her vignette of Mr. Rawls, the neighborhood handyman who shows up in a moment of crisis to fix her fence and teach a few life lessons in the process. Jennifer Jordan provides a meaningful portrait of the college professor who led her to her chosen profession with his stories, anecdotes, and testimony to the power of the word and craft of the men and women of the Harlem Renaissance. Orian Hyde Weekes touches on the topic of the nurturing support of a surrogate "father" figure from an unlikely source in "A Few Good Men."

These are the unacknowledged heroes that we want to applaud, support, and encourage. They are necessary to each of us, invisible to most of us, and taken for granted by too many of us, including the women who have loved and lived with them. My feelings of love and appreciation are shared by the women within these pages and many of my sisters who were too busy with other projects to submit material for consideration but were kind enough to offer their words of support and encouragement, to "get back to the desk and keep at it."

The 30 essays and memoirs here were culled from more than 120 submissions. They confirm my belief that they are just a hint of the broader story of Black men's lives and the positive relationships that have existed for so many decades. We must record their life stories or risk denying a significant part of our identities if we do not acknowledge them. To cherish, to hold dear, to harbor fond feelings and gentle memories of, to look upon with fondness and favor—these statements are rarely, if ever, expressed in the same sentence as one in which African-American women describe their relationships with African-American men.

Some of us do like, no love, Black men. If you want bad news brothers, look elsewhere. These life experiences are brought to you by the women who know and love them best, the women who have shared their lives and their struggles, experienced their pain and disappointments as well as their triumphs and small victories.

The portraits here are not always flattering, and few, if any, fall into the *"Father Knows Best"* romanticized image of white fatherhood that television offered us in the fifties. Yet it is a valid perspective because it is written by the people who know these men best—the women who have been loved by them and have shared their struggle to achieve comfortable, respectful lives and who have endured the same denigrating experiences of racism. These are the memories of the daughters, wives, sisters, mothers, and best friends who have been influenced by their presence.

This anthology is an effort to extend the same praise, gratitude, and respect to such men as we have often offered our mothers. We hope that such an offering will give credibility to the three out of four Black men who do support us and will reverse some of the tide of negative information that is overwhelming us. These are the men we cherish, an accolade that is not usually conferred on Black men. Consider it a valentine and a peace offering; a gesture of admiration to Black men by the women who understand their attempt for respectability and manhood when the easy action would have been to give up. It is long overdue.

Foreword

Marcia Gillespie,
Editor-in-Chief, MS. magazine

*Y*ears ago when I was the editor-in-chief of *Essence* magazine, we ran a writing contest for college students. The title of the winning essay, a prose-poem by Julianne Malveaux, was "Black Love is a Bitter Sweetness." While reading *Men We Cherish: African-American Women Praise the Men in Their Lives*, the title of that contest-winning essay, and all that it implies, kept dancing through my mind. The essays in this book bear witness to the complexities of race and gender, to the ugly realities of racism and sexism, to our personal hopes, particular needs, strengths and weaknesses, family histories and ties. All the baggage we as women inherit and take on in the course of our lives resonates in the relationships with the men in our lives, and in many instances the men missing from our lives and the men we miss. Just as it resonates on the pages of this bittersweet praise song.

The title of this collection may lead some to assume that these essays are mere sugar-coated paeans to "good Black men." They'd be wrong. The women writing here of "the men they cherish" aren't engaging in fantasy. The words on these pages don't always go down easy, and the men they write about don't seem too good to be true. The men are not flawless idealized figures, and the most intimate stories center on ordinary folk. Some of the men are being praised here for simply doing the best they could, for the "small" daily victories of refusing to be bowed or embittered by racism, and for their willingness to shoulder their responsibilities to family. But there are dreamers and gentle men, achievers and strivers and lost men who were more shadow than substance here too. *Men We Cherish* is about us and the many textures and flavors of our love for our men—fathers, husbands, sons, friends and lovers, our brothers and The Brother—sans the rose-colored glasses.

These essays, each in a different key, speak of the profound effect men have on women's lives and how powerfully important the presence of good men in our lives can be. Whether writing about men at the core of their most intimate relationships or men as a group, the women who have contributed to this volume remind us of the importance of our connections and the power of affirmation. Their praise songs are shaped by fragile connections and powerful bonds, missed opportunities and enduring memories. It's women struggling to understand, and sometimes forgive, the men in their lives, to unravel their mysteries and our own. It's unvarnished woman talk about the fear we often quietly swallow—the fear for the safety of the men we treasure, in a world where the lives of Black men and boys are too easily destroyed. It's about all kinds of love and loving—loving because of and in spite of.

In writing about men, we women almost invariably write about ourselves—our needs, dreams, vulnerabilities—and this book is no exception. Here, a diverse group of powerful women writers not only write about the men they cherish, they also share their dreams and bare their hearts to us. This is a book men and women should read together and talk about to each other.

Men We Cherish

Part I

Fathers
and
Grandfathers

What I Came For

Faith Adiele

Ever since that day three months ago when I returned home to Boston from a vacation and found a letter from my father, a man I've only known for four years, I have been fueled primarily by two emotions—anger and guilt. I had been fairly angry four years ago when I visited Nigeria, his home, and we met for the first time. More than anything, though, I was hungry to discover my cultural roots. We danced about politely, uneasily, for a year, the situation aided by my welcoming stepmother, my American mother's letters, my adoring younger half-brothers and sister, my proud aunts and uncle. By the time I moved into the family home, I was content to focus on learning how to be Nigerian, how to be the illegitimate American daughter of a prominent Nigerian politician. By the end of my year my new father and I appeared to have achieved peace. He hugged me as he put me on the plane and promised to stay in touch. When I returned home to the United States, he wrote regularly, providing letters of introduction to expatriate Nigerians here who I had been too intimidated to befriend. I began to feel halfway Nigerian, surprised at the feelings of guilt whenever I was tardy in my replies. And so now, here he was—this new father I had requested—and all the responsibility that comes of family.

His letter, more a note really, was clearly a follow-up to an earlier letter I hadn't received and therefore difficult to follow. I read it several times before the information sank in. I gathered that my new father was in the United States for medical treatment. He mentioned his pacemaker and his eyes. He had arrived in Nebraska, of all places, while I was away on vacation, and had tried to contact me. "I thought I would have had a letter or telegram from you by now," he wrote. Guilt. He made no mention of coming to visit me in Boston or of us getting together. Anger.

After checking with the postal officials for the earlier letter that I never received, I leaned against the wall of the post office, the beige envelope with a Nebraska postmark dangling from my fingers. People stretched above, below, and around me to reach their mailboxes. It was too much information to assimilate. My father was in America. What's more, he had been here two weeks already. I wondered if he had come alone. African elders rarely traveled solo; perhaps my half-brothers and sister were with him. My heart skipped a beat; perhaps I could talk him into leaving one of them behind with me. *My father was in America*. He was also in poor health and had just undergone serious surgery. Stranger still, having come halfway across the world, he had set down in the heart of America, bypassing the East Coast entirely. I knew he had gotten his original pacemaker in Nebraska when he was there on sabbatical in the seventies. Had the University of Nebraska arranged something with the Nigerian government? He hoped to be leaving soon, his letter said. Did that mean he would leave without seeing me?

"Are you all right?" a woman asked, glancing at me a couple of times as she spread out her mail across a nearby counter.

I smiled blankly. "My father's here," I explained.

She cocked an eyebrow and returned to sorting her mail. "That's nice."

No, you don't understand, I wanted to say. This is big. He's never been *here* since I've known him. He's not American; he lives in a country under a military regime. He's here, but he's far away in Nebraska. He's here, but he's sick. He's my father, but I don't really know him. He's here, and who knows when he'll ever be back again.

That night at home I read the letter several times. I decide to call him in the morning from the office. In the meantime, I call my mother and my best friend Mike. Both tell me to go to Nebraska.

"But he didn't mention it," I agonize. "I think it's one of those things a *true* Nigerian daughter is instinctively supposed to know. I think I'm supposed to fly out immediately when I learn of his arrival . . . though it could be that I'm supposed to await his summons. I don't know what to do."

Just go, each urges me. You'll feel better.

"Of course," Mike advises, himself an expert on building relationships with absent fathers, "you'll get there and realize that like all fathers, he's essentially incapable of dealing with you on your terms, and after a day you'll be wondering why you ever thought this would be a good idea. But," he ends, the eternal optimist, "at least it will be out of your system, and you'll know you did the right thing."

My mother is more hopeful. While my father, her first college love, was still in the United States, she remained friends with him so that I could have links to my Nigerian heritage. After he was summoned home during the Nigerian civil war, she studied African history, encouraged us to write, and, finally, supported my trip to Nigeria. "It will be a great opportunity to bond with him," she enthuses about this latest development.

"Just the two of you alone in Nebraska with plenty of time on your hands." Before hanging up she offers her cure for just about anything: "Remember to take lots of books to read."

It takes until noon of the next day to psych myself into dialing the number of the boarding house in Lincoln, Nebraska, where my father is recuperating. A pleasant-sounding woman answers the phone and searches the house.

"No, I'm sorry," she says when she comes back. She sounds like she means it. "Magnus isn't here. He must have gone over to the hospital."

It strikes me as odd to hear him called "Magnus." In Nigeria he was "the Reverend" or "the Doctor" or "the former Commissioner" or "the Honorable." When speaking Igbo, family members call him "Pa-Emeka" ("the father of Emeka," the first-born son). My mother always refers to him as "your poppie." I have never heard him called by his given name.

I ask if he is coming back, and she assures me that he has just gone to a follow-up appointment. I leave my telephone numbers with instructions for him to call collect. "Tell him his daughter called from Boston," I say, and I can sense the woman on the other end of the line respond. Perhaps she listens just a bit more intently or copies down my numbers a bit more carefully or volunteers more information. Whatever it is, I feel the effect of those words all the way from Nebraska. Not only am I calling long distance from a well-known city, but I am the next of kin. I feel giddy with the sudden power of it. How many times before have I been able to admit publicly, *I'm his daughter*? How powerful the feeling of legitimacy!

"I've been out of town," I explain breezily, "but I'm back," the implication being: And now everything's all right.

Less than an hour later, my father is on the line. "Queen," he shouts, lapsing immediately into the pet name he gave me four years ago, "is that you?"

The instant I hear his booming, delighted voice a quiver of emotion dislodges itself from somewhere deep within my body and climbs my spine, warming my cheeks and voice, catching me off guard. My ambivalence about making the call fades away, and I find myself laughing and calling him "Daddy" as if it were the most natural thing in the world at age thirty to be chatting with my father in America.

I get a thirty-minute response to my question "How are you?", that meanders backward and forward in time, encompassing the actions and well-being of a host of unidentified individuals on numerous continents. When there's a lull in the conversation, I blurt out my second question, "Daddy, did you come alone?"

He is indignant. "Of course not!" he declares, and I can imagine the wide, sweeping gesture he makes with his arm. My heart begins to thud, torn between praying for my sixteen-year-old half-sister, my favorite, and the discovery of a completely new relative. He recovers his composure, then announces with great dignity, "I traveled with God."

I bite the insides of my mouth to keep from laughing. I really wanted my sister but can't help wondering where God was during all this mistaken midnight rerouting to Houston he has described. As we prepare to hang up I promise to call him later that night from home.

He seems gratified. "You will?" he asks. "What time?"

I explain that I have a class until nine, which is eight o'clock his time.

"Yes," he says eagerly. "I believe it is an hour difference, so when it's nine o'clock there, it's eight o'clock here."

"Yes."

He continues, "And when it's eight o'clock there, it's nine o'clock here."

"Er, no," I correct. "Boston is always one hour ahead."

He ignores this. "And that means that when it's seven o'clock there, it's six o'clock here, and when it's six o'clock there, it's seven o'clock here. And when it's five o'clock there, it's four . . ."

I decide not to argue. A good Nigerian daughter never questions her elders or talks back. More importantly, there's no arguing with him. I promise to call at eight o'clock his time. It's going to be a long visit.

That night I announce my intention to come to Nebraska the next week. "It's all set," I tell my father. "I've booked my flight."

"Really?" Dad says, as if I had just embarked upon a fascinating story. "Is that so?"

I'm not quite sure what this means, but he sounds impressed. I launch into my carefully prepared speech about how—here in *America*—one needs a certain amount of lead time to order one's life. He listens, murmuring "yes, yes." After I finish, he tells me not to come.

Hurt, I demand to know why. The hell with being a good Nigerian daughter.

He gives me the same cryptic, only-an-African-elder-can-know-all response that drove me crazy during my year in Nigeria. It is a declaration, meant to be delivered in public while wearing chief's robes and holding an animal skin fan, not an explanation. "I have my reasons," he says over and over. "This trip is not about a visit. This isn't the time."

I'm thirty years old, I want to say. You're sixty-two and broke, we're separated by an ocean, a hemisphere, and a military dictatorship. If not now, just when exactly do you plan on dropping by for a real visit? I say nothing.

He then launches into a long, incoherent story in which the distances between Lagos and London, London and Boston, Boston and Chicago, Chicago and Nebraska all figure prominently.

He seems indignant that Boston to Chicago is nearly the same distance as Chicago to Nebraska. I understand his annoyance at having been routed so far into America, so far from everyone. After all, he has Auntie Adanma in London, me in Boston, and apparently some distant cousins in Chicago. Why, then, Nebraska?

He is convinced that the phone lines are tapped and refuses to say more, only hinting that "certain people" will meet up in "certain locations" that are more readily accessible than "other locations." I am left to assume that Boston and Chicago are the accessible locations in question, and that he and I are the certain people who will meet there "when the time is right."

I try to break it to him gently that I don't think anyone is tapping the phone. No one in the United States gives a damn about a long-deposed politician from Nigeria who has forsaken politics for religion. They don't seem to care that one of the world's largest democracies has been under military rule for nearly ten years now. He laughs. "Oh Queen, Queen," he says, and I can see him shaking his head. "You're so young. You don't understand."

That much at least is true.

After that first delirious phone call to my father in Nebraska, I spend the next three months either on the phone or avoiding the phone. Usually my father is content to have me check in, ask after his health, and listen to a few minutes of jokes or Bible verses or details of his ailments. He is often witty and high-spirited, and we laugh a lot. And yet, try as I may to call every other day, something always comes up, and I start to put it off. Sometimes I spend entire weekends procrastinating, devising reasons that it's a bad time to call, and yet I am miserable and guilty when I don't. Once I go two entire weeks without contact, and he leaves several frantic messages. When finally I call back he sounds merely tired. His only reproach is to say,

"How now, Queen? Why so long?" I blame a hectic conference and travel schedule, and that is the end of it.

*W*henever there is something I particularly want to know, I enlist my mother's aid. She calls him—this almost-forgotten boyfriend of hers she can never actually forget—reluctantly, with questions about the family tree. My theory is that, as an elder and not a dutiful Nigerian daughter, she is freer to ask questions than I. She calls me back. "You owe me big," she grouses good-naturedly, offering the few coherent answers she could ferret out of him. "This took two hours out of my week-end, and who knows what I got. The man likes to talk!"

We compare notes. As I suspected, he is much more forth-coming with her, but information on individuals and dates is still foggy. Often his answers contradict ones he has given me just days before. He is sharp, however, and his elusiveness seems more a function of intent than forgetfulness. It is as if he has mastered the art of verbal scramble, has invented an entire lan-guage to accommodate to the lines being tapped. Or is it simply that his is a purely African conception of time and truth? All time exists side by side, the living walk with the dead. Did his mother, the grandmother I never saw, die when he was a child or when he was thirty? He tells my mother one date, me an-other. In his world, where ancestors and descendants alike get rerouted to Houston, both seem possible.

Before she can lecture him for not making arrangements to visit me in Boston, he tells her of his intention to visit after his medical attention is complete. "He says you two have already arranged it," my mother reports to my surprise.

I hang up, my left ear throbbing, red. I've spent three hours on the phone with my father and two with my mother.

How did I manage to come from such talkaholics? I complain to Mike. No wonder they broke up. They had to—neither could get a word in edgewise!

The state of his health appears to be a mishmash of misdiagnosed ailments, hypochondria, poor medical practice, and poorly followed advice. From my vantage point in Boston, I can't figure out a thing. The original plan was to replace his pacemaker and remove the cataracts from one eye and then from the other, with a week's recovery time between each procedure. After the first eye operation, the doctors discover he has glaucoma and never should have undergone surgery. The eye worsens, and after a month hasn't recovered. His recovery from the heart surgery is equally problematic. A doctor finally mentions the possibility that they might have neglected to take out the old pacemaker, which had migrated across his chest to the right side, when they installed the new one. ("You'd think," Mike muses, "that at the end of the day they'd count the number of pacemakers on the operating room tray.")

Dad is understandably furious. "I could sue them," he shouts. "And they know it. Only I'm not like that. I'm only here to get what I came for and go."

He has started to talk like this. His speech is full of his good intentions, his religious demeanor, and how he has been put upon by others. He was one of the few clean politicians in the notoriously corrupt Second Republic. Others embezzled from the government and accepted kickbacks, squirreling away oil money in Swiss bank accounts or building fancy houses abroad, but he did his job. Always he refused to get carried into political machinations, even when he was arrested. I feel the weight of these past months in Nebraska over the phone lines. How he must feel to be seriously ill so far from home, without real family, clan, community, country, with only a long-distance stranger daughter. To try as an elderly black man to deal with arrogant doctors and the American medical system. To have lost one eye and gained an extra heart. To have become a political exile in absentia, as yet another coup sweeps Nigeria into a leadership vacuum and the government that originally promised to pay his medical bills ceases to exist. I understand his anger but have no idea what to do. I put on the speaker phone at work and do paperwork until I sense a shift in tone.

One day he announces that writing is not a profession. In Nigeria, he says, writers are always arguing over this and that. I laugh. How can he say such things when Chinua Achebe is his neighbor and boyhood friend? When writers like Wole Soyinka were jailed for opposing the government's attack on our tribe during the civil war? He reminds me that I shouldn't let time waste but should get started on a higher degree. I remind him that I am in fact halfway through a master's degree program, in writing. He repeats his premise that writing is not a profession. He has decided that I should just forget about that and "get cracking" on my chosen profession.

What, I inquire quietly, would that be?

He explains how my interests in things international and political (he must be confusing me with my mother) will be well served by a career in international law. "I've told all the doctors here how you are doing such good work there at Harvard with the Nigerian students and such, and studying international law."

"Nice try," I mutter. Though I am annoyed that he seems to think I might actually drop my program to follow his advice, I am also amused. I call my mother. "Guess what my 'chosen profession' is?" I ask.

She starts giggling before I can even tell her.

*A*s the weeks pass, friends ask me what I plan to *do*. This angers me. "What do you mean, what am I going to do?" I reply hotly.

"I've seen this man once in my life, and I was the one who made it happen. He'll be gone in a few weeks. He lives a hemisphere away. What's *he* gonna do?"

After two and a half months he has tired of Nebraska, of diagnoses that go nowhere, and of his hand-to-mouth existence. He wants to be in Chicago by the first week of October, the week Nigeria is scheduled to return to civilian rule. He has an open ticket from Chicago to Lagos, with a stopover in London to meet with Auntie Adanma's doctors. We plan to meet in Chicago for four days. He has letters and gifts for me from the rest of the family and wants to discuss "my future." I will help him prepare for his return home. It is the only weekend all fall that I don't have to be out of town at a conference. I book a flight to Chicago and make reference to my arrival every time we speak.

The week before I am scheduled to depart he still hasn't received his doctor's authorization to travel. When I call he seems vague and won't commit himself to an arrival time. "I can't guarantee that I will be there," he says. "We can only try for this time."

My anger comes to a head. Doesn't he know this isn't Nigeria? I rage to myself. That you can't just summon someone at the last minute? There needs to be advance warning to book flights, inform employers, prepare for missing classes. Doesn't he know that I'm busy; I'm broke; I'm scared? He seems to expect me to obey, to know the rules, but no one raised me to be a dutiful Nigerian daughter. I don't know how to maneuver someone through an airport in a wheelchair, how to negotiate a strange city with a blind man, how to parent a parent I've only known for four years, three of these in absentia. These are things I never learned, things I never wanted to learn. When do I offer to pay his expenses, when do I call relatives and enlist their aid, when do I override his protests? For twenty-six years I was raised as American. I never laid eyes on him. How can he expect me now, at age thirty, to know how to be?

11

When I call back later that night he declares his intention to sneak out of town to meet me, hospital bills unpaid. I ask if it is safe for him to fly; what do his doctors say? "I have to be there," he insists. "I have no choice. You have the ticket and we can't make you lose your hard-earned money!" He seems happy to have the decision forced on him.

*I*n the air over Chicago, it hits me that this will be the first time the two of us are to be alone together. (Not that being with him is like being alone in the traditional sense of the word. He preaches the way other people breathe. There is nothing like one-on-one conversation. He is with one person the same as he is with a congregation.) My greatest fear is that, in the absence of the rest of the family, he will want us to pray together. I tell myself that I can handle his rambling, sometimes witty monologues, even his paranoia about being trailed by political enemies, but I refuse to participate in any pre-dawn family prayer meetings.

Half of me—the American half—resents the whole situation. The other half of me—the Nigerian half—thrills at the thought of this opportunity to continue my education on How to Be Nigerian. An opportunity to serve a function, to have purpose. I'm excited to be doing something, buying things, going places, making plans and reservations. To be taking action, rather than continuing the long, helpless, painful phone calls to Nebraska. I look forward to being swept into an unknown world where I pay his bills, make his calls, do all the things a Nigerian child would do—the important work of being a member of an extended family. We will be task-driven: to arrange his flight to Britain, to contact Auntie Adanma in London, to get news on the political situation in Nigeria, to shop for everyone back home, to stock up on his medication. Secure in my role, I will stride purposely forth, speaking authoritatively, garnering cooperation and support. I am taking care of my father, I will say. A renowned political exile and priest. I am attending to family business.

Then the wheels of the plane hit the tarmac and the cabin roars and vibrates with the impact of the earth and I start to cry. As long as we were talking on the phone, we existed in limbo. There was always the possibility that the Nigerian military would in fact hand over power and allow free elections, the possibility that someone had been mistaken about the date of my grandmother's death and would give her thirty more years to live before dying again. There was always the possibility of another day, another call to Nebraska. Now that we are about to meet, I am suddenly convinced it is the last time I will see my father.

I arrive at O'Hare, Terminal One at 2 P.M. on October 2, 1993. My father is scheduled to arrive at Terminal Five at 1:40. It takes me a full thirty minutes to speed-walk from one huge glass terminal to the other, panting in my winter coat, seeing visions of my blind father clutching his heart and crying out for me. Signs everywhere warn you not to take the luggage carts out of the terminal. The only thing stopping me from breaking the rule is my inability to find one. I drag my bags from one security checkpoint to another. I collapse on the occasional motorized walkway beneath neon sculpture, disregarding the soothing computerized female voice out of some futuristic film that exhorts travelers to "Keep walking, keep walking." By the time I reach his arrival gate, hot and out of breath, everyone is gone. The luggage carousel is similarly abandoned. I rush back and forth. Finally I find him in the special service room sitting in a wheelchair in front of a bank of uniformed airline workers, his back to me. He wears a tan corduroy beret and dark wrap-around shades over his glasses. I burst in, crying "Daddy!"

"A-*heh!*" He acknowledges my arrival by immediately launching into his side of the quarrel he is having. No greeting.

The airline staff people all look visibly relieved at my arrival. A tall white woman, who is leaning over the counter arguing with Dad, tells him that they need the wheelchair back immediately. Dad clutches the chair and insists that the airline staff in Nebraska promised him special help with traveling and with transporting his luggage. "My doctors arranged everything. Look!" He waves a sheaf of medical documents at her. "I just had a heart operation!"

An affected blond boy eavesdropping from behind the counter rolls his eyes. I glare at him, and he gives his ponytail a toss. The woman says in a loud voice that the airline is not responsible for transporting his luggage, no matter what his medical condition. The wheelchair attendant, a young Black woman, seems reluctant to kick him out of the chair. The first woman throws up her arms. "Ah," she cries, turning to me, clearly prepared to dump the whole thing in my lap. "Are you traveling with him?"

"No, no!" Dad cuts her off, like a dog set on a bone. "She has nothing to do with this! What would you do if she were not here, with me sitting here just as I am in this wheelchair, unable to move?"

Eventually I negotiate another half hour in the wheelchair. Together the attendant and I manage to corral Dad's luggage. He has African-sized suitcases, built for carrying back riches from industrialized nations. There are five altogether, each huger than the next, weighing nearly a hundred pounds each. It seems ridiculous to take all five to a hotel for four days and then bring them back, but they are too large for a locker and the airline refuses to check them. Fighting the urge to cry, I call a series of cheap hotels near the airport and book the first one that has free shuttle service. "See if they have a nice Chinese restaurant," Dad suggests. While we wait, the attendant turns down her radio and ignores the calls that come in. When she finally leaves she refuses my tip. "I will pray for your people," Dad calls out after her.

I stand across from the Black clerk at the Chicago O'Hare Grand Inn and regard my African father in the dingy lighting of the lobby. Stuck in this underequipped hotel run by Pakistanis on a highway strip mall near what could be any airport in America, I realize something. I have done this myself. I found my homeland, allied myself with my people, fell in love with my siblings, forgave a father who never came looking for me. I finally understand what my friend Susan means when she says I did an amazing thing by going alone to Nigeria at age twenty-six. I created family and created it so authentically that a stranger could recognize it on my face. For all that I may rail against Dad's expectations, I am the architect of this relationship. I have constructed nothing less than my own commitment to it.

I organize the van driver, the desk clerk, and the hotel manager to drag Dad's five huge bags to our room in the Chicago O'Hare Grand Inn. The room they give us is near the lobby, at the front of the hotel, and pitch-black. Heat pours out of the radiator. When I pull back the floor-to-ceiling drapes, the room is flooded with the noise of highway traffic. I call for another room, and so our strange caravan of Pakistanis, Nigerians, and American Blacks dragging giant vinyl suitcases along the shag-carpeted corridors resumes. Dad declares the second room perfect.

After checking the beds and bathroom for cleanliness and assessing how steady Dad is on his feet, I tell him I'm going out to the pay phones in the lobby to call the airline about his flight to London. Only part of my motivation is to avoid the hotel charge on phone calls; I fully intend to make a brief call to my mother for moral support. "Wait!" he cries, struggling with his clothes. "Tell them about my condition." He claws at the layers of shirts and sweatshirts, his diminished strength all too evident. I feel like crying.

"It's okay," I say, trying to quiet him. "It's just the reservation." Still he wrestles with sweater after sweater, finally managing to hoist them all up and expose his chest. He has lost much weight; his slack mahogany skin is sagging toward his belly. His chest, still raw from the two sets of operation scars, looks as if a lion has attacked him: three long scratches on the left side, where the new pacemaker was installed; three on the right where the old one was removed.

"See," he says, tracing the grooves in his chest with swollen fingers. "Tell them about me."

I remember the first time I saw his pacemaker—the outline of his pacemaker, rather—through the skin of his chest. It was three years ago, at the end of my stay in Nigeria. We had all been goofing around together—he, Emeka, Okey, Adanma, and I—and he had his shirt off. There was not much left to him physically—some tufts of wiry black hair sticking out beneath a beret; little feet pointing inward; a tiny frame, so reduced in size. I saw the raised rectangle over his heart and stopped in my tracks. I had never given much thought to the occasional mentions of his pacemaker. Imagining perhaps a microchip, I had never thought that a pacemaker was an actual machine that could be observed with the naked eye. Seeing it there in his body, so primitive and artificial, I had to sit down, panting as if I were the one out of breath, the one with the fluttering heart.

I suddenly realized how arbitrary it all was, that I had managed to find my family and that my father was still alive, his very life kept going by a box in his chest. I asked myself, What if I had been just a few years later? And again I asked the question, Why hadn't he been the one to order his life—to come in search of me—once his very existence became the function of a piece of machinery? These were questions so large they couldn't be asked of a man who couldn't even say when his mother had died. When there is only so much time, there are only so many questions. The question is really how to put some questions and anger aside. How to begin here, where we find each other. How not to make others pay for their mistakes. How, as he put it, to "get what I came for and go."

*B*y the time I get back from telephoning the airline and my mother, who tells me it will all be worth it in the end and suggests possible topics of conversation, dredging up every thirty-year-old detail she can remember about my father, the entire surface of the hotel desk is covered with stacks of paper. He closes the top desk drawer, and I catch a glimpse of crumpled tissue, slips of paper, a jumble of U.S., British, and Nigerian coins. It is as if my father has been inhabiting this room for months. He reminds me of Tati Rauha, my mother's eighty-year-old aunt, the way he keeps checking his documents, mainly duplicate copies of his medical records, fastening and refastening layers of rubber bands and plastic bags around each envelope.

He has also lined up all his shoes against the wall near his bed. There must be five or six pairs, though we are only in town for a few days, and he can't even really walk. They are short, wide shoes, meant for short, wide feet with high arches—just like my mother's. No one can figure where my long, narrow, flat feet come from. The shoes look like tiny boats—open, worn, calling for feet.

I ask why he has unpacked everything, how we can possibly reassemble all five cases. With a wave of his hand, he informs me that "God will pack." Eying the massive suitcases that fill the room, I have a sinking feeling that I will end up being the one helping God out in a pinch.

I'm amazed that in my short absence he has managed to scrounge through five huge suitcases to find all his shoes and line them up so neatly. It reminds me of a British woman I met in Indonesia traveling with her little son. They were perpetual world travelers who didn't have a home. The first thing they did each time they arrived in a new place was find a windowsill or shelf where the boy would line up his little cache of toys. Once his toys were arranged, the place—wherever it happened to be—became home.

It also reminds me of Mom, always making lists, always organizing her tiny corner of the world, puttering around on short, stubby feet talking to herself. How odd that my parents—who spent less than two years together, more than thirty years ago—should end up being two of a kind.

I wade into the chaos he has created for himself in our hotel room, and he beams at me, wanting to know if I've located a Chinese restaurant yet. "They knocked while you were gone," he says. "But I didn't answer." This time he doesn't sound quite so paranoid. Though it was probably just the Pakistani manager checking to see if the new room is acceptable, I feel no great confidence in our safety.

. . .

I awake in the morning to find my father kneeling next to my bed in the dark, asking God to watch over me. "Good morning, Queen," he says when he has finished, struggling to his feet and patting my forehead.

I am exhausted. It is the first time he and I have ever slept in the same room. All night I was restless, my sleep shallow and full of dreams. I shower and then call the front desk to find out about breakfast. It turns out that they lied about the on-site restaurant. "We *have* a restaurant," the clerk corrects me. "But renovations." That accounts for the huge hole in the lobby. The nearest sit-down restaurant is on the other side of the highway, a few blocks down. While he chooses from among his selection of shoes, Dad turns on CNN for news about the upcoming return to civilian rule. There is nothing. In this particular way station, apparently, Nigeria does not exist.

Over breakfast my father tells me about his trouble with the pacemaker. "You have to understand that it doesn't eat everything you eat," he says. "It likes low calorie stuff." He makes a face, and we both laugh. "It doesn't know *what* to think about *garri!*"

I nod, understanding the pacemaker's dilemma. It took me the entire year in Nigeria to learn to eat *garri*. People can no longer afford the staple food (yam), and a meal of fermented cassava weighs heavily on the chest.

He opens his Bible, which he has carried with him to the restaurant, clutching it as we scurry across the highway, and takes an empty packet of Carnation Sugar-Free Hot Cocoa Mix from between the pages. He hands it to me. He asks if it is possible to get more. "Of course," I say so heartily that Dot our waitress thinks I am calling her and arrives, armed with a smile and a fresh pot of decaf. "I can easily get more!" I turn the carefully preserved packet over. He must have brought it with him all the way from Nigeria. On the back he has written in spidery script, "Be thou O God exalted, above the heavens. Let thy glory be above all the earth."

On his way back from an airport run, the Pakistani driver sees us walking down the highway and stops to give us a ride back to the hotel. "Oho!" Dad shouts, scrambling almost easily into the van, pleased to see him. "It's that big fellow from yester-day!" He thanks the driver repeatedly and then asks about "his people." I do the translating from Dad's perfect yet heavily ac-cented English to the Pakistani driver's minimal and equally accented English. It turns out that the driver's people are in Scotland; he is the only one in the United States. "Hmm, a Pakistani in America whose people are in Scotland," my father muses as we disembark. He claps the driver on the shoulder. "Well, good for you, young man!" The driver nods, his bewil-dered smile mirroring the anxious crease between his brows. After handing us out, he rushes to load the next set of bags for the return to the airport.

Everything having to do with the Chicago O'Hare Grand Inn seems to please my father: the service, the overheating, Dot in her green ruffled apron at the restaurant down the street, her inquiries after his health, the bland food she chooses for him. "This is a nice hotel you have here," he tells the clerk as they sprawl in the sweltering lobby, praying for guests. "Very quiet." He thanks everyone, stopping strangers in the hallway and dis-pensing blessings like the pope.

"Your father seems to like this hotel," the Pakistani man-ager says one morning when I am hiding out in the abandoned lobby. He sounds surprised.

"Yes," I answer. "He certainly seems to." We smile at each other, each too polite to wonder why. I spend a lot of time in the hotel lobby and taking walks. Dad never questions my absences. Sometimes I call my mother from the lobby pay phone and ask her to call him so he won't feel lonely while I'm gone.

When I get back to the room one afternoon, he announces that I need to belong to a church. "I can suggest some if you need," he says. "I asked your mother. She said she has a church. I think she said Congregational, or was it Baptist?"

Though annoyed at being told to get religion, I stifle the urge to laugh. My mother has little patience for organized religion, even less for Christianity.

He continues. "No, it was Congregational. She didn't used to believe when she was young, but now even she has come round. She used to call herself agnostic. I said, 'Jo, if you must, call yourself atheist, but there is nothing like agnostic.' And she said . . ." He interrupts himself, deciding to forgo their ancient argument. "But anyway, now in her old age, she has become Congregationalist, which is fine."

"No," I interject, finally fed up. "She's not a Congregationalist; she's Unitarian and has been for a long time."

"Ah yes, that's it. Unitarian."

"And so am I."

I can't tell if he heard me. Already he is praying.

On the third day we have our first quarrel. "There are two things that are important," he announces over breakfast after Dot has delivered his beloved applesauce and refilled my coffee. "You need to study French and get a Bible. French is very useful. You know I speak French; I can go anywhere. And it's very necessary to have a Bible to read."

"That's funny," I say. "You don't even take the time to know me . . ."

"Queen," he interrupts, reproachful, "are we quarreling?"

I can't hear him. After three days of living close together in such dark, stuffy quarters, with his constant prayers and complicated stories, with the incessant television news coverage of every country but Nigeria, I can't help myself. "You don't ask first if I have these things. You just say I need to do them." After three months of guilt and anger, the words are bursting to get out of me. "For your information, I've studied French and traveled in French-speaking countries. I also have a Bible, which I've read."

"Queen, what are you saying?" He is half crushed, half indignant. "These are just things I am saying are important. If you have already done them, fine. But how would I know? How can I ask these things? One cannot ask such things."

Ha! I snort in derision. One cannot request simple information and yet one can dictate religion and career and education! I enjoy the heat and purity of my anger. In Nigeria I could never talk back. Surrounded by an inscrutable culture that revered elders, I wanted ever to be the dutiful Nigerian daughter. I needed him. Here, I realize in a drunken, giddy flash, he needs me.

"Oh!" he mutters to himself as if severely put upon. "I just *said* . . ."

*O*n our last night together he makes good on his threat to discuss my future. He has clearly been prepped by the rest of the family; I know the elders are distressed by my lack of a husband, and I recognize phrases used at the family council before my departure from Nigeria. At that meeting he had been the one to tell them to let me be, that I had not been raised among them and so could not be expected to know their ways. He sits on the edge of the flowered bedspread and rubs the bridge of his nose beneath the thick glasses. He seems to be as nervous as I am. "This is not something that can be discussed on the telephone or in a letter," he begins, "but now that I am in your life, it is something we need to consider."

After our argument the day before, I am determined to say nothing. My plan is simply to wait him out. No matter what he says, he is leaving soon. I start reassembling the five suitcases, wedging in his collection of shoes, the packets of hot chocolate, my gifts for the family. Somehow God hasn't shown up for the task.

He continues, talking more to himself than to me. "A master's degree can be gotten anytime," he says. "It is just better to finish it and be done with it right away." As usual, I have no idea what he means. Is this a concession to my degree in writing? "Now, they have asked me to find out about your plans but I say these are things that cannot be asked." I feel a flash of gratitude. I choose the sturdiest suitcase and pack it full of medications; it had taken my grocery money for the entire month to get his prescriptions filled that morning at the discount drugstore down the street. "Of course," he says, "one needs to be planning for a Ph.D. and a husband." I expected this much. This is standard Nigerian advice for women. "For of what use is a doctorate without marriage?" he asks the bedspread. "Or a marriage without the doctorate?"

He leans over my packing and peers at what I am doing. He exclaims over the watches and calculators and cassette decks for my brothers and sister, the scarves and lingerie for my stepmother, the chocolates for the rest. "Queen," he says, "you've really outdone yourself. You've remembered everyone. You are Christmas."

In the third suitcase I come across several dozen styrofoam cups, numerous packages of paper dinner plates, and the entire

Lincoln, Nebraska, yellow pages. "Oh no," I say, holding up my hands. "This stuff has gotta go!" The telephone book alone weighs five pounds. He refuses, claiming that paper products are hard to come by in Nigeria and the book was a gift. I argue that it's cheaper and better to use real cups and plates and that he can have no possible use for the Lincoln, Nebraska, yellow pages in Nigeria. "That's not the point," he objects. "It was a gift. You don't throw away a gift." I explain that the airline will charge exorbitant fees for excess baggage on both his flight to London and the one to Lagos. "No matter," he declares. "God will provide."

Just like God is packing, I think to myself. He finishes "our talk" about my future with a quote from Ruth in the Bible, forgetting to ask me anything about my plans.

I am able at last to track down the distant Nigerian cousin who lives in a nearby suburb, and as Dad talks to him on the phone, I steal one photocopy of each of his medical records. The cold medical language is unsettling: *The subject is an elderly black male, obviously suffering from dehydration and major weight loss.* Other diagnoses include glaucoma, prostate problems, traveling pacemakers. I slip the papers out of their bound packets and into my journal.

Dad brags into the phone receiver about me. "She found us. She is the one." He then switches to my mother. "Her mother was an Africanist. I was the president of the international students; she was the secretary. They asked me to speak about Africa at a big conference, then later we went into the cafeteria and she was there at the table and was asking all the questions." He snaps his fingers. "Only a first-year student and she was asking about this, and that. 'What about the United

Nations? What about Ambassador so-and so?' She knew more about Africa than most of the African students."

We decide to go out for Chinese for our last dinner together. "I want to take you to a nice Chinese restaurant," Dad keeps insisting. "I really enjoy going out for Chinese food." The Pakistani driver looks more anxious than usual at our request but insists that there is a nice Chinese restaurant en route to the airport. After driving for miles, he drops us off at the Holiday Inn, the last stop before the airport. Once again I feel like kicking myself for choosing the Chicago O'Hare Grand Inn.

The restaurant turns out to be a steak house. The desk clerk at the Holiday Inn has never heard of a nice Chinese restaurant in the area. He suggests Mexican, Indian, pizza, ten different varieties of fast food. Dad shakes his head. The clerk makes some calls and comes up with one name in a nearby town. He writes down the address and calls us a cab.

By now it is dark. The cab drives for miles into increasingly suburban territory. When the meter hits fifteen dollars and all we can see are miles and miles of trees, I tell Dad that we should just give up and turn around. Just then a mini-mall appears at a wide spot in the road. It consists of a laundromat, an empty, fluorescent pizzeria, and a storefront Chinese restaurant.

"A-hah!" Dad cries, pleased. "Here it is. No need to worry." He scrambles out and heads for the empty restaurant.

Great, I think to myself. Plenty of cornstarch and maraschino cherries. As I hand the driver the fare he glances around. He looks pissed to be in the middle of nowhere. "Sorry about this," I apologize, overtipping wildly. He speeds off without a word. I wonder how in the world we'll ever find another cab in this one-horse town.

The restaurant owners are nearly as thrilled to see us as Dad is to see them. After much mutual greeting and exchanging of blessings, we choose a rickety table near the back. From the look of it, the place is to a good Chinese restaurant what the Chicago O'Hare Grand Inn is to a good hotel. I ask Dad what he wants and he tells me to order. "I can't remember what I used to like to eat."

This surprises me. He talks about Chinese food so much that I assumed he was a gourmet who knew exactly what he wanted. "Oh no," he says happily. "I only had Chinese food once before, back in 1979 before we went back to Nigeria!"

The food turns out to be exquisite. After my initial shock, I begin to inhale the mounds of hot chilies, the tender morsels covered in tangy sauce. After a week of tasteless applesauce and mashed potatoes, I am ravenous. Dad eats little, slowly, perhaps memorizing each flavor to carry with him for another seventeen years. When the check comes, he insists on paying, digging into his reserves for the first time. The Chinese owners bow us out the door and call a cab. One arrives immediately and speeds us quickly, efficiently back to the hotel, Dad prattling happily all the way home.

Before we go to bed he shames me by reviewing the family medical history. (So there was no need to steal.) "This is what you need to know," he says, and I scribble in my journal as he narrates: He is allergic to chloroquine, codeine, aspirin (or as he puts it, "all the quines and all the dines"). My brother Emeka is allergic to aspirin, my brother Okey to everything. Everyone in the family is prone to stomach upset (how my mother and grandparents will welcome an explanation for all those years of mysterious childhood stomachaches!). Both he and his brother have cataracts.

In the morning we have the same driver to the airport, the anxious Pakistani Scot in his tie and zipped-up bomber jacket. By now he is used to us. He lifts Dad into the van, this time with the faintest of smiles, and then the five suitcases. When I check again, the smile has given way to mild bemusement.

My flight leaves two hours before his. I take him to the

airline counter and check him in. The airline won't authorize a wheelchair until closer to departure time but they promise an attendant will come get him and his carry-on. I end up paying two hundred dollars in excess baggage fees when I am only able to finagle a waiver for the suitcase of medicine. God once again pulls a no-show. I call Auntie Adanma in London and tell her his arrival time. Though he is impatient to get home and look after the family, she tells me that he should plan to stay some time with her. The workers are on strike in Lagos in response to the military's refusal to give up power. The airport is closed. I give him what cash I have left and set a time to call him in London. I apologize for not seeing him off safely, for leaving him there. "Nonsense!" he says. "I'll be fine." After he thanks me for everything and wishes me safe journey, he grabs my face and kisses my cheek.

I hop the shuttle to my terminal and watch him fade from sight. I think about our conversation on the way to the airport that morning. As we settled into the back of the van, Dad had seemed for the first time almost shy.

"If I had come to Boston," he had asked, "where would I have stayed? In a hotel or in your apartment?"

"In my apartment, of course." Even I knew that Nigerian elders didn't stay in hotels. "There's plenty of room."

"Eh? Is that so?" I described the dimensions of my place. "What of your roommate?" he had asked.

"She's very nice," I'd explained. "She's rarely there, but she took me to the airport to make my flight here."

This evidence of civilization in America had pleased him, as I knew it would. "I will need to remember to ask you her name so that I can greet her," he had declared.

"Sure."

He sighed, shifting his right leg closer to me. "I forgot to ask for the number of this place."

"Here." I had taken the hotel's card out of my wallet and

handed it to him. "You can have this." I grimaced. "But why would you want to remember this place?" I intend to forget this seedy motel, though it has been comforting having him on this side of the globe. It has made the family seem closer, especially during this time of political unrest, when everything I hear about Nigeria is bad. It has made me feel more legitimately Nigerian, more legitimately torn between two worlds, simply more legitimate. And for all that I need him to go home now, for my sanity, for his, I am acutely aware that as soon as he does, once again the Nigerian part of me will be alone on this continent.

Perhaps he understands this. He had frowned. "We must remember," he said. "Ten years from now we can visit this place and remember we spent four days here."

Perhaps in his own way he is just as sentimental as I. He the father, with his new American lion heart. And I, the daughter, my wet face surprising me, the stolen medical records and flattened instant cocoa wrapper pressed between the pages of my journal like scripture.

Same Coin, Different Sides

jonetta rose barras

It began as an ordinary evening. My grandfather arrived home
as sunset turned to dusk. A houseful of women and girls, we
greeted him with the usual fanfare of kisses, questions about
his day, and a search for possible surprises he may have
brought. He surrendered his Lykes Brothers Steamship shirt
quickly, the collar marked by the marriage of dirt and New
Orleans-induced sweat. By day, my grandfather—who I call
Daddy because he plays that role in my life—chauffeured
around steamship executives; by night, he blew his soul into his
alto and soprano saxophones, making memorable Dixieland
jazz. Years before I was born, he formed his own band, and by
my teen years the group had become famous—a movie couldn't
be filmed in the Big Easy without a cameo appearance by his
group. This particular evening, however, Daddy didn't have a
gig; his short, doughboy physique and slicked-back salt-and-
pepper hair were ours for the night. We eagerly anticipated
laughter, a sip of Scotch and milk out of his silver cup when my
grandmother and great-grandmother weren't looking, and lies—
beaucoup lies, which he called stories. I loved the story about

Marie Laveau, the legendary voodoo queen, for whom Daddy said he ran errands, collecting items she needed to cast her spells. Once he saw a man actually shrink, and another time one fell in love with a woman he'd just met. Of course, these were told with the usual exaggerated descriptive elaborations, which I have never been able to match or repeat with quite the same rhythm and intonations.

Our reveries halted abruptly when Daddy opened the door to his closet and discovered that three silk suits, his .38 pistol, and an alto clarinet were missing. (I'm unsure how he knew there were precisely three fewer suits that evening than there had been in the morning, since he had a closet full of them.) "Who took them?" he asked quietly.

We knew, but said nothing. It wasn't the first time my brother—the eldest of my grandfather's four grandchildren— had stolen valuables from the family. My mother knew her son had become a thief, a drug addict, and generally disrespectful, but she stored the dirty secret in her mind's purse. I certainly knew. When I was twelve years old, he stole my $200 trumpet and sold it for $75. I learned this quite by accident: One cool fall morning, I took my ritual walk to the bakery a few blocks from my house (my mother and I had to have doughnuts and hot chocolate or coffee in the morning). The owner, an older Black man of undistinguished looks, casually asked if the next time I came in I could bring the case for the horn "your brother sold me." Startled and ashamed, I ran from the store nearly blinded by the tears streaming down my face.

On this evening, there was no masking my brother's sin, no escape from accountability. When he arrived home, my grandmother was sipping from her usual glass of Imperial whiskey as she sat on the sofa near her mother. Daddy was in his easy chair. My two sisters and I were watching television in our room, but we came out when we heard the screen door close, convinced that what was about to unfold would be infinitely more dramatic than anything on TV.

My brother, even as a teen, towered several inches over my grandfather. No one looking at his golden skin, deep black eyes, and even blacker wavy hair would judge him a rogue. But he manipulated women and was expert at feigning innocence. He shifted into his usual routine, but Daddy wasn't buying. Without warning, Daddy's anger exploded; his fist hit the side of my brother's head, sending his body to the floor. I thought the boy was dead. My oldest sister started to go to his aid but thought better of it. My great-grandmother simply put her face in her hand, a quiet solicitation for divine intervention. My grandmother continued sipping her drink, seemingly unaffected by it all.

After several tense moments, my brother recovered from my grandfather's stinging right hook and pulled himself up off the floor. My grandfather ordered him to retrieve every item, warning him that the clock would be ticking. If he didn't return at a reasonable hour, his bloodthirsty grandfather would be on the streets. In less than two hours—which seemed remarkable to me, since my brother traveled by public transportation—he returned with three silk suits, the .38, and the clarinet. None of them looked the worse for their removal. My brother never stole anything else from the family.

That none of the women in the family intruded in the exchange between my grandfather and brother was born of our understanding that the moment belonged to them. The space in which they communicated, fought, and resolved their conflict was, at that moment, a male zone. I'd witnessed it before—the coded language men use to communicate to each other. Regardless of how many books are written such as *Men Are from Mars, Women Are from Venus*, women still are unable to translate the jargon, the cadence with any real accuracy or fully understand

and appreciate the meaning. It comes through when men talk about their women or quietly expose their fears to each other. The male zone is sometimes impenetrable, but there are also times we women offer no access.

On the day that my granddaddy sent my brother to the floor, there was another factor that restrained my actions, though I hardly understood it then. I had a deep-seated contempt for my brother; only recently have I come to recognize all the variables at work that summer evening. I questioned the male role model my brother presented, though I surely didn't speak in those terms. He was unlike the other men in my family. He wasn't like my Uncle Amos, who nearly worshiped my Aunt Loweska and couldn't strike a dishonest chord if his life depended on it. He was different from my Uncle Cephus, though they were both tall and dashing. The men in my family surrendered their egos to their women, choosing to wrap them in a certain warmth. Sometimes I imagined it was the same love they had bestowed on their mothers. My brother, on the other hand, somehow lost early in life that critical link of respect and love with my mother, and therefore found it difficult to replicate this in any relationship. Women were, for him, objects, vehicles on which his ego could ride to its next stroking. My grandfather—well, he wasn't a saint, but sometimes I could swear I saw a halo around his head. On that night, I unconsciously recorded the comparisons as grandfather and grandson faced off.

*I*n some respects, my brother and my grandfather were different sides of the same coin. Daddy called me "Li'l Rabbit"; my brother called me "the Black Sheep." The two nicknames exposed the nature of their characters and their opposing perspectives on me. Where Daddy, maybe as a feature of age, was tolerant, patient, difficult to ruffle into disagreement, my brother was restless, dissatisfied with everyone, perhaps most with himself. Daddy had the good fortune of being reared in a house with men—his father and older brother; but my brother never consistently had a man around from whom he could learn the inside secrets of malehood, if there are such things. Daddy cherished women, especially my grandmother. His love of my grandmother and his mother-in-law came through in small ways, such as the time he took to be sure my great-grandmother—his mother-in-law—had her favorite foods or a ride to church and the gifts he brought back to my grandmother from the trips he took with his band to England and other parts of Europe. Once he arrived with a huge box and placed it before my grandmother. Excitedly, like a young schoolgirl, she opened it, only to find another box, and another and another. Finally, she reached a small box, which she promptly opened to discover a diamond ring. Daddy had sat quietly by as she opened each box, waiting to see the smile that stretched across her face when she opened that last box and receive the warm, wet kiss on his lips. Those everyday gestures seemed to be worth the near fortune he must have paid for the ring.

The gift box my brother brought to every woman contained lethal levels of abuse. Take, for example, Sandy. A tall, lean, caramel-colored woman, Sandy wasn't pretty but she wasn't unattractive. She was only in her teens when I met her, but already she had two small children—shy and beautiful, although it was clear they were poorly cared for. My brother's Creole heritage was undeniable and won Sandy's recognition. It wasn't her looks that caught his attention but rather Sandy's generosity with her public assistance check. Whenever the first of the month rolled around, my brother was first in line. Within two weeks, Sandy's meager income had been consumed, and my brother disappeared. Sometimes she came searching for him at our apartment, seeking advice from my mother in the process. I often told her to quit him; told her she could do better. Told her that women set the standard in a relationship. But Sandy loved my brother more than she loved herself.

My brother's disrespect for women didn't end at the door to our three-bedroom project apartment. He tossed around abusive language, mostly at me, as if we were playing catch. He thought me too independent and too confident. "You think you're better than everybody," he often complained. The self-confidence I displayed came from the love bestowed by my grandfather. My sisters and I blossomed in his spotlight, and we were often the objects of his affection. We learned, by observing his interaction with my grandmother, the responsibilities of a husband and a father. From this we girls crafted our own make-shift definition of what it means to be a man.

*D*uring the 1995 conference of the National Association of Black Journalists, I attended a national workshop conducted by Max Rodriguez, publisher of *QBR, The Black Book Review*, which focused on journalists who have become book authors. One well-dressed young Black man asked, Why aren't there more books about us—about and by Black men? My mind quickly ran through the names of Black male authors like Darryl Pinckney, Randall Kenan, Richard Perry, Walter Mosley, and Kalamu Ya Salaam. I realized, however, that the young man's question suggested a deeper problem, one of definition. He implied that many of the books he saw didn't reflect the Black male experience as he knew it.

This struggle for definition is at the core of the battle raging in many African-American communities. It spurred my brother's descent from adorable son to thug. Without a father at home and unimpressed by my grandfather's machismo, my brother cobbled together a patchwork definition of manhood out of the ragged miens of the boys he ran with. His confusion presaged a broader disorder in the Black male psyche that can be traced to the aftermath of the civil rights movement of the late 1960s and early '70s, when African-Americans entered into a newly integrated world but left behind some very hard-earned lessons.

While legions of Blacks in this post-civil-rights world found high-paying jobs, fancy houses, and open doors to Ivy League schools and corporate board rooms, a larger number lost their souls. Given a small measure of freedom, many Black boys and men slowly and methodically turned their neighborhoods into armed camps, where it became difficult to discern friend from foe. An endless line of African-American men could be found on an endless number of corners in nearly every Black community. They were not engaged in any cultural ritual beyond passing around bottles, cigarettes, and stories about their sorry condition. Those who had homes were all too often pounding their fists into some woman's face or, even worse, whipping the hell out of some child.

These are not the imagined creations of racists, hoping to perpetuate negative images of African-Americans; these are scenes from life in the neighborhoods of Washington, D.C., New Orleans, Los Angeles, and New York City—places where I have walked. They are reflections of a people struggling to define community, family, womanhood, and manhood, a people attempting to define themselves—separately and collectively—as both different and equal. It is a struggle Black men have lost so far.

The truth of this conclusion may be found in the statistics. In 1991 the homicide rate among African-American males was eight times higher than among white males, according to a 1996 report issued by the Kellogg Foundation, "Repairing the Breach." Kellogg also found that of the more than 7 million Black families in this country, nearly 50 percent are headed by females. Finally, nearly 50 percent of the 1 million persons in America's prisons are African-American males.

"It is little wonder that many African-American males give up in hopelessness. Nor is it little wonder, as African-American males feel themselves abandoned by much of society, that they give into the growing rage they feel," said Bobby Austin, who edited the Kellogg report. "The tragic consequences of this rage are everywhere around us, both within and outside the African-American community."

*T*he Million Man March, sponsored by a coalition of religious and secular organizations, chief among them the Nation of Islam and the African-American Leadership Summit, held on October 16, 1995, in Washington, D.C., was the equivalent of my grandfather's right hook. It became the locus of the start of a genuine self-assessment of Black manhood, including answering the question of what it means to be a man, based on African-American culture, history, and current communal needs. Does it matter if a man wears a bow tie, or any tie; if he wears Afrocentric clothing; if he refers to a woman as "Ms."; if he opens doors; if he stands up on the bus for old ladies and women with children; if he finds a way—however meager—to provide food, clothing, housing, and an education for his family; if he defends his home against violence by those within the community or from outside; if he becomes an active participant in the political system; if his respect for women extends beyond those in his immediate family to females he encounters on the street?

Nation of Islam leader Louis Farrakhan made the point that Black men had to be held accountable for what has transpired in African-American communities around the country. My brother, were he still alive, would have laughed at Farrakhan and the idea that any one person could be held responsible for the actions of others. In the public housing project, he operated by the rule of every man for himself, unless, of course, a person was a part of your crew. Then there was a sense of family and responsibility. Anyone outside the closely woven fabric of the group, however, could simply go to hell.

Interestingly, Daddy and the men in his neighborhood saw themselves as responsible to each other and each other's women. If Daddy wasn't around and the lawn needed cutting or my grandmother needed a ride somewhere, there was a man on Mexico Street she knew she could call, who she knew would respond favorably. Once she wanted to repair a Christmas decoration on the roof. I volunteered to help, but she refused to permit me to climb on the roof. Instead, she sent for Mr. Thompson, a neighbor, who came promptly, climbing the ladder, making the fix, and going back to his television show without even a minor complaint. He knew, as did my grandmother, that my grandfather expected the men in our community to come to his wife's aid when he wasn't around; he was never disappointed. There never was any doubt in my grandmother's mind that she could depend on the men of her community.

Daddy could not believe that men needed a national march to inspire them to accept their responsibilities or to understand who they were. Issues of definition and place for him were solved more than half a century ago. At eighty-seven, it isn't just his body that is old. His values remain secure in what some might call an ancient tradition that evaluated a man not by external features and material trappings but by the substance of his character, his care of his family, and his defense of community.

*G*rowing up in New Orleans, I learned valuable lessons from Daddy and my brother about being a woman, lessons that chaperon my relationship with myself; they still anchor me in a Southern women's tradition, while casting me as an uninhibited explorer of the world. I know that a woman who wears a man's pants too long forgets her own geography, the curve of her hips, the softness of her legs, the lyrical quality of her voice — the seemingly insignificant features that capture her essence, setting her land apart from that of men. I have also come to understand that being feminine doesn't mean being weak or dependent; and while a woman can demand, and should expect, equality, she will never be equal to a man, nor he to her. Thank God.

I also learned that women set the standard for society. They indicate their value-encoded yardstick by what they are willing or not willing to accept from men. If women determine that Pampers are a measure of fatherhood, men will buy or steal the disposable diapers by the boatload, plop them on the table, and consider their job done. If there are no rules involving the care of children or support for the home, then it necessarily falls to the women to lead the household; if "bitch" and "ho" become acceptable terms of endearment, then men will use them, even with women who have not bought into the nomenclature of the street. If women decide that thigh-high, skin-tight dresses and finger-waved hair are presentable attire, men will gravitate toward women who sport that look. Women get just what they ask for—as Sandy did with my brother, as my grandmother did with Daddy.

The abdication of responsibilities by Black men in America is a logical outcome, given the low performance requirements set by African-American women. The fact that my brother continued to steal from us until my grandfather tried to half kill him falls at my mother's feet. Had she consistently demanded more of him and refused to bail him out or offer excuses for his corrupt ways, the harvest would have been less bitter.

I remember as a teenager living in the Florida public housing complex, my brother, in the throes of negative project experiences, coming home with a group of guys. I worried about what was going on, especially when all of them piled into the bathroom. I knew they were using drugs. I couldn't watch as he disgraced our family's home and exposed my young nephews, who were visiting, to this kind of episode. So I knocked on the door, demanding entry. My brother brushed me off, saying he'd be out in a minute. I promised to call the police, if he didn't come out at that moment. Never one to issue idle threats, I dialed the emergency number and reported that my brother and his thuggish friends were shooting drugs in my mother's apartment. "Come quick, please." The police arrived at the front door just as my brother and his crew had exited through the back door. Later that evening, my brother walked up to me, anger seething in his speech and stare, and asked me what kind of sister could I be. "The kind that respects myself and will make sure you do the same," I said, rather arrogantly but without guilt.

Though the animosity my brother projected that day became a thick fog that I couldn't quite escape, he never brought his friends into my mother's house again—not for any reason. Like my mother, women today churn out excuses—societal pressures, racism, unemployment—for the male failures in their midst. These external forces may explain some things, but they excuse nothing.

• • •

I make no excuses for the demons that possessed my brother most of his life. Nor do I unduly exalt Daddy, although he remains as high as any man could ever be on my list. My acceptance of both of their contradictions, foibles, sensitivities, and raw callousness helped me sculpt a truer image of malehood.

Kahlil Gibran in his book *The Prophet* has a passage about friendship: "When you part from your friend, you grieve not; for that which you love most in him may be clearer in his absence, as the mountain to the climber is clearer from the plain."

In my early adult life, I detested my brother and struggled hard to be sure that I did not find myself in the embrace of a man of his kind. As I have grown older, though, I realize that each of us has two selves constantly in battle; the trick is to dance longer with the better self until the other grows disgruntled and leaves. My brother danced too long with his darker self, but the other was there waiting to have his dance card punched. This realization permitted me to love him despite his seemingly innumerable faults. Daddy's right hook may have protected our material possessions, but it didn't save my brother; he died at twenty-seven—an argument over some biblical scripture, was all my mother was told.

Several years ago, Daddy had a stroke, which prevents him from playing his saxophone and clarinet. He still calls me "Rabbit"; my daughter is "Li'l Rabbit Number Two." His mind released long ago memories of that summer evening when he sent his only grandson falling to the floor.

Until the Million Man March, I, too, had placed the episode in the far reaches of my mind, frightened that its exposure would cause too much pain. Instead of angst, the remembrances born of the march have brought great comfort, deeper under-standing, and fuller appreciation of these two men and of other men I have known and continue to know. Equally as important, however, I rediscovered the Southern woman inside of me and began an indefinite, unabashed celebration of her.

Sweet Summer

Bebe Moore Campbell

I was seven years old, sitting on the front steps waiting for my daddy to come and take me to summer.

I can't remember when this waiting for my father began. Was I four or five or even younger? All I know is, it became and end-of-June ritual, an annual event, something I could set my clock by, set my heart on. I don't know whose big idea it was to divide up my life the way they did. Summer, Daddy. Winter, Mommy. Actually, Mommy had me winter, spring, and fall. That was a sensible plan, I suppose, a sensible plan for a little girl, but gradually it began to dawn on me that their division had me lopsided, lopsided and lonely: a girl who sat on the steps in June and waited for her daddy.

It wasn't my ritual alone, of course. I was like a lot of northern Black children making the annual trek down south to the Carolinas, to Georgia, Alabama, or Mississippi. Across Philly in the summer of 1957, hundreds, maybe thousands of Black kids were packed and waiting to be driven to wide open spaces, barefoot living, outhouses, watermelon patches, swimming holes, Grandma. Daddy.

A green Cadillac whizzed by, and my heart gave a quick jump inside my chest. Maybe . . . No. Wasn't him. Wasn't he, I thought, correcting myself mentally as my mother's voice invaded my private thoughts. I turned around and took a quick look at the front door. Coast was clear. I stuck my wet thumb back in my mouth and covered it with my other hand, just in case Nana or Mommy came outside. My mother was paying me ten cents a day not to suck my thumb and I'd already collected my dime. The rhythmic sucking flooded my body with tranquility for a minute until the urge for even greater pleasure made me bold and I took away my "cover" hand, reached up, and started pulling my ear with it. Ahhhhh. I hadn't been sucking and pulling for a good ten seconds when a green Buick slowed down as it approached my house. I jerked my hands away from my face, wiped my dripping thumb on the inside of my shorts and stood up, craning my neck to see if the person driving the car was my daddy. Daagone. The look-alike vehicle slowly turned the corner. Wasn't he ever gonna get here? I sat down, slipping my thumb back into my mouth. My right fingers rubbed my ear vigorously, so that all I could hear was a thin noise going thick-athickathickathicka, as if somebody were playing weird music just for me.

I sucked my thumb, pulled my ear, and grabbed one of my plaits. Nana had combed my hair into three fat braids that morning as she sat on her bed and I sat on the floor, the back of my head between her open thighs. She dipped her fingers into a bright yellow can of Nu Nile hair conditioner. Nu Nile was a gummy grease, a conk in a can. It smelled so good, like peaches cooking. Once when I was little, my cousin Michael told me that it was really candy and I should eat some, and I believed him and swallowed a big glob of it. And he fell on the floor laughing. That sort of turned me against Nu Nile (but not against my beloved Michael). "Nana, please don't put that stuff on me; it's too greasy," I whined, trying to wriggle away, but Nana clamped her thighs shut around my chest and I couldn't move.

"Don't you want your edges and kitchen to look nice?" Nana asked. Nice meant straight and slick. The absence of naps was nice. Nana clipped a white barrette with little combs in it around each plait. I didn't have bangs (I asked Nana to cut me some, but she told me, "Bangs! You want to look like Mamie Eisenhower or something?"), and my high forehead was damp from sweating and a little greasy near my hairline. Nana said Nu Nile made a kitchen behave. Nu Nile mowed down my kitchen.

Bumpety! Bumpety! Bumpety! I bounced my butt from step to step to make the time go faster. When was he coming? When? My heart and all activity stopped at the sight of every dark green car that passed by. I thought about the next day, when I would be in North Carolina, miles and miles away from Mommy. How come, I wondered, sucking and pulling, how come I got to be with my daddy only when school was out? How come, I thought, bouncing from step to step, my thumb in my mouth, my fingers in my ear, Mommy and Daddy and I didn't all live together?

The heat from the brownstone steps warmed my bottom. A trickle of sweat dripped slowly from the top of my neck to the small of my back. I'd been sitting in the sun for two hours, getting browner and sweatier as I waited. Behind me I could hear the ruckus in my house as my mother and Nana prepared for my journey. In the kitchen my grandmother was frying chicken for the long ride south. A cake was baking, and the sweet, doughy odor got tangled with the fragrance of frying chicken, and both wafted through the house all the way to the front door. Nana was singing, "Ain't nobody's business if I do-oooo," while she baked, not fast singing, but a constant, happy tempo that filled her kitchen as much as the smell of food. In the living room Michael was sprawled across the dark green velvet throw pillows that Nana kept on the sofa, pretending he was soooo interested in watching Bugs Bunny running away from some angry cartoon man, but I knew better. Michael's eyes were vacant and he wasn't talking to anybody. He ran his mouth all day long, so I knew something was bothering him. Upstairs my mother was packing. From time to time she would come to the front door to ask me if I wanted to take this doll or that toy or book with me. When I would say yes, she would say, "You do? Really? You think you're going to need this? You don't really need this, do you?"

I held my face in my hands and gulped in the scent of the Jergens lotion I'd soaked myself in earlier that morning. I didn't want to go to North Carolina looking like Queen Ashy Mae. Looking up and down the street, I didn't see a green car in sight. I went inside and climbed the stairs to my mother's bedroom.

"When is my daddy coming?" I hadn't meant to sound whiny, but that's the way it came out.

My mother looked up from the big tan suitcase on her bed, crammed with my socks and underwear and every piece of summer clothing I possessed, and gazed at me, halfway smiling. "In a little while. Are you in such a hurry to leave your mommy all alone?" She sniffed a little, pretending she was crying.

"Uh huh," I said, laughing. I didn't really want to leave her. Why couldn't she come with me? But I knew better than to ask that question. Mommy would only tell me that she had to go to work, and I knew that already.

I watched cartoons with Michael for a little while, but then my thumb-sucking monkey crawled up on my back and I knew Michael would be only too happy to tell my mother if he saw me. So I eased on out the front door, sat down on the steps, and resumed my sucking. I scanned the street. No green cars. Bap! Bap! Bap! I hit the edge of the step with the back of my heel. Where is he! I settled myself on the steps, straightened my bright pink shorts, and tucked in my short-sleeved pink-and-white top. Bending over, I brushed off my new white sneakers. I wanted to look nice for my daddy.

I had sucked all the juice out of my thumb; it was milk-white and wrinkled. I got up, pushed open the front door, and yelled inside. "Can I walk to the corner?"

"Do you mean 'may'?" my mother yelled back.

"May I walk to the corner?"

"Yes, but keep an eye out for your father's car."

It was mid-morning on a Saturday and Sixteenth Street was already crowded and noisy. Several people had opened their windows, and I could smell eggs and frying bacon as I walked down the street. My new sneakers squeaked as I walked. They made me feel tall and bouncy. Across the street, Mrs. Lewis was coming down the steps, a metal shopping cart clattering behind her. A frail woman, she stopped to catch her breath every time she descended one step. She waved wearily to me as I called out my hello.

Mr. Crawford, who owned the house three doors from ours, was doing his usual Saturday sweeping. He was the president of the block club, a tall, angular man with crinkly gray hair. This morning his hair was covered with a stocking cap. He was so intent on making his sidewalk spotless that he didn't look up when I passed until I said, "Hello, Mr. Crawford." Then he seemed startled, as though I'd awakened him from a dream.

"Oh, hello there, uh, uh, uh, Sugar. Where you goin'? Grandmama know you out here?"

"Uh huh. I'm waiting for my daddy to come take me to North Carolina."

"Oh, now that's nice," Mr. Crawford said, pausing from his sweeping to lean on the broom. His face brightened, and the thin outlines of a smile appeared. "North Carolina is my home, too. What part you goin' to?"

"My grandmother lives near Elizabeth City. Do you know where that is?" I asked excitedly. Mr. Crawford's revelation made me feel close to him and much closer to my destination.

"Sure do, baby. That's just down the road from Fayetteville. That's my home." Mr. Crawford was absolutely beaming. "You gone stay a long time?"

I shook my head. "Only till school starts. Then I have to come home."

"Well, that's a long time."

"It's not so long."

"Well, you have a good time. Don't let them mosquitoes eat you up, hear? Mosquitoes is bad down home."

When I got to the corner I turned right around and headed back up the street. Any minute he'd be cruising down 16th Street, looking for me and honking his horn. What if he was outside my house right now, honking away, and I wasn't there and Nana and Mommy didn't hear him? Maybe he would drive away and leave me. A legion of demons suddenly appeared at my back. I ran back to my house as fast as I could, almost bumping into Mr. Crawford, who was bending down over a dustpan. "Have a good time," he called after me. I didn't even turn around, just kept on running.

He wasn't even there. Daagone. I sat down wearily on the top step, panting like a dog, except I kept my tongue inside my mouth. I was just about to suck my thumb when Nana poked her head out of the door and handed me a napkin with a piece of pound cake inside.

"You want soma this?"

"Uh huh."

"What do you say?"

"Thank you, Nana?"

"You're welcome."

I bit into the cake; it was soft and warm. My anxiety dissolved as I concentrated on the sweet lightness in my mouth. The crumbs fell on my blouse and shorts, and I stood up to brush them off. I was flicking off the bits of cake with my fingers when I happened to look in the street. Somebody was parking a green Pontiac right in front of our house. Heat pulsed through my body and pulled at my stomach, almost like a cramp, except I didn't feel any pain, just needles and pinpricks, bingbingbingbing, racing from my middle to my feet, my groin, my heart, and when the trail led to my mouth I let out a little scream. "Daddy!"

I rushed down the front steps, flung open his car door, and nearly threw myself into my father's chest. I felt his strong arms around me, the stubble of his whiskers grazing my forehead. I looked up and there he was. A big red-brown man in a blue short-sleeved shirt and dark pants. He had on a short-brimmed light-colored hat that sort of angled down over his forehead. "Hey, how's Daddy's little girl?" he whispered.

"Fine," I said. Then everything around me got hazy. Who is this man, I thought, wriggling out of his arms into my seat? His face was out of focus, a mystery. I glanced quickly at my father. He had round, clear eyes. He looked at me, coughed, then looked away. "Be . . ." he started, but didn't finish. Who is he? "Da . . ." I started. What should I say? We sat there silently, searching desperately for a road that would lead us back to where we had left off on our last visit.

My father coughed some more, then swallowed. He looked at me carefully, scanning every inch of my body. "Your hair grew," he said finally, holding one of my plaits in his hand. "Lemme see your legs, kiddo."

I knew what he was looking for! I knew! I moved closer to him and held up first the right and then the left leg. I looked at my father's round, smooth face, studied his wide nose (just like mine), his full lips, until they became less and less strange to me.

Yes. I was used to that face. His hands felt warm and comfortable on my legs. Old friends, those hands. He ran his fingers along my thin calves. "Those sores healed up pretty good, huh?" he said, giving my left leg a little pat. "The mosquitoes are bad this year. Have to get you some repellent."

"Mommy packed some."

"Oh."

"Did Lassie have her puppies yet?" Lassie was my grandmother's dog.

"Yup. She had five or six of 'em. Mama gave 'em all away 'cept for one."

"Ooooh, Daddy, can I play with the puppy?"

"Well, sure you . . ." I looked up at my father. His eyes were blinking quickly. He licked his lips rapidly, then he smiled; it was like a nervous twitch.

"Oh, there you are, Bebe." My mother peered into the car window. She looked pretty even with the stiff little smile on her face. She didn't usually smile that way. My mommy and daddy looked as frozen as the dummies in Wanamaker's windows.

"Hello, George. How are you? How was your trip? Can I get you anything?" Her words rushed out in short breaths, as if she'd been running for a train or something.

"Hello, Doris." Daddy's voice was louder when he spoke to my mother. He sounded as if he were trying hard at something, doing chin-ups, maybe. Perhaps he was pretending he was as big and strong as his voice, I thought. I looked at the special hand brakes on his car. Then I looked at my father's lifeless legs. "I'll take a big glass of water," he told her. My mother went back into the house and returned quickly with the water. When she handed my father the glass their hands didn't touch.

Nana and Mommy loaded the trunk of my father's car, the two of them struggling with my big old suitcase, while Michael quietly watched. Nana put the chicken and the cake in a bag on the back seat, along with a pillow and a blanket for when I got sleepy. Michael hung back a little, folding his arms across his chest and not talking at all, until Nana gave him a little push, telling him, "Give Bebe a kiss. She's getting ready to go and you won't see her till September. Go on now. Don't take all day."

Michael kissed me quickly on my cheek. "You gonna write me?" he asked. His voice was soft and strange, and I knew instinctively that he felt left out. I was going off with my daddy and he was staying at home with the women. Michael's daddy never came to take him anywhere. I felt sorry for my abandoned cousin.

"I'll write you some good letters," I promised him. Michael's eyes were still downcast.

Nana and Mommy kissed me good-bye about fifty million times before it was finally the last, truly last kiss.

"Be good," my mother admonished me.

"You drive safely," Nana said to my father. Her voice was like a stern teacher's when she said that.

"I will," he promised her.

"We'll just go holler at Eddie and them right quick, okay, chickadee?" my father said as he rounded the corner, heading for my Uncle Eddie's grocery store. I nodded. Daddy steered with his left hand; his right arm was around my shoulder. I played with his fingers.

My Uncle Eddie's store was full of people, as usual. Nobody paid me much attention at first as I stood silently in the doorway. Then Aunt Marie saw me. "Well, look who's here," she said to Uncle Eddie, who was grinding up some steak for an old man with a thin swatch of hair in the middle of his head and just enough teeth to make me wonder, Was he gonna chew that meat or just suck the juice? With my Uncle Eddie, work always came first. He never stopped what he was doing, just looked up quickly and smiled at me, a fast, lopsided grin, then said to his customer, "My niece. She's a smart one." I showed every tooth in my mouth when Uncle Eddie said that. The man looked at me and started laughing, "Huyahuyahuya." When the man had paid for his hamburger, Uncle Eddie turned his attention to me. "Say, there, BeBe. You on your way down home, huh? See, ole Uncle Eddie knows where you goin'. Don't even hafta tell me."

I giggled. "My daddy said for you to give us two bottles of soda. Grape and cream."

"Soda, huh? He give you some soda money? I ain't in the giveaway business."

I held out a dollar. Uncle Eddie took it and handed me the sodas and some change. "Where's your ole big-head daddy anyway?"

I laughed again, feeling good that Uncle Eddie was teasing me and that I could see his lopsided grin. "He's outside."

When Uncle Eddie went outside I chatted with my aunt for a while and then with my Uncle William, my Aunt Edith's husband, who worked part-time at the store. Presently Uncle Eddie returned. "Your daddy said for you to come on if you want to go see Grandma." He held out his hands. There were bloodstains from the meat on some of his fingers. His hands smelled like fish and raw meat and . . . sweet things. Good ole Uncle Eddie. Now it was my turn to grin. There was a Baby Ruth in one hand and a lemon Tastykake pie in the other. "Which you want?"

"That one," I said, pointing to the candy bar.

Aunt Marie called from behind the counter. "Tell him you want both of them." She was laughing.

Uncle Eddie handed me the candy bar, then he gave me

the pie. "There. Don't ever tell nobody Uncle Eddie didn't give you anything." When Aunt Marie started laughing again, louder this time, I did too.

"Whatcha wanna do this summer?" Daddy asked as I got back in the car.

"Eat crabs!" I said solemnly.

"That's what we gonna do."

Out of the window long stretches of rowhouses went by in a blur until we were no longer in the city. When we reached the highway Daddy opened our windows all the way and the breeze whipped between us so loudly we could barely hear ourselves speak. He drove very fast. I wasn't afraid. I could tell that my daddy liked feeling the power of his car sailing across the highway. I knew he claimed that power, attached himself to it somehow.

My daddy was powerful, too. The summer before, we had been careening down the highway when we swerved a little and started bumping. "Damn!" Daddy said, sucking his teeth hard. He looked at my startled face. Daddy didn't usually cuss around me. " 'Scuse me, baby." He pulled the car to the side of the road and stopped.

It was dark outside. I was scared. "Whatsa matter?"

"Flat tire."

I could hear the crickets as soon as Daddy opened the car door. There was a full moon. Daddy leaned into his wheel, reached behind him and grabbed his chair from the back, and yanked it through the front door. He opened the chair, pulled it close to him, then hopped into the seat without bothering to put the pillow down. He rolled around to the trunk and took out the jack, a spare, and a flashlight.

"You can stay there," he said, when I started to get out. I squealed as the car started jerking up, up, up. It was hard to watch him from where I was sitting, but I could see his thick arms, his muscles flexing in the moonlight. Sweat was dripping behind his ears.

He changed that tire in five minutes. A car slowed down, but he waved it on. That surprised me. When he got back in the car I said, "Daddy, you changed that tire all by yourself."

Daddy said, "Sure. Whatcha think?"

I was halfway grown before I realized it was my father's determination to see himself as strong and capable that had him changing tires in the night. He wanted me to see him that way, too.

We drove for hours, eating chicken wings and thighs, nibbling on the cake and the Baby Ruth and drinking cold sodas as well as the lemonade in the thermos Nana had packed. After a while I took off my shoes and socks and tossed them onto the floor in the back. Daddy unbuttoned his top two shirt buttons, pulled a rag from behind his seat, and began swiping at his damp neck. I read aloud to Daddy from *The Story of Harriet Tubman,* and then we listened to the radio until the station started crackling like dried-up fall leaves. As the day wore on, the June breeze turned silky; it was like a gentle pat across our faces. All the while we drove, Daddy and I had our hands on each other. My daddy's arm rested on my shoulder; I held his wrist. We were on the edge of summer.

It was almost dusk when we reached Route 17. I could smell summer on that road. The lush, heavy oak trees on either side of the one-lane highway grew so thick their branches stretched across the road to each other in an embrace, making a dark, leafy tunnel of the road. "Look, Daddy, the trees are kissing," I said. He laughed. To our far right, beyond the dense leaves and branches, the murky waters of Dismal Swamp lay still and foreboding. Grandma once told me that before the Civil War slaves swam across the swamp to escape north, and I thought of the runaways as the stronger night breeze whistled and rattled against our windows. Maybe their ghosts came out at night, as haunting as the Turtle Lady, the green phantom who lurked in North Philly looking for children to eat. But I didn't see any ghosts, just water. The night air held a chill, and Daddy and I rolled our windows all the way up. The trees loomed alongside us as tall as dark giants. All of a sudden I saw fading daylight again as the kissing trees thinned out. There in the clearing the words "Welcome to North Carolina" and below that, in smaller letters, "The Tar Heel State," blazed out in blue and red. Almost summer. My bladder filled immediately.

"I gotta . . . I have to go to the bathroom."

"Can't you wait? We'll be there in fifteen or twenty minutes."

"I gotta go now, Daddy."

The car slowed, and he pulled over to the side of the road near a deserted picnic table surrounded by a grove of pine trees. "Lookahere. Go duck behind that first tree. And Bebe, uh, uh, you better pull your shorts, I mean your panties, else you're gonna wet yourself." He laughed a little. His eyes crinkled up. From the prickly, thin sound of his laughter I knew he was embarrassed. I went behind a tree, about twenty feet away from the car. I heard Daddy yelling. "Lookahere. Watch where you step. Might be a snake in there." I peed fast. When I got back to the car I could hear a trickling sound. He was emptying his urine duct. "Might as well go too," he said.

The sky turned inky and crickets began to sing their brittle nighttime lullaby. Route 17 went right into Route 58, the heart of South Mills. The town was a collection of a few houses, a post office, and a justice of the peace. My cousin Ruby, Aunt Lela's daughter, and her family lived there. We stopped at her house for a split second, long enough for my plump, pretty cousin to hug me and for Daddy to shoot the breeze with her husband, Snoodlum, and drink a great big glass of water while I raced around the yard in the dark with their two sons, Johnny and Jimmy. Then we had to go, because I was getting antsy. Summer was up the road apiece, waiting for me.

From Ruby's I could have walked to Grandma's blindfolded, the land around me was so familiar. I could have followed the smell of the country night air so weighted with watermelons, roses, and the potent stench from the hog pens. We crossed the bridge running over the canal that bordered South Mills. A sign announced that we had entered Pasquotank County. On either side of us, spread out like an open fan, were fields of corn, soybeans, peanuts, and melons. White and brick frame houses broke up the landscape. Some belonged to white folks, some to colored. We reached Morgan's Corner, and my stomach started quivering. It was where I bought my Baby Ruths and comic books! As my father's car slowed, my eyes scanned the fields of corn and soybeans for the opening to Grandma's. There it was! The car nearly stopped, and we slowly turned into the narrow dirt lane. We jostled and bounced over the muddy ruts, the motor churning and sputtering as the tires attempted to plod through waterlogged ditches, a result of the last rain. Daddy drove slowly and carefully. "Sure don't wanna get stuck up this lane," he muttered. My stomach was churning just as desperately as the wheels on my father's Pontiac. We lurched out of a deep gulley and glided into the front yard. Finally it was summer.

Grandma Mary was sitting on the porch waiting for us, as I knew she would be. She could outwait anybody. She told me having babies gave you patience. Grandma had had twelve children; one baby died at birth. "You have to wait for the pains to start, then wait for them to go, all that waiting with nothing but a rag to bite down on," she said. She stood up when we drove into the yard. "Hey," she called, walking toward us. My father had barely parked before I was scrambling out of the car and

Grandma caught me up in her fat ole arms, hugging and squeezing me. She had a smell, deep in her bosom, like biscuits and flowers and I don't know what all else. That's what washed over me. I turned around to see my daddy pulling his wheelchair out of the back of the car and placing it between his open car door and his seat. He gave a huge lunge and hopped from the driver's seat into the chair. Then he pulled out the pillow he sat on, hoisted up his body, and stuffed the pillow under his behind. He rolled over to the ramp in front of the house, pulled himself up, and went inside, yelling, "Hey," to Mr. Abe, Grandma's second husband, and "Hey there, girl," to Bunnie, my Aunt Susie's teenage daughter; Aunt Susie had died a few years earlier. I heard Mr. Abe answering back. Mr. Abe had been singing, some old gospel song that only he sang and nobody else. I hadn't heard that song in a year, a whole year. As soon as he answered my father, he started up with his song again. I stood on the porch with Grandma, soaking up Mr. Abe's song, trying to hear it not as last year's song, but as a song of this summer. I stood on Grandma's porch and listened hard. Mr. Abe's song was my bridge; if I could cross that bridge I was back home. I started humming.

Our Papa's People

Bessie and Sadie Delany

On February 5, 1858, our Papa, Henry Beard Delany, was born into slavery on a plantation owned by the Mock family in St. Marys, Georgia, on the coast near the Florida border. He was just a little bitty fellow—seven years old—when the Surrender came in 1865. "The Surrender" is the way Papa always referred to the end of the Civil War, when General Robert E. Lee surrendered to the Union at Appomattox Court House.

We used to ask Papa, "What do you remember about being a slave?" Well, like a lot of former slaves he didn't say much about it. Everybody had their own tale of woe, and for most people, things had been so bad they didn't want to think about it, let alone talk about it. You didn't sit and cry in your soup, honey, you just went on.

Well, we persisted, and finally Papa told us of the day his people were freed. He remembered being in the kitchen and wearing a little apron, which little slave boys wore in those days. It had one button at the top, at the back of the neck, and the ends were loose. And when the news of the Surrender came, he said he ran about the house with that apron fluttering behind him, yelling, "Freedom! Freedom! I am free! I am free!"

Of course, being a little child, he did not know what this meant. Back in slavery days, things were bad, but in some ways getting your freedom could be worse! To a small boy, it meant leaving the only home you ever knew.

Now, Papa's family were house niggers, and the Mocks had been very good to them. We remember our Papa saying the Mocks were as good as any people you could find anywhere in this world. That's a generous thing to say about the people who *owned* him, wouldn't you say? But he said that not all white people who owned slaves were evil. There was great variety in the way white people treated Negroes. That's what Papa told us about slavery days, and it's true now, too.

Mrs. Mock thought a heap of Papa's mother, Sarah, who was born on the plantation on the fifth of January, 1814. Why, Mrs. Mock had even let Sarah have a wedding ceremony in the front parlor. It was a double wedding—Sarah's twin sister, Mary, married at the same time. Oh, it was said to be a big affair! Of course, these weren't legal marriages, since it was against the law for slaves to get married. But it was a ceremony, and Sarah was joined in matrimony to Thomas Sterling Delany. This was about 1831. Their first child, Julia, was born on the first of November, 1832. Altogether, Sarah and Thomas had eleven children, and our Papa was the youngest.

Thomas was a handsome man. To what extent he was white, we do not know. We were told he was mostly Negro. The family Bible says he was born in St. Marys, and the date of his birth was the fifteenth of March, 1810.

Sarah was obviously part Indian; she had long, straight black hair but otherwise looked just like a Negro. When we were children we always giggled about her photograph, because her hair looked so peculiar to us. We never knew Papa's parents because they died when we were tiny. Why, Sarah died on the eleventh of September, 1891, just a few days after Bessie was born.

Thomas was part Scottish, which is where the Delany name came from. We have been asked, over the years, if we are any kin to Martin Delany, the Negro army officer during the Civil War. We are quite certain we are not, having discussed it with a historian once. People assume that we are related to him because we spell Delany the same way. A few of our relatives spell our name with an "e," as in "Delaney," which is really an Irish spelling. Others spell it "DeLany" with a capital *L* in the middle. Papa insisted we spell it "Delany." He said, "That's the way my father spelled it, and that's good enough for me."

Now, of course, we haven't any idea what our original African name was. But it doesn't worry us none. We have been Delanys for a long time, and the name belongs to us, as far as we're concerned.

The Mocks let the Delanys keep their name and even broke Georgia law by teaching Papa and his brothers and sisters to read and write. Maybe the Mocks thought the Delanys wouldn't leave, after the Surrender. But they did, and they each didn't have but the shirt on their backs. They crossed the St. Marys River and set down roots in Fernandina Beach, Florida. Papa told us that each day they would wash their only shirt in the river and hang it up to dry, then put it on again after it had dried in the sun.

Those were hard times, after slavery days. Much of the South was scarred by the Civil War and there wasn't much food or supplies among the whites, let alone the Negroes. Most of the slaves, when they were freed, wandered about the countryside like shell-shocked soldiers. Papa said everywhere you went, it seemed you saw Negroes asking, begging for something. He said it was a pitiful sight.

He said those folks didn't know how to be free. It was like if you took the hen away, what do you think would happen to those chicks?

Most of the slaves became sharecroppers, living off the

land owned by whites. The whites fixed it so those Negroes could never get ahead. Wasn't much better than slavery. The whites were able to cheat the Negroes because very few Negroes could read or write or do arithmetic. And even if the Negroes knew they were being cheated, there wasn't a thing they could do about it.

The Delanys were among only a handful of former slaves in those parts who didn't end up begging. Papa was proud of this, beyond words. They survived by eating fish they caught in the river and gathering up wild plants for food. After a while, they built a home, some kind of lean-to or log cabin. They were smart, but they were lucky, and they knew it. They could read and write, and they hadn't been abused, and their family was still together. That's a lot more than most former slaves had going for them.

Papa and his brothers all learned a trade. Following in the shoes of one of his older brothers, Papa became a mason. His brother was known in the South for being able to figure the number of bricks it would take to build a house. People would send him drawings and that fellow could figure out in his head exactly how many bricks it would take! Saved people a lot of trouble and money. Another of Papa's brothers was said to be the first Negro harbor pilot in America, and his older sister, Mary, taught school, mostly at night to poor colored men who worked all day in the field.

The Delanys were Methodists through and through. Papa was already a grown man, in his early twenties, when one day the Reverend Owen Thackara, a white Episcopal priest, said to him, "Young man, you should go to college." The chance to go to college was so fantastic it boggled Papa's mind, and of course he jumped at the chance, even though it meant giving up on being a Methodist. Reverend Thackara helped Papa go to Saint Augustine's School, way north in Raleigh, in the great state of North Carolina.

Well, Papa did not disappoint anyone. In college, he was a shining star among shining stars. He was as smart as he could be, and blessed with a personality that smoothed the waters. He soon met a fellow student named Nanny James Logan, the belle of the campus. She was a pretty gal and very popular, despite the fact that she was smarter than all the boys—and became the class valedictorian.

I'll Call Him Daddy

Marcia L. Dyson

Mama moved to the South Side of Chicago after her second summer visiting there with Aunt Sis, her mother's only sister. The dazzling lights and late night street life lured Mama away from her small hometown of Brazil, Indiana, near Terre Haute. Her round baby face, little pug nose, chubby cheeks, and dancing eyes caught a lot of attention. So did her full hips and big, short beautiful legs hidden by her one decent social dress, that fit her tight in the waist.

She wrote numbers in Aunt Sis's policy business and cooked, cleaned, and ran errands from the big house off Wabash Avenue. It didn't take her long to figure out that her meager earnings from Aunt Sis were "slave wages." She freed herself by taking a job for better money with a big policy lord named Buddy. Mama met Daddy at Buddy's station.

My father was a lady's man, a long, skinny, chocolate-colored man nicknamed "Duke," since he always looked good and was decked out in a new suit every time she saw him. A railroad man by day and a gambler by night, Duke was not one to be committed to relationships. It took three years (and two daughters) for Daddy to marry Mama. I was their third daughter—the baby of "Duke's girls." He left us before I reached my second birthday.

After Daddy's departure, Mama took a job at Brown's Restaurant, where she worked as a short-order cook and waitress six days a week. She left work and came home to tend to us and her chores at the end of her ten-hour shift. She was too busy struggling to worry about how she would manage beyond the immediate moment. Lucky? Blessed? I do not know what to call our good fortune when Matthew Perkins Smith (Doc) came into my Mama's life. He walked into Brown's one day for a hot meal, and he left with Mama's address. Shortly after that he had himself a ready-made family. Doc had never been married, nor had he fathered any kids. He didn't give a second thought to Mama's past marriage, her brood, or that she had ended her education after two years of high school. Or that she was nine years older than he was.

After serving several years in the armed forces, Doc had moved from Maysville, Kentucky, to Chicago to attend the Illinois College of Podiatry. He worked full-time at the Chicago post office to put himself through school. He was tall, brown, and handsome. His thick, coarse hair formed waves that flowed back off his face. His bushy eyebrows graced deep-set, dark eyes that danced. A heavy mustache framed a voluptuous mouth that generated gentle smiles and boisterous laughter. He looked frail next to Mama, with her thick, short body.

Doc's mother had died giving birth to him. Heartbroken, his father died two weeks later from a heart attack at the age of forty-two, so Doc was adopted by his father's sister, Jane Smith (Aunt Jane) and her lifelong best friend, Mary Holmes (Mama Mary). Both women were educators and had attended school together, from the elementary level to Kentucky State College. The state of Kentucky prohibited Aunt Jane from adopting because she was single, but Mama Mary was married and was able to gain legal custody of Doc. The two women raised him together. He got his gentleness, kindness, discipline, spirit of co-operation, and love from these loving women. As the gospel song says, "If you've been blessed, it feels like heaven. If you're blessed, pass it on."

I have been blessed by having Doc in my life. Daddy had placed his daughters on the margin of his world, but we were the center of Doc's existence. Duke dropped by now and then for a visit but, as Mama said, he was there to show off how well he was doing and brag about what some new woman was doing for him. Doc was the one that provided us with the staples of life and many pleasurable memories.

"Can we go to the parade?" I would ask Doc. Mama would pack us a big lunch, and the entire family would walk to the Bud Billiken Parade. On the first Saturday of each August, the Bud Billiken Parade kicked off, sponsored by the *Chicago Defender* newspaper (an African-American-owned daily). It was created to celebrate the lives and futures of Black children. It was, and still is, the largest African-American parade in America. Smoke from barbecue pits that started heating up early in the morning lined the parade route and stung my eyes as we walked and looked at the vendors' goods. I loved to eat, and my short, porky body was proof.

"Don't buy her all that junk," Mama warned Doc.

"What do you want, baby?" Doc would ask me, ignoring Mama's dictate. Smiling, I pointed to the candy apple, cotton candy, and snowball vendors' carts.

The loud music from the bands accompanied the baton twirlers, who periodically stopped in front of the screaming crowds. They waved the batons like magic wands and threw them high, high into the air. Everyone held their breath until the batons landed in the twirlers' hands. Without missing a beat, they continued along the parade route, dancing and twirling the batons to the pulsating beat of the drums.

"Do it, baby." "Yeah, let it all shake." These and similar quips were directed at the teenage girls.

"I could do that," I muttered enviously and in awe.

"You sure can, baby," Doc would answer, with me hanging on his shoulder to see over the crowd. "You can do anything you want to."

As we continued to walk, I started switching to the distant drum beats. The pleats of my white short skirt, with attached bloomers, swayed to the movement of my hips. I held on tightly to Doc's hand with my sticky left fingers. We would get home very late. I would obediently go to bed and have the most wonderful dreams. The dreams were a welcome retreat.

After my Daddy's departure, I had become a bed-wetter and often had nightmares when Daddy would come visit us, usually getting into bitter brawls with Mama. Yet Mama had to be the disciplinarian in our house. Doc just did not have the heart to spank me or my siblings.

"Matthew, Marcia just got you wrapped around her little finger," Mama would protest. He never denied it. I was an angel that could do no wrong in Doc's eyes.

"Oh, Marcia didn't do that." "Marcia could not have done that." "That's my little baby." Only once did he even try to chastise me.

I had repeatedly gotten out of bed, saying I had to pee. To get to the bathroom, I had to go through the living room, where the television was. I kept hanging back in the room until he told me to go back to bed.

"I got to pee again," I said in response to the irritated look on his face. By the fourth trip to the toilet, my bathroom story had worn on Doc's nerves.

"Who do you think you're fooling?" he demanded.

"I do have to pee," I lied.

He knew I was lying. I was trying to watch TV. Doc jumped up off the couch on the fifth trip and asked Mama for her strap. He grabbed me with one hand and the belt with the other. I wiggled in surprise, and giggled at the same time, when I saw Doc's fruitless attempt at spanking me only land two harmless blows. The third hit caught Doc on the arm. "Damn!" he muttered as the strap dropped to the floor. He retreated into the bathroom to moan.

"Get your little butt in the bed," Mama demanded. I shrank toward the door but not fast enough for her. "Girl, if you don't get in that bed and stay in it, I'll beat you into an amazing grace and give you a new opportunity for salvation." When Mama got religious with her threats I knew I was an arm's reach from a whipping. I ran.

"Are there big hills in Kentucky?" I asked Doc one day.

"Big ones and little ones, but plenty of both," he answered.

The only person I could relate to Kentucky was, of course, Daniel Boone. I never imagined life for Black folk outside my community. Brazil, Mama's hometown, was mostly white. All my questions gave Doc an idea one day.

"You are going to Maysville!" Doc proclaimed one morning just before school was out. I was eight years old. We were all excited about riding the train and going someplace new. Doc had made Maysville sound exciting and adventurous.

"Watch after my girls," Doc asked the Black train porter, as he pressed a tip into his palm. Mama gave my older sister,

Geraldine, charge over us and handed her the wax-paper-lined shoeboxes that held our fried chicken and pound cake lunches.

As it turned out, Maysville might have been Mayberry. The folk were dull, and there was nothing to do for Black folks. The only activities were watching fireflies at night and finding creative ways to dispose of Aunt Jane's green beans.

"Don't she cook anything else?" I lamented to Doc when he called to see how we were doing.

"That's the only vegetable she fixed for me," he responded. I could hear the smile in his voice over the phone. The only pleasure I got from the trip was from looking at photos of Doc as a child. I laughed at the photos of him as a baby in a dressing gown and as a young boy in bloomers and was awed by the handsome photos of him in high school and the photos he sent to Aunt Jane while he was in the service. There were not enough photos to entertain us, though, and we could not wait to go home.

"Do we have to visit again?" I asked Doc as I got off the train.

"Not if you don't want to," he said, a little disappointed that I was not pleased with my vacation. Aunt Jane and Mama Mary came to visit us instead. Besides, they wanted to see Doc, who was too busy working and attending podiatry school to visit them.

I didn't know podiatry from psychiatry, so whatever Doc was learning at his school didn't matter to me until the day he came home and replaced our cheap shoes with the ugliest brogans I had ever seen in my life. To my ten-year-old eyes they were like combat boots.

"Those are boy's shoes. I'm not wearing those things," I told Doc as he struggled to get the shoes on my feet.

"Oh, shoot!" I lamented as he finally managed to tie the laces.

"Watch your mouth, Marcia," Mama snapped.

"They weigh a hundred pounds," I whined. "I can't walk in these." My complaints were useless.

"You don't appreciate these now, but later on you will," Doc tried to explain. "You won't have to suffer from corns, hammertoes, calluses, or bunions," he informed us. I couldn't have cared less. All I knew was that they were ugly and the kiss of death even for my limited fashion sense. I did not appreciate the foot-care lesson. When I was successful at wearing them out, Doc would come home with another pair.

Doc did more than protect my feet. He didn't take lightly to Daddy's cavalier attitude about providing for his daughters, but he never argued with Duke. Doc was very civil to him when he did come around and was always gentle with us; slow to anger as the biblical saying goes.

This was not the case, however, when I came home from school one day, horrified after a young man had tried to force me into the alley near our building. I was twelve and had begun losing my baby fat. "Come with me or I will sic my dog on you," the man had told me, while holding tightly on to the leash of a fierce-looking Doberman pinscher. There were two things that my older sisters had taught me: how to fight and how to run. I ran like a bat out of hell into our apartment foyer and up the three flights of stairs, yelling and screaming. Mama and Doc had warned us about cussing, but every profane word I ever heard, and whispered out of Mama's hearing, came rolling off my tongue with amateurish fervor. "Oh, my damn, my hell, my shit!" I shouted while sobbing and calling for Doc and Mama. Mama flung open the door.

"The man . . . and the big mean dog . . . Oh, my damn . . . ! . . . Oh, Mama . . . out there . . . in the alley . . ." I tried to catch my breath to tell her what had happened. Doc overheard my frightened speech as I talked to Mama. He was still in his pajamas from working the night shift, but he jumped out of the bed.

"Where is the nigger?" Doc roared as he dressed hastily. Before I could retell my story, Doc ran past me and was down the stairs, but the man and his dog had disappeared. Doc could not bear the thought of any man touching his girls. Not only did Daddy not care enough to ask about any such problem, I didn't care enough to tell him.

*L*ike most Black families, our financial situation was bleak. Daddy was doing well, however. "Living high off the hog," is how Mama described Daddy's good fortune, which he did not pass on to his daughters. He never gave Mama any money to support us. The burden rested solely on Doc's shoulders and, thank God, Doc's shoulders were broad. While Daddy was living lavishly, Doc was struggling with his newly opened podiatry office. I was twelve years old when the practice opened. Doc bought the podiatry equipment at a used medical supply store. Mama put white semi-sheer curtains at the window that read: DR. MATTHEW P. SMITH — PODIATRIST. The phone number, HU 7–2739, was painted in gold and black.

Doc's patients were mostly old people. One woman, Mrs. Riffie, came faithfully every month. She loved to have her feet soaked in the hydra-pool and get her corns and bunions treated. She took a liking to Doc and Mama and all of us girls. When Mrs. Riffie's husband died, she gave Doc his car.

"You need something to get those children around in," she kindly told Doc. Her husband's grayish blue coupe was as old as dirt. It wasn't flashy like Daddy's 1963 champagne-colored Lincoln Continental with leather interior, but we had a car! The fact that Doc had never owned an automobile and that neither he nor Mama knew how to drive was the next problem. Mama urged Doc to get driving lessons. Reverend Lomax, who had worked with Doc at the post office, volunteered to teach him.

"Get out of the way," Doc hollered out of the car's window. He started the car and took off the handbrake. He cautiously drove down Seventy-second Street while my sisters and our friends and I followed along next to him on foot. We all laughed as he jerked down the street. We could hear the cussing under his breath as he neared the corner and stuck his left arm out to signal a turn.

"Go on now," he warned us again. He kept driving like he was in a funeral, so slowly that we could actually walk alongside the automobile faster than he drove. We made Doc so nervous that he almost drove onto the sidewalk.

"Damn!" he muttered as he miraculously managed to get the jalopy around the block and back in front of our apartment. Wiping the sweat from his brow, as did Reverend Lomax, Doc promised never to set foot inside the car again. He gave the car to my oldest brother, Jimmy. I was disappointed that Doc didn't keep the car, but I had to admit to Mama that I would have been too scared to ride with him anyway.

I scarcely remember Daddy in my life during my teenage years. I do not remember him giving me birthday or graduation gifts. I cannot recall him phoning me and asking me what I would like for Christmas.

Doc and Mama struggled to make our Christmases joyful. One Christmas, Doc spent $89 (a fortune on his income) on a surprise gift for us. On Christmas Eve, he became sick with the flu. My sisters and I took turns feeding and taking care of him after Mama left for work, still wondering what the surprise gift was. Despite a fever, Doc got out of bed on Christmas Eve, while we were asleep, to put it together. When we awoke and saw a bright red Flyer wagon under the tree, we didn't show much excitement or gratitude for the gift. Without a car, though, we needed something to haul food from the store and bring the laundry upstairs. This was the practical Doc, giving a gift that worked, literally.

"Oh, something to carry groceries in," we chimed unappreciatively, trying to sound happy.

The wagon lasted for years. It carried the groceries, the clothes to and from the Laundromat, and on some occasions, siblings and friends. It carried the discarded pop bottles we collected to redeem for two cents each.

*B*y the time I entered the eighth grade, Doc's podiatry practice was growing. He was able to move us to Chatham, a stable middle-class Black community that had prospering Black businesses. We unpacked our belongings in the third floor apartment at 8223 South Langley Avenue. The apartment was bigger than any place we had ever lived before. Doc replaced the red wagon with a light-weight shopping cart.

Being middle-class was new to me, and I was faking it well. I wore one of my sister's graduation dresses to my eighth-grade graduation. I had learned to be as careful with the pennies as Mama was and didn't want to waste any of Doc's hard-earned money. When I did ask for money to buy something special, I was never denied. I worked part-time throughout high school and paid for most of my clothes and other needs out of my own meager paycheck. I wanted Mama and Doc to have time and money for some pleasure in their lives.

When Doc joined the Illinois Podiatry Association, he and Mama began to enjoy a real social life. Once a year, Mama would make special matching outfits for her and Doc to wear to the holiday parties. As I snapped photos of them with my Instamatic camera, Doc released his humor. "Come here, baby," he once told Mama as he grabbed her by the waist and guided her in fancy footwork to the imaginary music in his head.

Despite Doc's wish for "his" girls to achieve great academic heights, only Beverly (the oldest of Duke's girls) and I managed to finish high school. Elaine's education was interrupted by teenage pregnancy and an early marriage. Doc's heart was crushed. He did everything possible to keep me from taking the same path.

Beverly graduated from high school at the age of sixteen. She was very bright, and Doc had hoped she would attend college. She postponed college for a year to save money by working at the post office.

"Rose, keep an eye on Marcia, now," Doc told Mama.

Doc kept his eyes on me, like a hawk watching its prey. I saw the deep disappointment over Elaine etched in his face. I was not going to repeat her history. I started a "Virgins Forever" club. The club had two members—my girlfriend, Corliss Arnold, and me. We both studied hard and became honor roll students. Doc was proud and watchful.

When I started dating, Doc was in a frenzy. Once, I had left a note telling him that I was going to catechism class after school and work. He didn't have any objections to my becoming a Catholic, as long as chastity was taught. Doc got home but didn't see the note. My boyfriend, Kirk, drove me home from the class because it was late and he didn't want me to take the bus. As he parked the car, Doc ran out of the house and snatched Kirk out of the car.

"Where have you been?" Doc snarled at Kirk. He proceeded to badger him. I ran in the house to retrieve the note and gave it to Doc. He read it between mean glances at Kirk. Embarrassed, he went back into the house, but he didn't apologize to Kirk. He did apologize to me.

"You have to watch that boy," Doc warned me. "He has those funny-looking eyes," referring to Kirk's beautiful hazel-brown eyes.

I forgave Doc for his rash behavior. Doc's anxiety over Kirk was replaced by his new concern about my changing attitudes toward society. I had exchanged Western ideologies and religious beliefs for the "revolution." Mama and Doc, who are very conservative, nearly had heart attacks when I declared that I was becoming a Black Muslim. I would sneak out of the house in miniskirts, with a long dress or skirt hidden in a brown paper bag. I would change clothes in a restaurant near the mosque, for fear of running into Mama on the street or Doc on the bus. The honorable Elijah Muhammad and his wife, Sister Clara, had invited me to live with them after I told them my parents did not want me to attend the mosque. They knew my parents were against their teachings, and I had become very close to the entire Muhammad family.

Mama and Doc employed Kirk to "talk some sense into my head." They were both extremely relieved when I finally left the Nation—until I got my next brilliant idea. I talked Kirk into becoming a radical nationalist, and we both joined the Black revolution movement.

Kirk and I followed his brother, Jimmy, and other close friends in joining the Topographical Center, a nationalist-based center that stressed self-empowerment, self-protection, and anti-government campaigns. We also decided to follow Jimmy's lead and get married—without the sanction of a racist government or church.

"What do you mean the legal system is nothing?" Doc asked. "What does 'the man' have to do with you getting a license?"

"You and Mama should come down and hear Brother Cl speak. He could explain," I stammered, referring to the leader of a Black revolution group I had joined.

"Who is this Cl character putting this s—t in you head?" he blasted. "What does the f——g Topographical Center have to do with you getting married so young anyway?" Doc continued, with his hands on top of his head, to relieve a throbbing headache.

"We, we . . . I mean, the organization makes its rules," I responded.

My answers didn't satisfy Doc. I tried telling him to open his mind to the oppressive state our people were in, explaining how the rules of the land did not apply to us. I also told Mama that the message I was trying to teach was deep.

"Deep? Girl, you're full of crap," she told me. She just didn't understand what was going on in the world.

I tried to reason with her and Doc. He felt that my agreeing to become Kirk's common-law wife made me common. I might as well have placed Doc in front of a firing squad and given the command to shoot myself. Mama eventually calmed down, perhaps because she recognized the look of "no return" in my gaze. Doc did not speak to me. I could not reach him.

On the day of our ceremony, every time the doorbell rang at Kirk's mother's house, where we held the marriage reception, I perked up. "Is it Doc?" I would ask Elaine. He never came. A few weeks later, when I went to visit him, he cried when I told him about the pain of his absence at the marriage reception. He held me tight. "I just didn't want it this way for you," he told me. I could hear him holding back the tears in his voice. He was relieved when Kirk and I got legally married the next year, after the birth of my son, Mwata.

Through the years, Doc had never said one bad thing about Daddy to us. Not even through his last years, when he was suffering with Alzheimer's and needed to be taken in by

Mama and Doc for a while. In 1992, Daddy was recovering from a heart attack, caught pneumonia, and died on a cold, wintry January day. Doc and Mama were the ones who paid for the funeral. As the eulogy was read and the faint praises were spoken, I wept, remembering the many tears Daddy had caused me. Every disappointment from him flashed through my mind, like scenes from a horror show. I wanted to forgive him for his absence, but I couldn't. I could only reflect on Doc's constant presence in my life. Instead of the sorrow I should have felt for Daddy's loss, the gratitude for Doc swelled within me. With a tear-stained face, I turned and stretched my hands to Doc, who was sitting behind me, comforting me with a gentle massage on my bowed neck. I spoke to him in a low voice, words of appreciation for his many years of being such a wonderful father to me. I motioned to him to come close and called him what I was never able to call him before—*Daddy.*

The Hottest Water in Chicago

Gayle Pemberton

My father died sometime during the wee morning hours of November 12, 1977. He had retired just a few months before and had been ill for longer than that, although none of us really admitted it. He was a "race man"—that is, for almost all of his adult life he worked for an organization that promotes racial equality. Because of the nature of his life, and because he was my father, I had always wanted him to write his memoirs. The whole family thought it a good idea and an exciting project for his retirement. It was agreed, just between my father and me, that I would help him write them.

In the early evening of November 12, 1977, I found three sheets of yellow legal paper on top of the television, sandwiched between a couple of *Good Housekeeping* and *Ebony* magazines. In my father's patented scrawl were the beginnings of his story. It went something like this:

> When I was ten years old I had a job cleaning shit off the boots of Black stockyard workers in Clarinda, Iowa. There were three kinds of shit on them: sheep shit, horse shit, and chicken

shit. Sheep shit is the worst of all and was nearly impossible to get off.

I haven't researched it myself, but I believe my father, and since reading those pages I have avoided sheep shit like the plague.

He hadn't had a chance to retire. He went from work to the throes of death. He hadn't had a chance to write more than those three pages. I will always wonder whether my reading of his work is correct: that for him, at least, talking about real shit was an appropriate beginning to the story of a life that was steeped in all kinds of it, both real and figurative, and a lot messier than the sheep variety. I will always wonder, too, because I never heard him say the word *shit*.

I cannot help him tell his story. I cannot tell it on my own, either. But I can ghost a tiny part of it now, even though I know of it in only the barest of ways. This part of the story meant a lot to him, and I think my father would okay my version of it, for we had planned to name the entire book after this episode from his working days. It's called "The Hottest Water in Chicago," and, naturally, it is for my father.

The setting is Chicago, of course, in the very early 1950s. Bigger Thomas has been dead for more than ten years; we listen to "Helen Trent" on the radio; we watch "Gang Busters" and "Boston Blackie" on our twelve-inch television—and the fights on Friday night, when my father lifts his portly frame out of his armchair, drops to his knees, and shadowboxes with the flickering images on the screen. We live in a housing project on the South Side, a very nice one as projects go. And when I saw it last, only a few years ago, I thought it had aged very well, weathering generations of youngish Black people clinging to the edge of the middle class, the bricks and glass and sidewalks still in place. We lived in Chicago only until I left the first grade. My sister, who later taught in its schools for a number of years, always said it was a good idea we left when we did; otherwise neither of us would have been able to read much now, and I certainly would not be able to write this.

I remember being at home with my mother, watching her iron one oxford-cloth shirt after another. She would pull each one out of the refrigerator, already sprinkled and damp from being inside a large plastic bag that had the hint of an odor of mildew. It took about twenty minutes per shirt, and her work was impeccable. Then she would fold them, professional laundry style, and pile them on the dining-room table, atop a sheet of newspaper. My father always needed two shirts per day: one for the day's work and a fresh one to wear at night to the interminable community meetings that kept him, throughout his career, away more often than home.

I would do my best to help, which sometimes meant concentrating on a drawing while I sat at a little table in the corner. At other times it meant playing laundry messenger by dropping the shirts onto the kitchen floor. One day—Mother ironing, of course—we were watching "The Bickersons" on TV, with Frances Langford and Don Ameche. At the commercial break, the show went off the air, never to return. Both my mother and I, separately, through the years, have sought corroboration for this major event, and we both have failed.

All in all, I don't recall much about my home life then, probably because things went smoothly. We ate regularly; I got Easter clothes and usually what I'd asked for from Santa. My sister, who is five years older than I am, terrorized me whenever a siren went off, with stories of the earth blowing up. And she tried her best to lose me when my mother would say to her, "Take your sister with you." No, nothing really remarkable. It took several years for me to learn that often my father had no more than a nickel in his pocket, that his paychecks were regularly late, and that my mother all too often had to fend off offensive phone calls from nasty, ill-mannered credit managers.

Most of my recollections of Chicago in those days are images from outside my home, and they are always painted gray. It's a scientific fact, you know, that Chicago is the grayest city on earth. It makes the gray of New York, or San Francisco, or Pittsburgh, or London, or Paris, or Moscow seem positively blue. Another reason I think of gray and Chicago probably has to do with the fact that I was much smaller then, closer to the pavement and the high curbs that seemed like mountains as I approached them. My father, taking my hand, would say, "Jump up!" and I still have a few tiny scars on my knees from those moments when my timing was bad.

The grayness had a sound track too: of sirens, for it seemed as if the whole city was in a perpetual state of burning, a habit formed in 1879. Of the El: we drove across Sixty-third Street on gray Sundays after church, turning onto it from South Parkway, now Martin Luther King, Jr. Drive, and there the El was a noisy, black, frightening umbrella, resembling a Mondrian painting gone out of control. Of streetcars: on State Street they were ready, I was sure, to jump the track as they careened through intersections, on either the left or right set of wheels, with their bells not sonorous but muffled, doing a frenzied *∂ink-∂ink-∂ink-∂ink-∂ink-∂ink-∂ink-∂ink-∂ink.*

There was no Dan Ryan Expressway cutting a tornadic swath through the city. The Loop was a full hour's ride away by streetcar and bus—Mother didn't like the El either—and I remember going there only when someone was coming to town or leaving. My mother, sister, and I would go to California in the summers to visit Nana and Papa, my mother's parents. We'd leave from Dearborn Station if we were riding the Santa Fe, or Union Station if we were taking the Southern Pacific or the Union Pacific. We'd pick up Grandma, my father's mother, from the Illinois Central Station because she came in on the New York Central or the Pennsylvania line from Ohio. I even remember going to the Rock Island Station for friends and relatives from Minnesota who came through Chicago, always on their way to somewhere else. The only other times I went to the Loop were when I was ill, which was often enough. Then, we had to take the El.

Chicago stank. The stockyards sent their bloody odors wafting through the summer evening air. The city dump blew the same smell, at least once a week, I swear, as that of a can of tomato juice that has been sitting in a refrigerator for five days. And there was another smell, one that persists today, after the dump and the stockyards have gone: of burnt potatoes. I have yet to discover its source.

I have other memories of Chicago, too: of being out at 1 A.M. with my sister the night Martin Luther King, Jr., was assassinated, and Chicago was burning, riding around in Scotty, her green VW, and seeing National Guard troops riding in jeeps with real live guns mounted on them; and of driving to Midway Airport, on the wrong street, as it were, and passing a building with a huge, white swastika painted on its side; of seeing Sixty-third Street as it looked the last time I saw it, with the street, the buildings, and the El in tatters. Dresden in 1945 looked better.

But those more recent memories are not important for this story. I mention them only to suggest that time passes very slowly and there is much in Chicago that never, ever changes. It is still gray; it still stinks; and it is still largely racially segregated.

*B*ut one morning in 1954, the owner of a hotel on Michigan Avenue, just south of the Loop, decided to make a change. The following is my scenario and, at this stage of the story, probably as likely as my father's since he never discovered any intentionality behind the act.

The Supreme Court has just ruled in favor of *Brown,* and this gets our hotel owner—let's call him Sam—to thinking: "Ya know, if they're gonna integrate the schools, I think I'll integrate my hotel. I've been turnin' away these boys, some of them in uniform from Korea, but it don't seem right to keep doin' it. I think I'll integrate this hotel."

It's Tuesday. My sister has chased me down the stairs once again. Mother is yelling at us to stop and to hurry because we're all running late. Daddy is up, drinking his seventh cup of coffee. He hasn't put on his tie yet, and he has the paper napkin folded around the collar of his oxford-cloth, button-down shirt, to keep the egg yolk from ruining one of Mother's masterpieces. I sit down and start consuming milk in large quantities. No one says anything memorable.

Soon Daddy says, "Gotta go."

I say, "Can I come?"

He says, "No. Gotta see a man about a dog." Which is what he always would say to my entreaty. And since I never could go, I at least wanted the dog—but we couldn't get one of them either.

He slips away from the table, grabs his tie, puts it on, puts on his suit jacket, pats my mother on her rear, which causes her to jump and extend his name to eight syllables. He gets in the blue-painted-over-maroon Mercury four-door, and goes to his office, some forty blocks north.

My mother starts a day of ironing.

My sister goes to school.

I plan to help Mother until kindergarten begins; I am on the afternoon shift.

It is a clear, gray day, a little chillier than usual for May 18. A steady breeze is blowing from the east, off the lake, as my father makes his way up Michigan Avenue. He swears at a few drivers, thinks about having to paint the interior walls now that I've been broken of my short-lived wall-drawing habit. He wonders if he'll get paid Friday.

There isn't much on his schedule today. Until eleven he's interviewing job applicants. One of the many things my father's organization does to further the quest for racial equality is to act as a broker for firms willing to hire Blacks. Applicants see my father, fill out forms, usually get some comments from him about the importance of promptness, shined shoes, and pressed pants, and then the white firm is contacted. This aspect of the business, I suspect, was not land office, but it kept my father fairly busy.

At 2 P.M. his superior, the director, summons him because a call has just come in from a man named Sam Somebody who owns a hotel on Michigan Avenue and who says he wants someone from my father's office to come down and spend the night. It seems the man wants to integrate his hotel. My father is delegated.

Small town Iowa in the teens and early twenties, as I understood it from my father, was a little different from other places. "It was broader in its thinking," he would say. Which meant that, as a young boy, my father met with very little discrimination. He went to grade school and junior high school with all the rest of the children in town. He visited their homes, played baseball, fought, cursed, and learned to spit with them. He shined shoes and became an expert on what could be found on their undersoles. He graduated from high school in Sioux City and then moved to Minnesota to work and to attend the university there.

Minnesota, in the twenties and thirties, was a little differ-

ent from other places, too. Although the Black community
there—as everywhere—was kept and did keep to itself, the
larger community was "broader in its thinking," he would say,
so attending the university was not primarily a matter of breaking down barriers. And employment could be found in some of
the farm-support industries in the Twin Cities.

There were, doubtless, many things my father chose not to
discuss with his children, or perhaps with anyone. I asked him
why we moved so often—four times before I was ten years
old—but I never thought to ask him why he hated funerals or
what kinds of discrimination he'd faced. He was never in the
military; his first visit below the Mason-Dixon line was in 1972.
I suspect there are a fair number of Black people from my father's generation who will say that Minnesota was devoid of
much unpleasantness. But whatever my father faced in Iowa,
Minnesota, or anywhere else, I'll never know. I do know that his
grandmother, Carrie Roberts, kept a scrapbook with all the
newspaper clippings she could find that had any reference to
"colored." Most of them detailed lynchings.

Now, at 3:30 P.M., my father calls my mother, making sure
there will be another shirt ready. He tells her he needs an early
dinner and a change of underwear because he is going downtown to integrate a hotel.

My mother says, "What?"

My father says, "I'm going to integrate a hotel."

My mother says, "What?"

My father asks if she is hard of hearing.

My mother says it sounds pretty stupid to her.

At 7:30 P.M. my father drives up to the address on Michigan Avenue. He looks at the facade of the building: five stories
high, about 150 feet wide. Hanging from the third floor level is a
large neon sign with the word HOTEL flashing on and off. The
sign is half a chevron, with smaller lighted printing below the

horizontal HOTEL. It says, ROOMS TO RENT PER DAY: NO HOURLY RATES. A Budweiser beer sign is in the window.

He gets out of his car and walks toward the door, shaking his head slightly, biting his lower lip. Once inside, he notices a dull light shining down from a filthy chandelier coated with the remains of hundreds of insects. To his left is a single walnut counter, the baseboard of which is splintered from too many feet scraping its edge over too many years. From behind the counter a man turns to meet my father, quickly turns away, and then walks toward a tiny office in a corner. He says nothing to my father.

My father waits at the counter, leans against it, pulls out a cigarette, and notices a faint aroma of Raid. At the sixth puff of his cigarette another man appears from behind the counter. He walks around it and out to my father, extends his hand, and announces himself as Sam, the owner of the hotel.

"Are you Mr. Pemberton, from the Urban League?" he asks my father.

"Yes."

"Well, good. You're going to integrate my hotel. Please follow me."

My father said the man was about five feet six inches tall, of a slight frame. He had short, black, very straight hair that was slicked down with a heavy, perfumy pomade. He wore shiny black shoes whose heels were run over on the outsides. And he was dressed in a blue serge suit that had recently been ironed, perhaps for the fifth or sixth time since its last cleaning. There were several spots along the sleeves and a large stain on the lapel.

"Let me show you the rooms," Sam says to my father.

They walk to a single door that opens onto a gated elevator. Smells of urine and alcohol permeate the small space. My father sighs.

Sam takes my father to the third floor. As they get out of the elevator, they are met by a single, dull EXIT sign, pointing to a stairwell to the left. There are three equally spaced, bare lightbulbs hanging from the ceiling. On either side of the long corridor are cubicles partitioned with chicken wire, each cubicle with a dirty mattress and a rickety nightstand. On each nightstand are aluminum ashtrays, two Dixie cups, a hand towel, and a hotel-sized bar of soap. Unwrapped.

My father coughs slightly, the smell of extermination catching the smoky mucus at the base of his throat.

"I see," he says.

"Every new guest is provided a clean, newly sprayed room," Sam explains. There is an uncomfortable pause as a ragged man passes on his way to the bathroom. The man mutters something inaudible, hawks, prepares to spit, and then suppresses it.

Sam says quickly, "You need anything, you come get me at the desk. Anybody bother you, you let me know. This is a friendly establishment. And, for your information, we have the hottest water in Chicago."

*M*y father said Sam beamed and rose on his toes with that line. End of story.

Because of the nature of his work, and the opportunity for it, I like to think that my father did at least one mitzvah each day. He came home tired the morning after he had integrated the hotel; he stayed in the bathroom an hour, and I could hear him talking to himself, occasionally chuckling. He came down to breakfast and surprised us with a line he reserved only for Saturdays: "And how are the sick and the afflicted this morning?"

He worked again on Friday; the paychecks were late. On

Saturday we all went to the new shopping center called Evergreen Plaza, where I ate my first soft-ice-cream cone. And it was now safe, now policy, for a Black man in Chicago to register at a particular transient hotel there, and find out whether the water could wash off the flea shit, roach shit, rodent shit, and human shit that was everywhere around him.

Twenty-seven years later I wondered what connection my father would have made between sheep shit and the hottest water in Chicago. I'm still working on that.

Mohamed Shaik

Fatima Shaik

It was the third day of our return trip driving from Ottawa to New Orleans, and the sun began to go down. The narrow, two-lane highway my father navigated was going to be dangerous soon because darkness would make the road's shoulder invisible, and the white headlights of oncoming cars would become blinding. Although there were many small motels along this winding stretch of road, there was no place for us to spend the night. "Colored" were not admitted in 1959.

I could feel the tension in my father's neck and shoulders as he hunched over the steering wheel. My mother got a wet face towel out of the ice cooler and gave him the cloth to put on his forehead to stay alert. I was seven years old and lay stretched across the rear seat of the Pontiac, watching through the rear window as the sky grew darker and darker. When the telephone poles sped past our car they made a sound like "why– why–why." Ugly white clouds crawled low in the sky and blocked my view of the distance.

I called out to my father, "What are we going to do?" He didn't say anything.

My mother frowned, put her finger over her lips, and said, "Shh. Daddy is tired and thinking."

Before that evening was over, my father showed me much more about living than about finding a place to stay in the divided South. He showed me that there were many ways to get around the barriers of racism. Now, more than thirty years later, I realize how many times my father had been thinking his way around the obstacles placed before him.

Many years before Dad began navigating my family along the narrow roads of the South, he had wanted to travel through the clouds as an airplane pilot. I saw pictures of him in our family album as a boy in short pants holding the model planes he had made. Other photos showed him in high school holding a different version of a plane, which won a competition. The prize was his first airplane ride.

He told me he rode in a bi-plane with an open cockpit. The pilot rode in front, and my dad shared the seat in the back with an older man. Although Dad was excited, the pilot was not. He hadn't even bothered to thread the safety belt shut, and Dad didn't know there was one. His fellow passenger put the buckle across both of them as the plane rattled and bumped to take off.

The sky was clear and New Orleans appeared in miniature, Dad remembered. The plane returned rather uneventfully to the Shushan airport. But Dad went home to his mother and sisters—his father had died just before Dad was born—with a firm notion that a new world awaited in aviation.

The summer of 1940, before he was a senior in college, Dad became one of the first young Black men the federal government sponsored to go to West Virginia State College to learn how to fly Piper J-3 Cub airplanes. With the Civilian Pilot Training Program, the United States was trying to build up a backlog of pilots in case of war. Six Black schools were included in the nationwide program. Dad often showed me the yellow clipping and photo from the Black newspaper, the *New Orleans Sentinel,* announcing that Octave Rainey, Adolph Moret, and Mohamed Shaik would be the first Blacks to learn to fly in Louisiana. As a child I never grew tired of hearing about them. Dad had pawned his saxophone to pay for room and board. The three men stayed in the dorm together. None of them had much money. They nursed each other's first-time homesickness. I memorized the way he described his first solo flight.

"My instructor had drilled me so often, I knew I could do it. Lots of guys were afraid to go up alone. But I just wanted the instructor out of the plane." Then he would slant his hand on an angle to show me the trajectory of the ascending plane, and school me on aerodynamics so that I actually thought I under-stood instead of just being a willing audience. "You see, those small planes were so light that even a little weight would hold them down. If the instructor got out, I knew I could really get up." He said the plane seemed to leap off the ground when the instructor left and handed the plane over for Dad to solo. "It was the best feeling I ever had," he told me often.

The year after his pilot training, Dad graduated from Xa-vier University with a degree in physics, but qualifications didn't much matter for a Black man in getting a job. He couldn't find work. The airlines didn't hire Blacks. Where there was work — in the post office, for example — Dad noticed that whenever he or any other Blacks passed the government exams, they were offered only mail handler positions. The better clerk jobs were always filled. Yet when all the Blacks, out of necessity, took the lowest paying jobs, suddenly the clerk jobs became available and were filled by whites.

Dad landed work delivering groceries on a bicycle. He would always add after the story ended that he felt lucky he had a job, so many people he knew did not. I only partly believed him. I always wondered why couldn't he get a job where other people qualified like he was were working. He could have worked for the airlines or airports. He had a degree at a time when many whites didn't, I insisted.

"It just wasn't that way in my time," he calmly reminded me. This was my first introduction to the seriousness of prejudice, not just the signs of WHITES ONLY I saw posted across the city or the segregated bus rides I took each day. Prejudice caused the vicarious pain I felt so very young when my Dad calmly spoke about his situation.

While he was still working for the grocery store, he saw an ad for civil service jobs in the post office. The government was looking for people to train as instructors in aviation mechanics. Of course, they meant whites. They would pay for whites to learn, he said, but they wouldn't hire Blacks who were already trained. Federal government jobs did not post WHITES ONLY, but experience taught most Black people the ads' unspoken intention. At the time Dad saw the ads, Blacks were not allowed even to attend the schools where the graduates of the flight instructor program would be teaching. He did not have to be told that Black candidates were really not considered part of the recruiting process.

In fact, there were few young men of any race in the United States who had college educations in engineering or science and who wanted to learn aviation. Dad told me that his mother looked at him, with his wavy black hair and tan skin, the young image of his father who had emigrated from India, and said, "If there is anyone, anywhere, flying or doing anything you want to do, you can do it too."

She had always told him that he was no worse or better than any other person because of his mixed race, so common in New Orleans that "Creole" became synonymous with that part of the South. Yet his African ancestors—acknowledged always by my family but not uniformly among most Creoles—held the most weight under the law. So, being law-abiding, Dad always lived on the dark side of segregation, except that one time when he applied for the government job as an aviation instructor. Dad told me that if there was a box on the application that asked about his race, he didn't see it. He sent in his application and was accepted.

When he got to Chanute Field in Rantoul, Illinois, they accepted him, he said, "as a rich foreigner." Because his name was Mohamed, people thought he was an "Arab." No one in the all white units expected that there were any Blacks in America with the abiding interest in aviation my father had. Also, no one that he came in contact with knew that Blacks came in such a range of shades, especially those from New Orleans. In fact, no one where he was seemed to know about educated Blacks at all, and he didn't feel the responsibility to teach them.

I always shared his bittersweet humor when he told about the relationships he had in Illinois. Dad was always outgoing, so he had many friends. When the young men would go girl watching and spoke up about who each thought was pretty, Dad said, he would often point to a Black woman and say, "I think she is." The men would laugh, "Shaik, you're crazy."

Even more oddly for an "Arab," as stereotypes go, one of Dad's best friends was Jewish. After a while they became roommates, ate together, and socialized at the Jewish community centers.

"I learned that people are people," he often said. "There are good ones and bad ones."

Dad hadn't wanted to be on the white side of the color line either. He said he didn't even try to "pass." He just let other people assume. He never gave up friends or family, or considered moving to any place where he would secretly go into another segregated world. He said, "I needed a job. All along I just wanted to be myself." Sometimes he didn't have that luxury, though.

When Dad was recruited by Tuskegee Institute in Alabama, the primary flight school was beginning to train the first of its famous Tuskegee Airmen. The school needed someone who knew government regulations to maintain the planes. Since my father was one of the few Blacks trained in military aircraft maintenance, he knew the ropes. He kept 120 planes flying all day every day at Tuskegee's Moton Field. He said that for his two and a half years at Tuskegee, there were no serious accidents due to mechanical failure.

The courage of the Black pilots was shown long before any flying combat missions, Dad insisted. After passing primary training at Moton Field, the men were sent to Tuskegee Army Air Base a few miles away. Dad often went there and watched the white flight instructors harass the men they were paid to teach. But those Black men took it, and they kept succeeding in their training despite their teachers' efforts to make them fail.

The war ended and Dad returned to New Orleans. The period of his young dream of flying was also about to end. My father began to work at a small airline company as a mechanic. He was hired because of his excellent credentials as an airplane mechanic and inspector. His new job was to check and regularly repair a midnight flight that landed at the small, local airport. Dad was sent to the company's home base in Minneapolis for a month-long training in procedures. He was sent back after less than two weeks because he already knew everything about them. When he returned, the airline's owner complimented him on his work. Then one night, the owner came to tell Dad that someone had discovered that Dad was Black. He hadn't tried to hide it, and when he was hired the owner didn't even ask or seem to care. Racists threatened to expose the airline as a company that hired "niggers" and close it down, however, and the owner said he couldn't afford that. He added that if Dad didn't quit that night someone planned to kill him. Dad picked up his tools and drove home.

"As a Negro, I had come to expect that kind of treatment," he said, when I asked once if he wasn't so angry that he could have burned down the airline himself. "It wasn't the owner's fault. In fact, I was surprised I had gotten as far as I did."

I was upset the first time I heard that story and each time it was repeated. I imagined my father walking away from the joy of his life. There was no point in him being dead, he said. He had a wife to support and he needed the money, he said. Those were the facts. They were irrefutable. They made me feel sad, though, and they still do, so many years later. At the same time, they drive me to think about the lessons of history and to tell my father's story of survival.

In New Orleans and out of aviation again, my father became an auto mechanic. Then he ran an auto mechanics' school. At night, he played jazz for a while with his cousin, Frank Crump. Once he drove a cab. Then he became a guidance counselor in the public school system for a steady paycheck.

He began working in a part of town where the grass was kept too high or was shaved too close into hard stubble around the cement one-story buildings. He used to come home to tell my mother and me that at that school he worked hard to keep the boys from calling each other bad names or fighting with their belts off, using the metal part to hit each other.

I clearly remember him saying that he got boys to stop fighting by telling them to hit each other if they wanted to keep white people happy. Sometimes I think that hearing this story so many times also kept me from pitching myself into the destructive behaviors so characteristic of oppression.

Some of the boys lived in the projects and others in small houses that looked patched and dusty. When Dad was driving me around some days he would stop and talk to their parents. I began to hear him give them advice and encourage the boys to attain the same goals that he had in school. Yet he never spoke to them about the one he was not able to reach, working in aviation.

Only privately did I hear him speak bitterly about what he could have accomplished, or what so many people could have accomplished, without the noose of a white man always dangling on the horizon. Still, I began to see him glow when parents and young men came up to him in the grocery store and said, "Thanks, Mr. Shaik, I'm doing better now." Or a mother would announce, "My son's got a good job now." Or, "He's going to college, God bless you." I glowed too, vicariously enjoying his accomplishment.

At night, I saw him still quietly and somberly reading books about airplanes and going through the newspaper for clippings. Often he took me to the library after school so he could search for the words that seemed to sustain him. That's when my family began traveling. First to Denver, where Dad took a graduate course in a college. The next year we began the long car trips to Canada.

A friend at the high school who worked with Dad encouraged him to take a course in the university there to keep his mind working while on summer vacation. Also, my mother, whose family name was LaSalle and who had grown up in the Louisiana town of St. Martinville, wanted to go to some place where she could speak French again. I remember seeing a newspaper clipping in the French Canadian paper *Le Droit*. It claimed our family was making the reverse trip of the Acadians, called Cajuns, who were thrown out of Canada because of prejudice.

I saw another reason why we went to Canada, however, when I looked in the faces of our neighbors and family as we drove away. The Cajun ancestors we had didn't count for much in the South, because our other ancestors were Black. We left our home, the place where prejudice reigned, to go somewhere that it might not, and our friends looked hopeful, frightened, and proud of our risk taking.

We went far, far away from the small segregated blocks where we were forced to shop and ride in segregation. We left the petty prejudice and massive racism we encountered on a daily basis in the land we called home to go where oppression by color wasn't the law or national custom.

Once, before I could read, I went to drink at a white water fountain at a supermarket in New Orleans. I remember a real look of panic on my father's face. Now I know it held all of the years of oppression, that he saw being repeated in my lifetime. He said, "You drink when you get in your own house." As I persisted he told me about segregation and how we were bound by it, but if we didn't drink water in public we did not have to obey the law.

Our other way of getting around the law was to leave it behind. So, every summer from the time I was four years old, we awoke at 4 A.M. one morning and packed the car with suitcases holding three months worth of clothes. We took sandwiches and soft drinks in an ice chest, sheets to cover the prickly car seats, a statue of St. Joseph for a safe journey, books, maps, and a flashlight. I settled into the back seat with a pillow and a soft toy just as the first blue tint of the sky showed. We left the dogs and the house with our watchful neighbors and family. And then we drove away.

The close single and double-shotgun houses ringed by cramped gardens on our blocks turned into those with more spacious plots on the avenues, which then turned into wide yards and fruit stands and swamps along the highway. Our annual car conversation noted that the air smelled different but fresher, that the roads, while crowded, were wider, that in the places where we were going we would be surrounded by whites who might not have encountered people like us.

In Canada we experienced a kind of freedom. No one stared at us or scrutinized us from the doors of shops when we walked by for fear we would enter. My parents had friends who spoke English and others who spoke French, as we did too at that time, and no one thought that it was odd that Blacks could be bilingual.

Strange to me then, that the issue much later when I returned to Canada as a young woman was the friction between the French and the English. The people of my generation advocated separating from the rest of the country to throw off their oppression.

I remembered Dad's words that "people are people," and wondered, does the pressure to separate versus that to integrate ever end?

*I*n 1957, my father entered the University of Ottawa. He became inspired by the seriousness and the open-mindedness of the men who taught him. He began to enjoy a new world of ideas and create many new ones of his own. He focused his research on the history of Negro education in Louisiana. Soon, he was on the way to his doctor of philosophy in education.

I watched him become less intense about the racism that trapped him and more intent on a goal outside oppression. He would eventually earn his Ph.D. and return to teach at Xavier, from which he had graduated. He would also, a few years before his retirement, become head of the aviation department of Delgado College in New Orleans. This same place had recruited him to teach during World War II when he was in his twenties, after having heard of his reputation as a pilot and mechanic. However, when he showed up for the interview, he was recognized as a Black man and was told by the administrator, "We made a mistake."

After we began going to Canada, Dad seemed much more sure of himself. He simply refused to let people treat us as inferior or out of place. Sometimes he would bring his six-foot-two frame directly in front of a white person whose job it was to keep Blacks out of a venue, and Dad would address him sincerely. "We want a table," or "We want to go horseback riding," or "We're here for the music." He began to do, in New Orleans, just as he did in Ottawa or New York; and, as in those places, we gained entrance. In retrospect, I think no one wanted a scene in those early years after *Plessy* v. *Ferguson.* Civil rights had not yet become law, but many people were pressing forward in different arenas for equal treatment. My father did the same.

I noticed an increasing amount of satisfaction growing in my father as I watched him testing the limits of racism and simultaneously making peace with his life by teaching and studying. We all learned so much when we took those trips to Canada in our sky-blue car. The people who would have harmed us dissipated as obstacles, just as so many white clouds that looked massive could be flown around, under, or over by the right pilot.

*B*ut that evening when I was almost seven years old, I was just coming to understand the many ways people were trying to ground us. We were returning to New Orleans on a narrow road in the dark and had no place to rest. The headlights of cars seemed to be coming right toward us. They buzzed narrowly past in a small, dangerous train. Every motel with a blinking vacancy sign had WHITES ONLY permanently lit under it.

My mother had used up all the ice we had picked up at the

last gas station to wet the face cloth for Dad's forehead. Hunched and tired, he appeared to me like one of the prize fighters he watched every Saturday on the television set, always calling me to the room if there was a Black one. I looked at my father and watched his eyes narrow, as he listed our possibilities: Sleep off the road in the car, prey to anyone, anything? Keep driving and risk dying in a car accident? Try to sleep somewhere where they might tell us we don't belong and arrest us?

Finally, he pulled off the road at a small motel with a very empty parking lot and some bungalows in a horseshoe shape. There was a big picture window, the front wall of a one-room house. It appeared like a movie screen, revealing a reception area. Inside was a pudgy, red-faced man and his mouse of a wife. They stared hard at our car as we parked.

My father directed me to stay in the Pontiac, and he pulled himself tall through the steel car door. I saw him adapt a particular gait, neither strut nor shuffle, more a walk with dignity and jive. I would come to recognize it when I got older in the ways of presidents and jazz musicians. I saw my father through the glass. I was afraid for him, for all of us. He faced the man and his wife. He nodded, and they returned his greeting. I saw him holding the map, telling them that we were going home to New Orleans from Canada. I saw that they were impressed but skeptical.

I saw them sizing up the depth of his tan, calculating his grain of hair, then peering past him into the car where I sat. I saw him bristle quickly, almost ignite over this threat, then I saw him redirect them with some talk. I knew it was not flattery, not bravado, but something entertaining and smart. I saw him stare directly into their eyes in a way that moved them to give him the key.

Dad was tired, and pointed when he told my mother and me what to take into the room. I knew then that we had gained entrance because the people thought we might be white and well-heeled. There was no pleasure in this trickery.

Before I went to sleep that night in a clean, tattered fold-out bed, I asked him: Why did race matter? Why did we live in the South? Why couldn't we just tell these people who we were?

Go to sleep, he said. It will be easier for you tomorrow. Just be who you are.

Granddaddy

Brooke M. Stephens

The news came with the sharp ringing of the phone at 5 A.M., jolting me out of a soft sleep. I grabbed it, ready to snarl at whoever had called a wrong number at that hour. It was Uncle Alvin from Toledo.

"Sorry to wake you, baby, but Clara just called. Dad died during the night."

A hollow stillness opened inside me and let the words sink in. It was finally over. Granddaddy had left us, just as he had said he would the last time I had seen him, a few weeks earlier. A steady composure seemed to grow and control me as I kicked off my electric blanket after a few minutes, not wanting to think about what it meant to lose him. The sky was getting light as I sat up and placidly began my part of the post-death ritual of funeral planning. I bit my lip and assured myself that it was easier to accept the inevitable. He was 105. It was his time.

It took less than twenty minutes to leave a voice-mail message for my boss telling him why I wasn't coming to work for a few days; phone the airlines and reserve three seats; and coordinate schedules with my cousin from Long Island and my aunt in

Peekskill for the next morning's flight to Mobile. I ignored the growing pressure in my chest through the hushed conversations and the attention to details, allowing the activity to block out my own concern about why I was so calm, but it should not have surprised me. We had done the same thing just two months before, when Grandmother Lillian had died.

The afternoon of her funeral, Granddaddy had folded his six-foot-four-inch frame into his favorite chair and repeated over and over to anyone within earshot, "Say good-bye to me now, 'cause I ain't gon' be here when you come back." We tried to humor him out of his grief and loneliness. "I've had enough. I'm ready to die now." I had leaned over him, stroking his salt-and-pepper hair, while Cousin Pat from Baltimore had held his hand and pinched his long earlobes.

"Oh, come on, Granddaddy, you can find yourself another wife. I've got some girlfriends who'd be glad to have a good man like you. You're still a handsome man. You got more hair than most men half your age, and your own teeth. If we get you all dressed up and take you dancing over at Peterman's, the women will fall in line waiting to get their hands on you." He had smiled at the mention of his favorite dance hall in the little logging town ten miles down the road, the one he always threatened to run off to and find another woman if we didn't treat him right.

"No, I don't trust myself to get married again, 'cause I can't see too good no more. I might pick somebody ugly, and even if I am blind, I can't live with no ugly woman." His rheumy old eyes, gray and clouded with cataracts, had filled with tears even as he laughed at his own joke. Nine weeks later he kept his promise and passed away in his sleep after telling Aunt Clara, as she put him to bed, "Thanks for being patient with me. It's almost over."

If he had lived another month he would have been planning his next birthday party, which was the family's excuse for an informal family reunion. The truth was Granddaddy's age and birthday were a long-standing family joke and a mystery to all of us. He said "yes" to any date you mentioned, teasing and agreeing with us so often that he probably had forgotten the correct date himself. We finally had to check census records to get an accurate year. He's the only person I know who outlived the seventy-five-year ban on the release of public information. He even lied to Grandmother Lillian, his third wife, when they got married. She thought he was sixty-two, when he was really seventy-five. We celebrated the event during school vacation, so all of the grandchildren could be there for the party.

For the last two summers, I and twenty-seven of my aunts, uncles, and cousins had showed up—teachers, bankers, doctors, engineers—from New York, Detroit, Chicago, Atlanta, Toledo, and Mobile for an impromptu family reunion on a Saturday afternoon in August. We laughed and hugged each other as we gathered under the large pecan tree in front of the white frame house that seemed so much smaller now. Two long tables with red-checked tablecloths were buried under acres of food. While we waited to stuff our faces we caught up on family gossip and repeated some of Granddaddy's stories.

"You remember the one about being ten years old when his mama told him he was 'field size' now, so he couldn't go back to school?" Cousin Pat started relating the tales.

"Yeah, 'I chopped cotton for fifty cents a day,'" Cousin Billy mimicked Granddaddy's voice. "'And when I was twelve, I started washing dishes in the logging camp for a dollar a day.'"

"Uh, hunh. 'I made biscuits every morning in a tin tub, putting the dimples in the top with my elbow,'" Cousin Peaco picked up the story, pounding the table the same way Granddaddy did to demonstrate his biscuit-making technique. "'Fed a hundred men every morning.'"

• • •

*W*hen Charles Garrette Stephens, Sr., was born in 1885, the ninth of eleven children, birth certificates weren't issued for midwife deliveries in sharecropper's cabins in Alabama. The family Bible had been lost, and the Monroe County courthouse burned down in 1912. Granddaddy traveled the logging camp circuit as far west as Louisiana, up to Tennessee and North Carolina, glad to have the work and excited by the camaraderie. He was unaware of the dangers until the day he saw a man cut in half by a wild swing saw. The accident terrified him, but even worse was seeing the man's body buried in a shallow grave, with only his first name, "Jim," scrawled on a flimsy raw pine cross since no one knew where he came from. It took Granddaddy seven years to save the $600 he needed to buy land and to pay taxes, get supplies, and have enough to live on until the first crop came in.

Charlie, as everyone called him, had lived in Monroeville, Alabama, so long that during the 1990 family reunion the local weekly newspaper had come to interview him about life in Monroe County at the turn of the century. His memory was clear enough to recall the days before the town had telephones, electric lights, and indoor toilets, and the nights when the Ku Klux Klan rode through the countryside terrorizing Negroes who complained about bad housing, poor schools, or unfair wages for cotton pickers. When he returned home after earning enough money working in the logging camps to buy his farm, he didn't leave Monroe County again until he attended my father's college graduation from Tuskegee Institute, twenty-eight years later. The only time he ever left the state of Alabama was when his sister in Detroit was dying in 1967.

More than one hundred relatives came from everywhere

for the funeral—Oakland, Ann Arbor, St. Louis, Cleveland, Dallas, Richmond—to pay their respects to the last of a generation that we had taken for granted, since he had been with us for as long as we could remember. The new young Black sheriff provided a motorcycle escort through the town. As the funeral cortege of thirty cars wound its way from the farmhouse to the church, in a small-town southern tradition that was new to me, traffic stopped on both sides of the road. All of the people in the town square stopped to watch. Men removed their hats. Women paused on the sidewalk and shushed children for a moment of silence.

A light rain was falling as we came out of the church, and everyone rushed to their waiting cars and quickly left the cemetery except Cousin Ricky and me. We stood together until his silver coffin was lowered into the red Alabama clay that he had farmed for sixty years. When the casket was finally covered, I took two yellow roses from the top of a floral piece, a fragile token of beauty to press into a book and hang on to for a while.

"It feels so final," Ricky said as we walked back to the car. "Like my childhood is really over now!" I knew how he felt. I didn't trust myself to speak, so I just hugged him and nodded, wrapped in my own memories but jealous of Ricky's. At least he had known Granddaddy as he grew up.

The rain had stopped by the time we returned to the farmhouse. Charlie's eight children, nineteen grandchildren, twenty-six great-grandchildren, and four great-great-grandchildren gathered outside on the grass along with a gaggle of cousins, spouses, and family friends that showed up and took pictures. We could have filled a city block, and Charlie would have loved it. His eyes would glow with pride at each family reunion as he looked at how his clan had grown each year. He was the ultimate patriarch, greeting and blessing us with a smile, a hug, and a joke.

After we sat through six rolls of film with five different photographers, I disappeared through the back door and changed into my sneakers to go out for a walk. I wasn't ready yet to gather around the huge tables covered with food and stuff myself in the after-death ritual of food and family nostalgia. Cousin Michael, a computer engineer from Detroit, saw me leaving.

"Come on, aren't you hungry? Are you sure you're all right?"

"I'm fine, just tired!" I whispered through clenched teeth, backing away from him. I wanted to be alone for a while, to think about what was happening. I headed down the gravel driveway, took a right turn, hurried down the road, and crossed State Highway 21 at an easy stride as several pick-ups and station wagons passed me. It was late May, and azalea bushes were blooming in front yards, rhododendrons were opening. The sweet scent of magnolia blossoms blended with the gas fumes from the heavy trucks. Steam was rising from the asphalt, so I took off my jacket and carried it over my arm. It didn't occur to me to think how strange a woman in a formal black suit wearing aerobic shoes might look to the farmers doing their Saturday afternoon shopping.

I walked purposefully, even though I wasn't sure where I was going. After two blocks I turned at the parking lot where school buses waited next to the Morning Star Baptist Church and came to a little white stucco building with bright red trim. The door hung dejectedly from the frame, with a large hole in the mesh screen. Large black letters painted on the side of the building said RADIO AND TV REPAIR. It looked wrong and out of place. We never needed a sign on Granddaddy's store to tell us whose business it was.

Outside was a wooden bench, worn smooth from years of teenagers sitting there and sipping orange Nehis or sucking on sour pickles while they flirted and waited for the school bus to take them home. Granddaddy had run this neighborhood store for more than forty years, long before the world had heard about 7-Elevens or Sunday sales at Wal-Mart. The store became a social center, with its own special camaraderie for every age group. Teenagers hung out here after school, dancing to the jukebox and munching on Baby Ruths. Old men gathered on rainy days to gossip about local politics and family events and swap exaggerated stories about past exploits that grew and changed with each retelling.

For a man who never finished third grade Granddaddy taught important life lessons that the kids didn't learn in the classrooms.

"Now, how do you know I didn't cheat you? Did you count your change?" If your change was less than a nickel he never gave you the pennies. "Aw, just take two Mary Janes and call it square." He had nicknames for each of his customers— Miss TuttiFrutti, Duffus Danny, Little Squeaky—and was generous to a fault with any widow whose husband had died in a sawmill accident and whose small pension check was never enough to feed the five or six kids that were left behind.

*O*ne Saturday afternoon I phoned the store for a quick chat and got a recorded "disconnected" message. I quickly dialed the number for his house, and he answered. "What are you doing at home?" I asked anxiously. "What happened to the store?"

"Wellllll," he mumbled. This was usually the prelude to a long story, so I settled back to listen. "You know I got that bump on my head when I fell on the ice out by the barn last year. I had a problem with my eyes and it never quite got better. Now Lillian has to do all the driving, and it's hard to read the paper. And one day, I gave somebody a quarter change when it should have been a nickel."

I had covered the phone with my hand and choked back a laugh. To me, a quarter was little or no money. Change for a parking meter or a phone call. But to a man who had been forced to leave school at age ten to go to work in the cotton fields for ten hours a day, a quarter was half a day's wages.

"If I can't see to count my money right, I ain't gon' trust nobody else to do it for me, so I just closed up." I fought a sudden surge of tears when I heard the rage and sadness in his voice. At 101, he felt that his body had betrayed him, and he thought he was being forced into early retirement. If he couldn't work, he didn't know why he was still alive.

*T*he sun was beginning to make bright orange streaks across the slate-gray sky as I continued my walk, taking the long way back to the house past the grocery store where I had met Granddaddy on my second visit to Monroeville. I didn't remember my first. I shuddered to think of how close I had come to not knowing him at all.

Until I was sixteen and needed my birth certificate to get my driver's license, my mother hadn't bothered to tell me that the man I'd been calling "Daddy" all those years, wasn't. She didn't exactly lie—but she never explained. After she told me the truth, my questions about my real father were answered with slammed doors, an icy stare across her coffee cup, and a very firm, "That's none of your business." We fell into a carefully choreographed silence, but I never stopped wanting to know. I got bits and pieces of information in furtive talks with other relatives, who exchanged shocked glances when they realized how little I knew. I spent less and less time at home after graduating from college because I couldn't participate anymore in the dance of denial.

Finally, in the summer of 1974, I went looking for my father's family. I'd had enough of the rumors, half-truths, and vague whispers that just led to more questions. I spent a weekend in North Carolina with Aunt Nell, Mother's older sister, who had shared a few secrets with me. After about six vodka tonics we got around to the subject at hand, and she told me enough for me to know that it was worth a trip to Alabama.

On a hot Saturday morning in July, I flew to Mobile and rented a car. I crossed the Tensaw River around eleven o'clock and headed up Route 65, flying past tall pine trees, red clay hills, and small towns with funny names I'd never heard before. Satsuma, Bay Minette, Perdido, Atmore, Uriah. They meant nothing to me. I wasn't searching for a favorite tree, an old schoolhouse, or some special setting to trigger a fond memory. I wanted a living, breathing testimony to my past. A live human being who could tell me more about myself than I could ever imagine wanting to know. I was looking for me.

Around one, I reached the center of the small town and shivered, thinking, This could have been home. It was Hicktown, U.S.A., redneck country Alabama style. The courthouse was the usual red brick with gold dome and clock tower in the middle of the town square. Somewhere inside it, I was sure, were the records of my short life there—birth certificate, divorce decree, death certificate, custody suit. Dusty pick-ups were parked at angles along the four blocks that made up Main Street, in front of the post office, general store, the bank, library, hardware store, and jeweler's. Except for an occasional Toyota or Honda, it could still be 1949 here. Maybe Mother did me a favor when she came back to get me, I thought.

I found the nearest pay phone and local directory in a small grocery store. I had only my father's name to go on.

Charles Stephens, Jr. Maybe there was a Charles Stephens, Sr. Would he still be alive? He would have to be at least eighty! I had visions of a senile old coot in a rocking chair, drooling tobacco, spitting on himself, and gazing off into a vague past that he could not share with me. Then I saw the name at the top of the page.

I stopped for a long moment, wondering what I would say. How do you walk into a stranger's life and introduce yourself as a long-lost grandchild? Would he remember me, or a worse fear, would he care? I took a deep breath and mumbled a silent prayer before I dialed the number. I noticed that I couldn't stop my fingers from shaking.

He answered after the third ring.

"Mr. Stephens, did you have a son who was a Tuskegee airman who died in a plane crash?" I asked. The question came out of nowhere. Silence. "Mr. Stephens?" my voice quivered.

"Yes," he answered cautiously. "Why do you ask?"

"Then that makes me your granddaughter," I whispered. I heard a quick intake of breath on the other end. Ohmigod! Had I given him a heart attack?

"Marilyn?" he said, softly. "Is that you, Marilyn?"

I blushed and giggled trying to find words. This man knew me! Only close family members ever called me by my middle name.

"Where are you?" he asked.

"At a grocery store—the Piggly Wiggly near the court-house."

"Oh my god," he shouted into my ear. "I'm on my way! I'm driving a yellow Ford!" and slammed the phone down.

My mind raced while I waited. What had I done? What was I doing standing in the sweltering heat of a small Alabama town in God-knows-where county, where I might have spent my whole life waiting for some faceless stranger I didn't know and wondering how different things might have been if I had grown up here? What do I call him? Grandpa? Grandfather? "Mr. Stephens" sounded too formal. Will I like him? Will he like me? What will Mother say? Whatever happened at this meeting, I knew I could never go back to being who I was before now.

The humidity was making everything clammy, but I broke out in a cold sweat as I tried to ignore the time-bomb seeming to tick in my stomach. I watched the afternoon shoppers going about their ordinary business, and I wanted to scream, "Look at me. Don't you know something special is about to happen here? My life is going to change! I found my grandfather!"

Within minutes a rusty-fendered old yellow Ford caked with red clay dust pulled into the parking lot. Out stepped a tall, broad-shouldered man dressed in khakis and wearing a wide-brimmed straw hat. He had strong bright eyes, thick gray hair, and a joyful smile. So this is what a grandfather looks like! I didn't know what to say—I'd never had a grandfather to talk to before. I waved to him, feeling too shaky to move.

He saw me. Without a word, he crossed the distance between us with a quick lanky stride, and before I could say anything he picked me up in his arms as if I were still the four-year-old girl who had been taken away from him twenty-three years before. He crushed me to him, laughing and crying for at least ten minutes as he kept saying, "Thank you, God. Thank you. Thank you. Thank you. Now I can die happy. All of my children have finally come back to me."

Wrapped in those strong arms and caressed by the calloused hands of this huge, loving stranger, I was humbled to realize that there was someone in the world who loved me completely without knowing anything about me, because I was family. When I looked into his eyes I saw that I had never left his heart. I had no idea who this man was, but I knew I was home.

"Granddaddy" took me back to his farmhouse, where I found a small shrine in his living room for my father and me. There were baby pictures of me that I had never seen, and ones of a man in uniform. I knew, without asking, that this was my father. Even I could recognize my face in his: the same nose, eyes, and forehead. A pair of bronzed baby shoes sat on a coffee table. I picked them up, dusted them off, and found my name and birthdate on them.

Later, we sat outside under a huge pecan tree on a white metal glider as chickens and kittens played around our feet. A cow was mooing in the large barn behind us. He talked for the next few hours and I listened. I finally got the courage to ask some of the questions that had brought me there, such as what really had happened between my parents.

He looked at me with a tranquil smile on his face. And he looked. He just sat and looked. He looked at me, through me, past me, inside me, with the steadiest, clearest pair of gray eyes and the most intense gaze I had ever fallen under. I could almost feel his eyes moving, tender and slow, across the contours of my face, gently touching my forehead, caressing the bulge of my brows, tracing the bump on my nose, stroking the hollow of my jaw. Searching my face for evidence of my father in me, reawakening the memory of the old me and merging it with this new me, this woman who had returned here after all these years. Recalling the little four-year-old girl and comparing me with the image of the child he had been carrying in his mind for years.

Instead of answering me, he disappeared into the house with a quick step and a look of mischief. He returned a few moments later with a faded velvet hatbox tied with a tattered red ribbon. Inside, wrapped in tissue paper, were a little blue coat, a faded white cotton dress trimmed in pink ribbons, and some hand-knitted sweaters — perfect fits for a two-year-old.

"Essie Lee just couldn't seem to part with them after you

left. Even when the other grandbabies came along." He handed me a blue-and-white knit cap. "It was the last thing she made for you." I was sniffling with tears as he began to talk about my parents.

"There was a war on at the time, and they were like everybody else was, scared to death and trying to live life in a hurry. Nobody really knew what to expect, and we were all worried about what we would wake up to the next morning. Charles was moving around all the time in the army, and Grace was trying to work and go to school. Unfortunately, those two young people said and did a lot of things that hurt each other. But they both loved you very much. Other than that, you don't need to know the details. I just hope your mother is happy now. You seem to have had a good life." His words were spoken with so much love and understanding that I didn't realize until three days later that I got no answers at all. It would be another fifteen years and many more visits before he would finally tell me the truth about how he had taken care of me for four years when my mother had abandoned me in the hospital and disappeared.

I will miss Granddaddy's stories, which were always full of loving lies and nonsense. "Me and my brother Webb came home from the logging camp on Saturday night and brought our money to Mama. After church on Sundays, we'd go walkin' and lookin' at the girls. They'd eye me with a big grin, sayin', 'Hey, Charlie, wanna walk with me?' Then they'd look at Webb, like they wisht he weren't there, 'Oh, hey, Webb.' When the railroad came through here we'd spend a nickel for a ride down to Burnt Corn and walk the seven miles back. Somebody's Mama or Daddy always came along to chaperon us but sometimes we managed to hold hands on the train. That's how I courted your grandmother, Harriet. Webb was always jealous 'cause he swore he saw her first, but the minute I laid eyes on her, I knew she was mine." I heard these tales hundreds of times, and even when

I could mouth the words along with him, I never got bored. When I asked him about his feelings about the racism he had lived through, he answered with the simple wisdom of his experience, "I did all this so you don't have to."

If I was in the kitchen, he would drape an arm around my shoulder and ask, "What do you think you're doing?" and start another story with a naughty grin and a wink of his eye. "I used to be a cook, you know . . . I lied to the head cook to get the job 'cause it was a raise in pay to a dollar and a half . . . messed up the first batch of bread and hid the stuff in the woods. Then this ol' wild boar came up to the camp next day covered with flour and batter. I lost a whole day's pay for that."

Then he would offer advice from his days as a short-order cook with a drop-dead serious look. "The secret for making a perfect yellow cake is to take some slime from the underbelly of a frog. It adds an extra-special taste and gives a real bright color to it." He'd break into hilarious guffaws as I stared in horror. Now the world he had created, full of down-home wisdom mixed with backwoods myth and outdated memories laced with bodacious humor, was gone.

Although his spirit has left his body, Charlie Stephens's legacy is still with us. It is obvious in Cousin Billy, who shows his flirtatious humor as he winks at every pretty girl he meets; in Uncle Alvin's gentle sensitivity wrapped in a constant stream of jokes; in Cousin Pat's gregarious storytelling; in Uncle Raymond's slow-talking manner when he gives you a firm "No! And that's all there is to it" on any idea that he thinks is stupid. Aunt Clara has his sweet smile, and Aunt Ethel can stare you down with his same no-nonsense attitude as she quizzes you, like a drill sergeant, about your job, your love life, your trips to the dentist, and are you saving any money.

As we sat in the airport waiting for our return flight, the careful composure of the last few days began to crack when it hit me that this would be my last trip to Monroeville. Grand-daddy wasn't here anymore. There was no reason to come back to this dinky little town, where they didn't even have a movie to go to when we didn't want to sit on the porch and listen to the crickets at night. A place where we complained about the smell of the hog pen, and the fireflies dancing in the dusk wasn't enough to distract us from our boredom, and the fresh pecans, sweet corn straight off the stalk, tender collard greens, field peas, and peaches were taken for granted as we picked them out of the back yard each day.

If it is true that a child's personality is molded in the first few years of life, then my sense of self was shaped by a man who had loved me enough to let me go, yet still welcomed me back with such an abundance of love when I returned that it fright-ened me. Granddaddy's generous spirit and boundless love and humor set a standard of appreciation and approval that spoiled me for any other man who would ever compete for my heart.

We boarded the plane and I sat shaking in my seat, the growing pressure in my chest finally giving way to the wall of tears that I had pushed away for four days. As the jet engines revved up, the vibrations rattled through my body and I finally couldn't hold back any longer. With a deafening blast at take-off that lifted us into the sky, I screamed as loudly as I could.

Part II

Brothers, Uncles,
and
Extended Family

A Macon Boy

Victoria Cliett

Recently, the pianist at my church had to go out of town, leaving my church with no one to play for services. A church member asked me if I played, and I said, yes, but only if I had the music. She shook her head and said, "We need somebody who can play by ear." Play be ear. I felt an indescribable sadness because until that moment I had not realized how much of my talent I had thrown away over the years. My Uncle Van could play by ear. In fact, if I had mentioned him to the fellow church member, she would have nodded and said, "Yes, your uncle can *play!*" That is how well known he was in our church conference. Uncle Van, Van E. Cliett, was my hero when I was a child because he could "play by ear." Playing by ear has a different meaning to me now than it did back then. Now, as I finish my studies on my doctorate in English, add books to my reading list and type papers, I'm afraid that I've become too formal, my talent stilted, and as with music, I can read only with words, only with notes. But Uncle Van could play anything from "Farmer in the Dell" to "Für Elise." Keys that sound lonely and plaintive under my fingers were a cabaret under his command.

In my family and in my church, Uncle Van was a legend. After he graduated from high school in 1957, he went to Oakwood College, where he met Richard Penniman, known as Little Richard, in the spring of 1958. He played in Little Richard's evangelical tour the summer of 1958, parting ways after six months. He came to Detroit in 1959 and played for the Burns Avenue Seventh-Day Adventist church. Because Seventh-Day Adventists worship on Saturdays, Uncle Van played at Baptist churches for extra money on Sundays. He left Detroit and moved to California in 1965, two years before I was born. He visited maybe once or twice, but growing up I would hear what a phenomenal piano player he was. In 1971 he married a woman with two daughters, but he still played for churches. He was separated and divorced from her in 1976. At that time, my mother announced that he would be coming to visit from California for a week in the summer. I could have laid palm branches all the way from the airport to our house, but I settled for submitting to the torture of my mother scrubbing every inch of my body.

We picked Uncle Van up on a Sunday evening. We children, me, my twin sister, and three younger siblings, were ordered to be seen and not heard. We gave Uncle Van the requisite sugar, then went to a steak house for dinner. The adults ordered ribs, my mother ordered hamburgers for me and my sister. I watched them as they deftly served the ribs from the slabs and held them by their fingertips. My father and Van talked and caught up, while smooth clean bones with slight traces of gristle piled up on their plates. I plotted during dinner on how to get him to play the piano that evening. I wanted to ask Uncle Van if he would play when we returned home, but the conversation was steady and I was prodded by my mother to finish eating.

After we arrived home, I asked him to play. "Maybe tomorrow," he said. My mother scolded me for bothering him as she ushered me to the bedroom to get ready for bed. In bed, I could still hear my father and Uncle Van talking. I could hear Uncle Van's voice in a steady stream, rising and falling in intensity, and my mother's and father's unbridled laughter, rising up the stairs, and I could tell without even seeing them that they probably had tears in their eyes and had fallen back on the couch in helpless abandon as Uncle Van told his stories. That is what my Uncle Van could do. He seemed invincible in his ability to pull a song or a story out of thin air and have it perform at will. Hearing the laughter, I was determined to play like my uncle. If I could play like Van, life would be at my command. There would be no song I could not sing, no memory beyond the reach of my fingers. Van's playing brought to mind a thousand songs and a thousand experiences. My mind brimmed over with every song I had ever heard in my life: a commercial ditty, a lullaby, the chimes of an ice-cream truck. And I wanted him to play all of it. I wanted to play it too. That night I dreamed of Uncle Van and me standing on stage together in the hot lights, an invisible but approving audience giving endless and over-whelming applause.

It was Monday afternoon, and I watched Uncle Van unpack groceries after borrowing my mother's car to shop. He put a bucket of chicken on the stove and unpacked 7UP, cantaloupe, a side of bacon, plums, a large bottle of Tabasco sauce, grapes, and candy bars: Snickers, Three Musketeers, Milky Ways, and Hersheys, spilling out like gold in front of my eyes. He put the chicken on a cookie sheet and sprinkled each piece with pepper and Tabasco sauce. He baked it in the oven while putting the fruit in the refrigerator. When he sat down to eat, he placed a fat chicken breast with most of the Tabasco-doused skin peeled away in front of me. I waited for him to say grace, but he offered none and began to eat, not even reaching for his glass until his chicken breast was a bony corpse. I took a swallow of 7UP after every bite, the small specks of pepper and Tabasco burning my throat. Uncle Van did not talk much, and I decided that he just wanted to eat. I also decided to wait a day or so to ask him again to play, as I coughed my way through the chicken.

On Tuesday afternoon, I saw Uncle Van by the piano looking through one of the duet books, but not once did he touch the keys. He came out to the porch with a glass of 7UP in his hand and sat down. I sat down next to him, hoping he would tell a story about his childhood. My images of the South, when I was young, were based on graphic depictions of lynchings in *Jet* magazine and stories of Black activists hosed against the wall, beaten by white sheriffs and bitten by dogs. Yet my father and Uncle Van never spoke of these things. Instead, I heard stories from Uncle Van about my father and the runaway mule, or the time Uncle Van had to help wash clothes and fell into the bluing. In some way I felt protective toward my father and uncle, two Black men who grew up in a place where their lives could have been snuffed out without a second thought by whites who saw their very existence as an aberration, talented men who grew up in the same small town as Otis Redding and Little Richard. Even today, it is difficult for me to see an archive photo of a lynching without imagining the rich baritone of my father choked out or my uncle's hands stilled and lifeless at his side. At nine years old, I was glad my father lived in the North, where I thought it was safe. How little I knew then.

"What was it like growing up down South?" I asked as I sat beside him.

Uncle Van huffed and ran his tongue over his square, even teeth. "Growing up down South is just like anyplace else. Maybe a bit slower."

"Did you know anyone who was lynched?"

"No."

"Didn't white people kill a lot of Black people?"

"They didn't kill anyone I knew."

"But aren't you scared to live down South?"

"Why do you ask that?"

"Because. White people hate Blacks down South."

He laughed and ran his hand over his Afro. He wore his Afro very high, but because he was losing his hair, it was starting to sink in the middle like a ruined soufflé. He put his feet up on the railing. He didn't say anything more, just flexed the ball of one foot and took a swallow of 7UP.

Uncle Van was gone for the next two days visiting friends. I asked my mother who he was visiting, and she told me it was none of my business. I asked her if he would play the piano, and she threatened me with a whipping if I bothered him about it again. When he came back, he resumed watching TV, sitting on the porch, and reading the newspaper, with an occasional phone call or two. He was in the kitchen splitting apart a cantaloupe when I came in from bike riding. I gave him a breathy "Hi" and opened the refrigerator, looking for something to eat.

"Want some cantaloupe?" he asked.

"No, thanks." I got a bowl of tuna fish and some bread. After making my sandwich, I poured a fat dollop of Alaga syrup over it. This was my father's favorite snack. I ate it too, when the urge hit me.

"Do you want to get married again?" I asked as I sat down to eat.

"I don't think so."

"Don't you miss your wife and stepkids?"

"She's not my wife anymore, and I miss the kids."

"Do you have a girlfriend?"

"No, I don't think I'll have a girlfriend anytime soon."

"Why not?"

Uncle Van looked up from his cantaloupe. "I do not have a girlfriend because I do not want one," he enunciated carefully.

"Then what do you want?"

"You can always get what you want. It's getting what you need that's the problem." He ate his cantaloupe and did not talk anymore.

Friday evening was always a big occasion at our house. Since we were Seventh-Day Adventists, Friday evening was a long preparation of clothes and food for the next day. My father and Uncle Van were setting out their clothes for church and my mother was at the ironing board pressing out the folds of our dresses. When Van laid out his shirt, she said, "I'll hit that with the iron, Van," and expertly whipped the shirt onto the board, leaning on it hard, with her elbow against the iron.

Dinner was the same as at the steak house, except that my mother talked more, bringing Van up to date about everyone at the church. My father, mother, and Van cleaned their plates twice while my sisters, brother, and I dallied around, our plates a bland palette of potatoes and corn. I could hear them talking in the living room after I went to bed. I heard the familiar, soft thump of the phonograph arm as my father started to play his records, and for a long while Mahalia Jackson, the Harlem Boys' Choir, and the Howard University Men's Chorale floated up and around me until I finally went to sleep.

Sabbath morning, we had a huge breakfast of grits, eggs with cheese, toast, bacon, and sausage. My father and Van wanted to have time to catch up with friends, so they left for church together. My mother, sister, and I arrived later. I was positive that my father and uncle were going to prepare a selection, and my mother could not drive fast enough to the church.

At the eleven o'clock service, the congregation was abuzz as church members greeted my uncle. Once, my mother had mentioned that my father and uncle were the most popular members of church and that everyone had been sad to see Uncle Van leave. He managed to sit down before the service began. During the remarks, the pastor cleared his throat and said, "Today we have with us an old friend, who is very dear to us. I am happy to welcome Van back to our congregation, as he is here visiting. As some of you know, he played for the Burns Avenue S.D.A. church for five years. He will not be able to play for us, but we hope that he will have a very pleasant fellowship with us this Sabbath." A collective groan of disappointment emanated from all around. I kicked at the pew in disappointment, at which my mother gave me a sharp smack on my thigh. Uncle Van sat with us at the end of the pew looking straight ahead, his hands clasped tightly together.

Uncle Van and my father did not come home after church. My mother informed me they would be eating with some old friends that afternoon. My frustration from the morning events boiled over, and I asked her why Van would not play.

"He's going through things. Be quiet and eat your dinner," she said.

I picked at my plate. "Going through things" implied mysterious trials, which required much prayer and crying. I know now that the separation and divorce had been tough for my uncle, spiritually and emotionally.

The Sabbath passed quietly. I took my customary nap. Uncle Van and my father still had not come back home when I awakened. After sunset, my siblings and I were allowed to watch TV for an hour and eat pizza before being sent to bed. Tucking myself in bed, I tried to console myself on not hearing him play the piano, but it was hard to extinguish hope.

In the morning, I saw his suitcase at the foot of the stairs. It was 8 A.M. and usually I was not up by then, but I heard my mother setting plates for breakfast.

"You could have stayed in bed. I'm just fixing breakfast for Van before your father takes him to the airport," she said.

"I wanted to say good-bye," I said, surprised my parents would allow Van to leave without seeing anyone for good-byes.

Uncle Van and my father came in from the den, where they had been reading the Sunday paper. We ate pancakes and sausage for breakfast. My mother asked Van if there was anything he wanted to take back and what kind of lunch he wanted. She decided at the last minute to go with my father and Van to the airport and went upstairs to put on nicer clothes. When my mother was ready to go, my father picked up Uncle Van's bag and began to go out the door.

"Wait a minute, Bert," Uncle Van said, walking over to the piano and sitting down. He sat with his head bowed for a moment, then began to play a gospel song I recognized as "Something Within Me." His fingers jitterbugged across the keys and the piano jumped up and talked back with an energy my sister and I had been incapable of producing, even with weekly piano lessons. My father sat in an armchair listening, his head nodding in rhythm. My mother leaned against the vestibule with her eyes closed, hand patting her thigh. Even now, I wondered where could it have come from, this rhythm that I thought was dead and gone, now coming back to give us something, to give hope. I was spellbound. After what seem like brief seconds, Van ended the song. His fingers raked almost every key, then stopped with a resounding thump. By the time I came out of my trance, Uncle Van had walked out to the car with my father. My mother instructed me and my sister to watch after the little ones. I watched the station wagon leave the driveway, go down the street, and turn the corner.

I ran to the piano trying to remember which keys to play, fingering them for a while. My piano teacher had never taught me gospel. There was nothing in my lesson books I could play that sounded even remotely similar to what I had heard. After much meandering, I gave up and let my hands dance wildly upon the keys, playing no song at all. I could hear my sister yelling from upstairs to cut the noise, but I didn't care. It was the rhythm that was important.

Uncle John

Norma Jean and Carole Darden

U ncle John was the oldest son of Charles and Dianah Darden. The dreams and hopes of the family centered on him, and he proved worthy of their confidence. From the beginning, John was a carbon copy of his father. Even in his youth, he was disarmingly self-assured and knew how to survive and to protect others. But from the age of ten, when he was unable to find medical assistance for his unconscious sister Annie, John had one driving goal, and that was to become a doctor.

At the age of thirteen, he was sent by Papa Darden to high school in Salisbury, North Carolina. Lean years followed as he worked his way through Livingstone College, medical school, and an internship on Long Island, New York. His was a long, hard struggle, but when he made it, he established a pattern the younger children would follow. Summer jobs, mainly on the railroad and ships, took John all over the country. But he always found his way back to Wilson to share what he had seen and learned of the world, and to encourage his brothers and sisters in their pursuits. By the time he was ready to put out his shingle in 1903, Wilson already had Black medical service, so

John went deeper south, settling in Opelika, Alabama, where, as the only Black doctor in a thirty-mile radius, he was greeted with an eighteen-hour workday.

His overloaded practice in that remote little town almost caused him to lose his fiancée, Maude Jean Logan, who questioned his long absences from her. But Uncle John's persuasive letter, which we found in Aunt Maude's Bible, saved the wedding day:

Sat. Noon

My own darling Jean:

Here on the very verge of our approaching happiness comes the saddest news pen could write . . . Sweetheart Jean, the condition of a half dozen patients demands that I keep constant watch over them for at least three days. Had thought to see you at the cost of their lives; but you would care so much less for me then . . . Won't you sympathize with me just a little, the responsibilities on this end and realize that no man under the canopy of heaven could love you more . . .

Soon after, John, making calls with his new wife in his horse and buggy, became a familiar sight on the narrow dirt roads around the Opelika countryside.

Emulating his father's diversified business tactics, John opened a drugstore on Avenue A, the main street of town. His brother J.B. had just earned his degree in pharmacy from Howard University, so he was recruited as a partner. The two brothers dispensed prescriptions, cosmetics, ice cream, and a lot of good cheer, and the store became a meeting place for the community. Local residents tell us that their Sundays were not complete without a stroll to the drugstore for a chat and a scoop of John's homemade ice cream. After the death of their mother, baby brother Bud, our father, joined the group and, at the age of nine, became the ace soda fountain man, specializing in a tutti-frutti sundae. Eventually Opelika proved to be too quiet for J.B., so, with John's blessings, he returned to medical school in livelier Nashville, Tennessee, leaving the oldest and the youngest brothers together. John was like a second father to Bud, who nicknamed him Toad because of his protruding abdomen.

According to Bud, John was a natural leader of men and was considered the guardian of minority rights. People brought him their sorrows, their joys, and news of gross community injustices. Long outraged at the lack of public medical facilities for Black people, he established a private hospital. It was a simple one-story wooden building, but many complicated operations were performed there and many lives saved. Like most country doctors, he had his thumb glued to the pulse of the community and became the town chronicler. He knew who had been born, who had died, and who had moved in or out. (Because of his two additional jobs as the Lee County jail doctor and a conscription doctor, he even knew who was incarcerated or who was inducted into the army.) Thus, he had firsthand knowledge of the jailing of people for minor infractions of the law, of assaults on defenseless females, and of the countless other indignities perpetuated on Blacks. During his time, the air was indeed permeated with clouds of sudden and irrational violence.

Once Dr. John's quick presence of mind was able to avert the lynching of a Black stranger. Bud remembers that he and John were in the drugstore when they heard a commotion coming from the street and upstairs, where John's brother-in-law, a dentist, had an office. Dr. John Clark came down to tell them that a stranger seeking refuge from a lynching mob had run into his office quite out of the blue. With no questions asked, John left and returned in a flash with a few fearless and daring Black citizens and the white Republican postmaster (a federal appointee in those days when Republicans were considered liberals). The mob had gathered momentum and was threatening to storm the building. But the postmaster, whom John knew to be sympathetic to the plight of Blacks, had arrived heavily armed, and he kept the mob distracted while John and his friends spirited the man out of town. The man's crime? A visitor from Chicago unfamiliar with local customs, he had almost lost his life for taking a seat in an empty white restaurant while waiting for directions to another town.

Afterward, some local residents conducted a campaign of harassment against John and Maude, who remained cautious, cool, and armed until the fervor died down. We asked Aunt Maude if John had ever considered leaving town. She answered that in the darkest days in the backwoods of Alabama, he had never wavered in his determination to remain in the community he loved and to aid others.

She also told us that the balance and harmony so sorely missing in John's hostile environment were supplied by his love of music, of religion, of gardening, and, surprisingly, of fashion. A meticulous dresser, he had developed an appreciation for good fabric and fit from his mother, the seamstress. He was a steward in his church, raised livestock and pigeons, and kept a beautiful flower and vegetable garden, as had his father. However, the talent that set him apart was his melodious baritone voice, and it is said that he could be heard singing a mile away.

In a life that had so many parallels to Papa Darden's, it is interesting to note that after John's death the local Black high school was named for him in appreciation for the many things that he had done for the citizens of Opelika.

My Little Brother, Jimmy

Carolyn Hart-Solomon

The first time I saw him I thought Mom had made a mistake. She had told me that she was going away for a few days and would bring back a wonderful gift for me. I held my breath, loving the idea of a surprise, especially this time, because I knew what it would be—the red tricycle I saw in a department store window when we rode the bus to downtown Birmingham to go shopping. We had looked at it on several Saturdays and admired the shiny black leather seat, the bright yellow tassels on the handles, the sparkling silver horn, and the little white basket with the brass plate on the front just waiting to have my name engraved on it. I began to dream of making every other girl in my first grade class jealous of me when I rode down Sixth Street or went to the park at the end of our block on weekends.

The day Daddy brought Mom home, I stood at the top of the stairs of the small apartment building in the Vinesville section of town where we lived, trying not to dance with impatience as Mom slowly got out of the car. She was carrying a large bundle. It was blue, not red, and from the way she cradled it in her arms, somehow I knew it wasn't my tricycle. My hopes withered in tortured confusion. Clearly, this was not what I had expected. At six years old I was the only child and the center of the family universe, and I liked it that way.

"Meet your little baby brother, James Henry," Mom announced proudly as she came inside and gently laid the bundle on the bed. I slunk along behind her in disappointed silence. She chattered on about how beautiful he was as she carefully unwrapped him and ended by telling me how wonderful it was to have someone different in the house. When I got a closer look at him I could see that at least he was red. Red and wrinkled and whining, and he smelled. When Mom changed his diaper, I saw how truly different he was from me.

For several days a steady parade of grandparents, neighbors, and friends—who usually doted on me—trooped through the living room to coo and gawk at James Henry, or Jimmy, as the new arrival was quickly nicknamed. Each of these well-wishers paused long enough to pat me on the head, pull my pigtails, or pinch my cheeks and tell me how lucky I was to have a little brother. That was my first acquaintance with the kind of acquiescent lie that grown-ups force children to participate in with their compliments and cajoling. My silence was interpreted as agreement, but the marvelousness of the moment escaped me. I did not take kindly to the presence of this interloper, who was demanding, and getting, more attention than I was. I couldn't possibly tell any of them how much I would have preferred a red tricycle, or a puppy—a cuddly cocker spaniel that would lick my face, adore me, and chase me around the playground. If we had to have another living breathing thing around, puppies were much more fun than babies. Who needed a little brother? I decided to play along with this game for awhile.

Babies weren't a new thing in our house. Mom taught kindergarten at a school in the neighborhood, so parents often came by to visit with their children. Sometimes she baby-sat for our neighbor, Mrs. Ramsey, who lived next door, or for Mrs. Lovingood from across the street. Each baby was different and they were fun to play with, but they always went back home with their own mothers.

After a few days, the novelty of Jimmy's presence changed from amusement to annoyance. He had to have his own special little bathtub. The burping and feeding routine quickly became a bore. When Mom insisted that I was too small to hold him and might hurt him if I dropped him, I really wasn't interested anymore. Where was the fun in his being there if I couldn't play with him? By the end of the month I asked her how long Jimmy was staying. I didn't like the answer I got. "Forever" was longer than I planned on allowing him to be around. My quiet lie of agreement slowly changed into the more pronounced emotion of resentment. I didn't know that these feelings were "sibling rivalry"—all I knew was that I didn't want him around.

Days went by when he was the total focus of attention because he was sick, or he was teething, or he had gained five pounds, or he was just there. One afternoon, I stood next to the bed watching as Mom dressed Jimmy, changing his diaper for the umpteenth time that day, and I wondered what I was supposed to do with him. I still couldn't understand why I needed a baby brother. Maybe someone else on the block would like to have him since I didn't see what we needed him for. He must have caught my bad thoughts. He let out a steady golden stream that arced straight up and out and wet everything in sight—including me.

The battle lines were drawn. If I was stuck with the blessing of being a "big sister," then he had to suffer for it. I became a bossy little tyrant whose mission in life was to make him sorry he had ever been born.

Over the next few years I became part-time baby-sitter, and my mother's constant mantra became: "Watch out for

Jimmy." "Take Jimmy with you." "Don't forget to bring Jimmy with you." "Give Jimmy some of your ice cream (or Coke, or pie)." "Stay here and guard your little brother." Guard him? I wanted to strangle him.

When he was old enough to go to kindergarten Mom came up with another brilliant notion. Let Jimmy go to kindergarten at the same school as I went to. That way he would have a new social experience, and guess who could look out for him. Her bright idea was social suicide for me.

My girlfriends had brothers and sisters, too, but they didn't have to drag them home from school every day. They could hang out after school lollygagging in the park, go to the library, or kill time at the candy store; I had to take Jimmy home. My weekend visits to my girlfriend Sylvia's house or my best friend's birthday party were interrupted or cut short or just plain canceled if Mom needed me at home to baby-sit.

One day I decided that I'd had enough. It was time to free myself of this snotty-nosed little whiner. On the way home from school, as we changed buses in the busy downtown traffic, I got my own brilliant idea of what to do with him. An elderly Black woman was standing next to us on the street corner as Jimmy and I waited for the light to change. She admired his chubby cuteness as he held my hand. When she grinned down into his grubby little face, I quickly said, "Here, you can have him!" and raced across the street, dodging an oncoming taxi. I made it safely to the other side of the street, feeling free for all of half a minute. Then I looked back at the puzzled woman and the screaming little boy. Jimmy was pointing at me, sending up agonized howls of abandonment, while the poor woman waved at me to come back. His screams, along with a vision of the whipping I knew I'd get if I showed up without him, made me slowly slink back across the street and reclaim the little creature. Seeing his terror and the tears in his eyes, I knew that I had gone too far. After that, I could never quite abuse his trust again. I was also relieved to discover that he didn't tattle on me when we got home that evening. Years later, when I guiltily apologized to him for the incident and shared with him how awful I had felt about doing such a thing because of his agony that day, it stunned me to hear that he had absolutely no recollection of the event.

As we got older, he learned how to get even. One Easter Sunday, I was chosen by my Sunday school teacher to recite a poem during the children's hour, in front of all the grown-ups in church. The whole family sat together—Mom, Daddy, Grandmother, me, and Jimmy—in the second row. Jimmy was seated next to Mom at the end so we wouldn't elbow each other during the service. When the minister called my name, with all my ten-year-old pride I smoothed down my brand-new dress and stood up. I was so busy smiling and looking ahead of me at the pulpit that I didn't see the little brown shoe that extended itself in front of my skinny ankles as I stepped out of our pew. I caught the smile of triumph on his face as I went down in a flutter of yellow organdy glory, petticoats and panties exposed, smashing my front lip against the edge of the seat. I managed to get up and recite my poem through a swelling lip, fighting back tears of rage and embarrassment. I returned to my seat and gave him a look, which I hoped was so full of venom that it would freeze his blood. The whipping and lectures he got when we returned home weren't enough.

That winter, I got a mammoth case of measles and stayed home from school for a week. On the third day of my fever, Mom let me sit up to watch television for a while. Jimmy came in after school, smiling and asking how I felt, with his hands held tightly behind his back. I should have been suspicious of his niceness right away, but the fever and the attention put me off guard. He said he had brought me a get-well present. Before

I could ask what it was, he extended his arm, offering me a fat dead rat that he held by the tail. Mom entered the room to see what was going on as I let out a round of screams. Jimmy dashed out past her, stuffing the horrible gift in his pocket before she could see it. She never did believe my story about the dead rat. After all, her "baby" wouldn't do such a thing. Yeah, right.

A week later, when I was well again, I deliberately left his new tricycle out on the playground in the rain, hoping it would get stolen. It did. Then we were finally even, at least as far as the issue of the red tricycle was concerned. I still hadn't forgiven him for the one I never got.

*T*he one person who managed to keep us civilized in her presence was our grandmother. Her constant stories and gentle manner were enough to humiliate us into behaving and respecting her unequivocal love for each of us. We were careful to keep our teasing and torture of each other out of her sight although it continued, non-stop, when we were away from her. Through her long fight with cancer, even when we didn't understand what was happening to her, we both knew she was special to us and we were special to her.

At eighteen, I was happy finally to leave home for the first time and to leave my cretin brother. I started going to college and hitched a ride home for the long Thanksgiving holiday weekend. In the few months I had been away, Jimmy seemed to have suddenly turned into an awkward, skinny twelve-year-old who was taller than I was. He seemed anxious to see me but resented giving up my bed, which he had started using as his place to study.

That night, Grandmother passed away in her sleep. Jimmy

was the one who hugged and comforted me after the hospital phoned us. We were both somber as the specter of death settled around us. Much of our hostility melted with our tears in the November rain as we watched her burial. The two of us knew that, somehow, we had negotiated a wordless pact of loyalty between us that day, as we shared our mutual grief and loss.

*O*ur relationship changed while I was away at college. I got involved in the student demonstrations and marches of the civil rights movement. My parents phoned every other day begging me, like most Black parents begged their children, to please be careful, don't get hurt, don't get arrested, or, worse, killed. Jimmy stayed home, frustrated that he had to watch it all on television, telling me how glamorous he thought it was and that he wished he could be out there in the streets with me. I got a kick out of his admiration and became his political and intellectual connection to the outside world. I funneled back to him all the new ideas and challenges that I was learning myself, in the freedom that came with leaving home for the first time and being on my own. Existentialism was my new thought pattern. I sent Jimmy dog-eared used copies of books by Sartre, Kafka, Camus, Gide, and Jean Genet. I turned him on to every Black author I discovered, since we had never heard of any—Richard Wright, Ralph Ellison, James Baldwin. I copied and mailed home to him any third-world political journals I could find.

When I came home for vacations and holidays, we had serious discussions about the racism we had grown up with and the buried rage we had been programmed to live with, growing up Black in a small Southern town. His political awareness emerged and became as radical as my own; he grew a monstrous Afro, wore his first dashiki, and considered changing his name to something African. At seventeen, he was excited when he joined me and my husband in a voter registration march in the streets of Atlanta with other students.

When he reached eighteen and was required to register for the draft, the Vietnam War was at its peak and was threatening our lives, his more than mine. We had heard stories about the insane body count and how many young Black men were coming home in body bags each month. Somewhere in the back of my mind I still harbored the notion that if anyone was going to get to do him in for some ridiculous reason, it wasn't going to be the U.S. Army, it would be me. What I could not admit to him or to myself was how much I loved him.

When he filed for conscientious objector status, I supported him completely. It was either that or run off to Canada, which we had discussed as an alternative. The problem was that none of us knew any people in Canada. We had heard that there were Black people in Canada, but we didn't know any and neither did any of our friends. The day he went down to report for his physical, I prayed that this was one exam he would fail. We laughed like fools when he was sent home by the army doctor because he was too thin! They took one look at his long skinny carcass and told him that he had to put on some weight and come back in three months. Jimmy went home and stopped eating, started jogging, and lost another twelve pounds. When he returned for his next physical, not only was he too thin, but he was also classified 4-F because of his chronic asthma.

My "little baby brother" had grown into a six-foot-four-inch human who was skinnier than a refugee from a war zone. He looked as though he could have been a political prisoner. I breathed a sigh of relief and got on with my own life while James—he insisted that he was no longer a little boy, so I had to stop calling him Jimmy—became a politically conscious radical young Black man who was willing to risk running away from home and country rather than be drafted and die in a war for a country that did not respect him. I just hoped that his loud mouth and strong ideas wouldn't get him killed in a street demonstration or a political rally.

The one new adventure I wasn't prepared for when he went off to college was his beginning to date white women two years later. I was mute with rage and confusion after he called to tell me about "Jennifer." How could he do this to me? I wrote letter after letter, all of which ended up in the trash, since I was disturbed by the depth of my own fury. I called Mom instead. I began to feel like James's alternate mother as the two of us commiserated by phone and hoped it was just another phase that he would soon grow out of. Experimentation with new lifestyles had become the watchword of the day, but this was going too far. I bit my tongue and tried to dismiss it as another defiant challenge to everything else we were changing. Hair, names, politics—why not lovers? How often had we discussed the white man as enemy? I wondered, why did he see the white woman as a separate category? I felt betrayed, hurt, and rejected, like most of my women friends. We had often watched the brightest, most talented brothers around us pass us by for the nearest blonde bimbo, without so much as acknowledging that we were even in the room. How could I tell my friends that my brother, who I loved and admired, was sleeping with the enemy?

I had gone out with a few white men myself and worked around several who had made overtures, but I wasn't silly enough to take any of them seriously, even though my marriage was falling apart at the time.

When James insisted on bringing Jennifer to New York to meet me, I made excuses for several weeks until I couldn't put it off any longer. I refused to let them stay at my apartment, lying about the place being painted. We met at an out-of-the-way cheap restaurant—I knew how broke they were since they were both in graduate school at George Washington University—for a Friday dinner after work; me in a button-down business suit, the two of them dressed like rejects from a Salvation Army thrift shop. The six years between us suddenly felt like six centuries, when I heard the generational way I criticized him. I blasted him with words like those Mom had shot at me when I had come home from college. "When are you going to comb that hair? And trim that beard." "Oh, God, I hope that tattoo isn't permanent!" Being a corporate snob, I was just glad that none of my business friends could see me with them.

I was cool to the point of being rude and deliberately insulted Jennifer by never getting her name right. I called her Gina, Jeanette, Joanie—anything to try to make her feel less than human. I ignored her when she asked questions and pretended I didn't hear her compliments about how professional I looked. The most sympathy I could manage was when he told me about being stopped and harassed by the cops on the New Jersey Turnpike. James said he figured they thought he was a drug dealer. I couldn't miss my chance to tell him I thought it was because he was with "Janice" here. Right on cue, she burst into tears. James was so hurt by my reaction that they didn't order dinner and left me there alone, feeling like a bad penny waiting for change.

When he phoned the next morning to curse me out and accuse me of being a Black racist, I told him he could just as easily find someone who could love him who looked more like me and his mother. It was the first time we had ever condemned each other's choices. We didn't speak to each other for several months. I could have been kinder, but generosity wasn't on the menu at that moment in my life. I used the excuse of not being able to forgive him for being with a white woman. I was really angry because he seemed genuinely happy, and I was jealous.

That spring, when they got married, James found a way to get even with Mom and me. We were both hurt and humiliated when he didn't invite any of us to the wedding. When their little girl was born a year later, my parents and I relented and apologized, for the most predictable of reasons: we wanted to see who she looked like.

We lost touch for a while. It hurt me to be left out of his life as his marriage and children kept him occupied. My job transfers and career moves took me too far away to visit on weekends and holidays.

Some of his other life choices shocked me. After their second baby was born, James chose to become a househusband for five years because his wife could earn more money. I had to re-examine my own feminist rhetoric. Wasn't this going too far? His wife brought home the bread and butter while he made beds, did laundry, clipped coupons and shopped for the Wednesday specials at Safeway, cleaned bathrooms, took care of two children, and went to PTA meetings. He also found the time to finish college, get his master's degree in psychology, and become the best damned gourmet cook I've ever met. When he did return to work full-time he started his career as a family therapist, which he has built into a thriving consulting business.

Despite the distance, thanks to cheap weekend phone rates, in moments of crisis we found time to talk. He shared his worries about where his life was going and how he rated as husband and father. I bent his ear about every new job, new man, and new life crisis that I met. He listened to all the gritty details and gave me his opinion, knowing full well that I would do what I wanted, no matter how stupid it might be.

Through the multiple relationships in which I have found myself over the years—one husband, two live-in boyfriends, and a parade of innumerable lovers and intimate friends—James was always there, supporting me in the emotional roller-coaster ride of my mood swings as I moved in and out of these liaisons. He was also there after the break-ups and had the sensitivity not to add a judgmental "I told you so!" when he had every right to do so. He's been there during jobs I hated, career moves that made me grit my teeth, and the average Black career woman's tribulations.

My brother has come to occupy a space in my head and heart which is coveted by all the other men who come through my life. He is the one man I know that I can trust unequivocally. He has earned the right and privilege to tell me truths I need to hear—and I will listen. Through the obstacle course of careers, kids, marriages, and divorces we have counseled each other with liberal doses of hard truths that would have started World War III if they had been uttered by anyone else. When he tells me I'm being obnoxious, I know it's for my own good. When I tell him he's being a shithead, he hears me. His wife once said to me, "He listens differently to you than to anyone else around him." And he should. Who else knows his flaws and shortcomings as well as I do? He knows mine, too.

After we both hit the over-forty milestone, the special nature of our kinship gradually became apparent to me. I have traded being a bossy big sister for a mutually respectful relationship. We are sibling, friend, parent, and confidant for each other. We have learned to forgive each other far more quickly and make special concessions to each other that surprise even us.

Who else would I loan my life savings to for his business without contract or collateral? (He paid me back with interest.) Blood loyalty and a bond of childhood bruises have created a trust that has outlasted the time when we sparred over who controlled the TV.

As Mom said that day when she brought him home from the hospital, having him in my life was a gift. And a lesson. No one else could have taught me the lessons of compromise and forgiveness, of tolerance, patience, and acceptance of who I am and who he has become. I think we are both better people for having grown up together. Lovers, spouses, bosom buddies, and even parents may disappear from my life, but he is the only constant witness to my development as a human being over time.

On a recent evening, when his wife was home with the flu, I was his "date" at a business dinner. I was proud to hear the praise offered by his professional colleagues when James received an award for some of the work he has done with at-risk children in emotionally abused families. It gave me great pleasure to realize that the whiny little four-year-old who dogged my every step has developed into a dynamic human being that I am proud to know. If we weren't related it would be a privilege to call him my friend.

Esco

Kai Jackson-Issa

Mississippi–Cherokee–African–South Side. Hands muscled thirty years in Chicago steel mills. That was Esco Winston, my beloved uncle. A short man, standing five-feet-four, bowlegged, squat, and powerful, like a buddha. His skin was brown copper, his face was petite and finely chiseled. He had a round, nearly bald head, which he covered in winters with a tweed kangol and in summers with a weathered, canvas fishing number. His perfectly clear eyes were alive with mischief and friendship. Dimples on his cheeks danced with the whimsy in his eyes. He grew his thumbnails outrageously long, to grip and sort the photographs that were his lifelong craft and passion.

Esco was my first role model as an artist. Like most role models, his presence was so subtle, so everyday, that I did not appreciate him as such until after he died. While he lived, Esco showed me that art is not luxury, not detached. Art is spontaneous and peculiar, as he showed in the story he told me of seeing little girl triplets walking down Forty-seventh Street on a Sunday morning in 1940, making him grab his camera and halt his car, in that order.

Esco taught me that an artist is a committed historian, as his documentation of his favorite subjects proved: Ella, Sarah, Duke, and Count at the Regal. The Robert Taylor and Ida B. Wells projects raised. Fred Hampton and the Panthers gunned down. Reverend Johnnie Coleman. The Muntu African Dance Troupe. Father Clement's and Holy Angels church. Haki Madhabuti. Harold Washington as congressman and mayor. Bud Billiken. Esco rarely charged his subjects for his pictures. When city trees felled rooftops after tornadoes, when winter potholes swallowed cars, or when landlords neglected plumbing and plaster, Esco was on call and never charged people for his sharp witness craft.

Art is family: his yearly visits to our houses to take portraits of us as we grew. His presence at holiday parties was steady, and always we young folks would grumble about how long we had to stand for his pictures. Esco had definite ideas about who should be where and how we should be posed, angled, and expressioned. One picture could take thirty minutes, and deviating from Esco's schema could make it take even longer. Afterward, Esco's flash would signal our collective laugh, and we would return to food and bid whist and gossip, more restored and drawn closer than we knew.

Art is patience. One day we ate turkey submarines spiced with sweet pickles, mayo, and onion on the lakefront. We were there for him to teach me how to work my new thirty-five millimeter. We watched the seagulls all afternoon. Esco told me how difficult it was to shoot them flying. He talked about sky lighting, motion, color. I thought he was being difficult and stingy with his craft, because he never touched the camera or taught me how to work it that day. Now I realize he was showing me the essential truths about photography, which have little to do with f-stops, lenses, and light meters, but are about the artist waiting until harmony with the subject is reached.

Esco had learned photography under the G.I. Bill, after serving in the army in World War II. He studied at Chicago's Washington Park with Margaret Burroughs and Gordon Parks. By day, he worked at the steel mills, but his heart had become a camera. I listen to my aunt, who remembers Esco as he was then, a life-loving Black boy, home from the war and with a bit of money for the first time. He began his habit of stashing his money in strange places—his shoes, socks, underwear. He wore custom-tailored suits. He carried a gun. He drank Weller's whiskey and smoked an occasional cigar. My aunt tells me: "After the war, Esco had bought a piece of car. He was gonna take us girls to Forty-seventh Street to get some fried pies. We didn't know any better, so we went. Esco was driving. All of a sudden he put both his legs on the steering wheel and opened up the door, then he snatched up a lantern that was in the middle of the street. We were terrified!" She tells me Esco made the girls laugh by climbing lampposts and jumping over corner newsstands. Esco had an apartment then. His "studio," he called it, but it was a space of ill repute to the rest of our family. There, the shades were drawn mostly, and pretty brown girls came by day or night, posing for free portraits on a green brocade ottoman.

I knew him some thirty years later. I first knew him as "Uncle," one of the many men always at my Uncle Andrew's house, sitting around the table in the cigar-thick kitchen, talking, laughing, and cursing into the night. My tie to Esco was not by blood, but by his seventy-year friendship with my Uncle Andrew. They met as boys in 1923 at the Forestville Elementary School, located in the South Side section of Chicago known as Bronzeville. Esco was a hungry little boy then, far from his home of Hazelhurst, Mississippi. He was so hungry one lunch-time that he couldn't help staring at the sausage biscuit Andrew unwrapped from a bit of wax paper. The boys' eyes met in lifelong friendship. Andrew shared his biscuit. The rest of their history together is that of men long dead: Gus, Mose, Happy, Kaho, Fletcher. To me, these names smell like whiskey and clean shirts and cigars and trumpets. They smell of good times and brothers beyond blood.

I really began to know Esco after my mother's death and my father's stroke. Esco was an angel after my deepest loss. When I doubted if I should leave home for college, Esco assured me that he would look after my father. He was a faithful presence at the airport when I arrived home on school breaks. Seeing him there when I entered the gateway steadied my frantic heart. He was the strong, healthy parent I wanted so much to depend on. I'm not sure what I was to him. The treasured child he never had? A late second childhood? Our love began during those years, in what proved to be the strangest relationship I've ever had with a man. Esco got more possessive of my time when I was home. He'd want to go out with me every day, leaving my house in a huff if I told him I was meeting friends, or, God forbid, my boyfriend. One day he told me, "Babydoll, you just don't know how I feel about you. I love you."

"I love you, too," I said, carefully ignoring his implications.

Then, pointing to his cheek, he asked, "Can I have a teeny weeny?" I gave him a kiss on the cheek.

I listened to Esco's sweet talk, always fleeting. He never ventured beyond a teeny weeny, either. He liked me to keep him company on his visits and errands, to listen to his stories over Army and Lou dinners of smothered chicken and macaroni. He spoiled me with shopping trips and spending money. He gave me the peace of mind to study away from home. I loved his attention. He was the impossible standard I used to measure my boyfriends and then be mad at them. When Esco took out his wallet, carefully undoing the many rubber bands around it (his technique for catching pickpockets), he usually gave me a few hundred dollars. I don't remember how I spent the money, and the lesson for me is a powerful one: Money exchanged that isn't earned by hard work rarely sticks to the hand. My profoundest lesson, besides how to graciously accept gifts from a man and keep stepping, was that people and relationships are, more than anything, complex.

Our relationship turned after a few years, when Esco began ailing with cancer. I tried to look after him, coming home once a month to be with him, to help straighten his apartment and grocery shop. Esco was proud until the end. He never wanted to admit I was there to help him, or that he needed help. He would go on like I was in town for a visit, and we would go to lunch, to museums, and around the neighborhood.

I feel privileged to have been loved by a Black man whose generation has faded, by a man who was not threatened by women, a man who enjoyed women's company so much that he never forgot the birthdays of my aunts and brought them birthday cakes and teased them about the things they did when they were girls. I knew how deeply Esco loved women by the way he treated his ex-wife, Viola. Esco had married late in life, well into his fifties. Viola was younger with a son, who Esco cared for and regarded as his own. The cooling of Esco and Viola's love affair is family lore. Viola, fed up, fired one single shot from her .38 into the wind of Esco's flight out to the back yard. Viola made a phone call, and a delegation of my aunts arrived, totally on Viola's side. They all knew Esco had funny ways.

Esco soon moved into his own apartment. When I knew

them, they had been separated for over twenty years. But every day, Esco would go over to Viola's house when she was away at work. He would do things for her, like take out the trash, water the lawn, let repair people in and wait there while they did their work. Sometimes he would take me along. I would watch Esco's face, searching for traces of sadness, resentment, or possessiveness. There were none. Esco had found a quiet place to be effective in Viola's life, and he was content. When her car died, he bought her a brand new one. One Christmas, during the same time he was professing his love for me, Esco took me to a jewelry store and I helped him pick out a diamond tennis bracelet for Viola. Later, when Esco was dying, he moved back into Viola's house. He rested in a bedroom across from hers, and Viola, a registered nurse, was there for him and took care of him until he died.

Esco lived in an apartment on Eighty-eighth and Stony Island Avenue, over a doctor's office. I knew the place well because my father used to live there, two apartments down. On my weekend visits to my father's, we'd always stop and see Esco. One day, as we stood outside the building, Esco rode past us at full speed on his bicycle. He was about seventy at the time. He laughed at our surprise, delighting in the mini-spectacle he caused on the sidewalk.

Esco favored loose, cotton Cuban embroidered shirts with many pockets, in cool colors of white, beige, and sky-blue. He was never without his Mayan necklace, a gift one of my aunts had brought him from Arizona. The piece was stunning, an inlaid brass, silver, and copper Indian figurine, hanging on a silver link chain and coming to Esco's midchest. That was the only piece of jewelry he wore. His pants were usually brown polyester, a bit flared and nicely pressed. His shoes were custom-ordered extra-wide rubber-soled walkers, always a bit run down. Esco was self-conscious about his wide feet. His style —

comfortable, not flashy, with just a splash of flamboyance in the necklace—spoke "elder," "Afro," "artiste." "I know I don't look like much of nothing," he lamented once, during our love days. The next day, he showed up for our dinner date in a tan, double-breasted Italian suit. He was immaculate and elegant, laughing all night at my shock.

Esco drove an ancient, royal-blue Pontiac two-door. He boasted that he didn't have to worry about anyone stealing it. His two-thousand-dollar Hasselblad cameras (the kind the astronauts used to film the moon, Esco bragged), rested on the floor of the back seat, packed in frayed vinyl carry-ons. The back seat was covered with manila envelopes filled with his pictures. Esco's driving technique, when I knew him, was hair-raising on a good day. He was an eclectic driver: cautious, cowboy, oblivious. I always rode looking down into my lap, my eyes fixed on his photos he wanted my opinion on. I never worried about us having an accident, though. I pictured his car blessed by his buddies of yore, gone from body but watching from the other side. I imagined that they rode on Esco's rooftop, protective and resplendent in open shirts and slacks or straw pajamas.

Esco took me to hear James Baldwin read from *The Evidence of Things Not Seen* at a bookstore. When we arrived, the small store was packed; a long line had formed outside. I don't know what most convinced the attendant at the door—the borderline-official presence of Esco with all his photography equipment, or Esco's quiet, relentless conversation. He let us in. I heard Baldwin read for the first and last time of my life. Later, Esco took a picture of James Baldwin signing my book. In the picture, I am gushing at Baldwin and telling him that I want to be a writer someday.

When my father lay dying from another serious stroke, Esco drove me to the hospital every day. He stayed in the lobby or the solarium, waiting to take me back home, sometimes the entire day. He always brought me newspapers, my favorite turkey submarines, and vanilla milk shakes.

The last time I saw Esco take a picture was on my wedding day. He walked me down the aisle. Too weak from his cancer to walk down the long staircase that led into the back yard, though, he met me at the foot of the stairs. He wore a deep purple Nigerian *buba* with gold embroidery, and he supported himself with a carved wooden cane. He had become honorary father and friend. During the ceremony, I turned and saw Esco's face, veiled by his camera, held by his unsteady, expert hands.

I helped to clean out Esco's apartment after he died together with Viola, my aunt Nerissa, and my cousin Phyllis. Our day was an unfolding of hilarious surprises. We found his fantastic collection of World War II–era dildos, pornography, and bejeweled Asian swords. There was his collection of pistols, hidden everywhere, inside socks, under couch cushions, in a kitchen cabinet—pearl handles, huge .44s, one tiny brass pistol that fit into my palm. We marveled that Esco had managed all those years not to accidentally shoot himself. The green ottoman from his earlier period of bachelorhood was covered by a bed sheet.

His copper collection. Plastic grocery bags filled with pictures. His long, beechwood table, covered with plastic boxes of Amway vitamins. A closet filled with pristine Dobbs' English hatboxes holding never-worn fedoras. That day, I came away with two poster-size pictures that Esco had taken of me. He had wrapped them in large trash bags and stored them behind his couch. They embarrass me, they're so big. I keep them now in the back of my closet. Here is testimony of his love for me, evidence of his painstaking command of light and detail, his will to bring out the best in his subject. Esco

Winston: helper, warrior, artist. Uncle, father, friend. I remembered and learned in the company of women that day, as we laughed and cried over, tried to section off, sift through, say good-bye to, what was left of the man we had known and loved.

Straight to the Ghetto

Connie Porter

For me, there is nothing like James Brown singing "Santa Claus, Go Straight to the Ghetto" to bring some spirit into a house at Christmas. In a trembling voice, punctuated by his renowned horns, he implores Santa Claus to:

> *Hitch up your reindeer*
> *—Unnh—*
> *And go straight to the ghetto . . .*
> *You know that I know what you'll see*
> *'Cause that was once*
> *Me . . .*[*]

Last Christmas I played this song while my family had dinner. Four of my eight brothers and sisters, their families, and our mother had come to my home in Virginia for Christmas. My brother Ronald thought that stomach-rattling funk was a bit too

---

[*] James Brown, "Santa Claus, Go Straight to the Ghetto," *Soulful Christmas*, King, 1968. Used by permission.

much to digest turkey and greens and dressing by, but even he had to admit he enjoyed it. Perhaps it moved him. It is such a cliché to say that the song moves us. But James Brown *does* move me.

As a child, my siblings and I watched hundreds of hours of "American Bandstand" and groaned every time some white boy or girl with long hair and no discernable sense of rhythm gave a song a high score in "Rate a Record" and repeated the phrase that the song had a "good beat you could dance to." Like any cliché, that phrase had little meaning. I always thought there had to be more to those songs. Somehow the kids with the slingable hair were just incapable of expressing what lay at the heart of the music.

As more Blacks danced on the show, with big Afros that stood out like halos and bell bottoms so wide you could hide a small child inside them, I thought things would change. They would tell me what those records were all about as I perched on my knees before the black-and-white television in the kitchen, but they said the same things the white kids did. With thousands of words to draw on, all they could come up with was something that had been said before! They made their counterparts on "Soul Train" look like geniuses when they went to the Scramble Board and unscrambled such challenging names as "The Jackson Five," taking home a years' supply of Ultra or Afro Sheen.

I'd hate to think what the world would be if we all held on to the indignation and the sense of keen disappointment adolescents feel. I can now look back on those dancers with more kindness. They are mothers and fathers now, raising children who rave and slam dance, who do the Butterfly and Bounce. Their daughters have learned nothing from their mothers. They are falling off platform shoes their mothers swore off years ago. Their sons have their fathers' hairstyles. The white boys are still slinging their hair, and somehow too few Black boys have grasped the idea that an Afro is a high-maintenance style, which needs to be shaped, oiled, and trimmed. A lopsided mass of hair matted on one side of the head is *not* an Afro. Every time I see a young boy in the mall with his hair looking like he just woke up from a bad dream, I feel like shocking him wide awake with a picture of the old Michael Jackson with an Afro the diameter and symmetry of a basketball. One could think these children are the way they are because of their parents. They spoke in clichés, so the children just tuned them out. The children never knew the stories of their parents' lives, so they are repeating their parents' history, bad clothes, bad shoes, and needlessly bad hair.

But I don't think these children didn't listen. Most of us know our history and repeat it in the form of family stories. In my family there is a story about my father. Even when he started to court, he still had to have my aunt, his younger sister, wait outside the privy at night because he was afraid of the dark. There is the story of my uncle, who as a baby was kidnapped by gypsies in Birmingham and was rescued just as they were leaving town with him. Then there is cousin Richard, who brought a raccoon, dead and skinned, head still on, to be cooked at a back yard barbecue.

When we get together, we tell these stories over and over; they are prayers; they are chants; they are songs that move us.

Anytime we repeat the cliché that a song moves us, I think what we mean is that it takes us to another place, to some other time when we were someone else.

What was missing for me as James Brown screamed through my house and my nieces and nephews giggled because they were eating by candlelight like people in movies, was my brother Michael. He had to work up in Pittsburgh and could not join us.

While I listened to the music and ate with everyone, I was also defying the laws of physics and moving back in time, back to the place where I grew up. Ghetto.

A few years ago someone told me not to say that, not to tell people where I grew up. I suppose the person thought since I was a writer, maybe I could invent a storied past. One that contained none of my family's stories. But that is where I'm from. The second youngest of nine children, I grew up in the housing projects in Lackawanna, New York, just outside of Buffalo.

Anyone from a large family, especially one with a big age spread in the children like ours has — over twenty years — knows that in such families you have more than one family. The older siblings have their family, the younger ones theirs. I don't remember my oldest two brothers, Midford and Malcolm Jr., ever living at home. They had both gone off to the navy before I entered kindergarten. It bothers me that I don't remember them. I was a baby when they left. Malcolm Jr. tells me that he would put me on top of the refrigerator and tell me to jump off. I would, and he would catch me. At least he says he caught me. I'd like to remember him, to have spent more time with him, to maybe have jumped off of higher things.

The brother I do remember, the one who was really in *my* family, is my brother Michael, the youngest of all the boys. When I am in the mall with the boys with the bad Afros and baggy pants, the boys with the braids, with the sneakers falling off their feet, the boys who talk loudly and stroll slowly, the boys too many of us are afraid of, I think of my brother Michael when he was a boy.

We were each someone else then. I was a skinny, dark girl in braids, my straightened hair shiny with Dixie Peach. He was a handsome brown-skinned teenager with what they now call the TWA—teeny-weeny Afro. He did not join in with my sisters and me when we held parties for our dolls, or spent hours in the summer in the back alley making dirt cakes, playing kickball, and roller skating on metal skates, our skate keys dangling around our necks, our feet tingling on the rough and uneven pavement. Somehow, I thought he would enjoy these things, not realizing he was almost a man then, not realizing that after he finished his paper route, and after he worked a second job, he did not feel like running like a wild child through the mild and windy blueness of a summer in Buffalo.

I think we played so hard, dug in the dirt so long, laid out in the cool grass eating Popsicles because we knew summer didn't last long in Buffalo. Too soon my mother wouldn't be able to hang sheets on the line, and we would not be able to surreptitiously run under them, drinking in their freshness. Winter would come in early fall, and there might be snow on the ground by Halloween, and still be snow on the ground at Easter.

It was when we wintered over, like sheep in a barn, that Michael and I played. I especially liked Sundays after Sunday school, after dinner, the dishes done, the floor swept, everyone else gone upstairs to watch the color television. Michael and I would stay behind and watch the end of the late football game.

The Bills would have lost the early game, even with O.J. He was someone else then, too. He was famous, not infamous, running through the mud in War Memorial Stadium. He was simply the best running back in the league on one of the worst teams. Despite O.J.'s efforts, the Bills would lose, throwing my brother and father into bad moods by four o'clock.

Watching the late game was a way of letting go of that funk, a way to cheer for a team that had a chance of winning. I didn't care too much for those games, though. They reminded me too much of the games from years before, when there was one television.

My sisters and I sat with our Sunday dessert, a bowl of ice

cream and a couple of Oreos, waiting for some game to end so we could watch "The Wonderful World of Disney." Our ice cream would melt as we waited for the last two minutes of the game to be over. When it wasn't over exactly at seven and Tinker Bell did not appear on the screen, one of us would yell, "Hey, Michael, turn on our show!"

"It's not on yet. There's still a minute left in the game," he would answer.

"No, it ain't. You said there was two minutes left five minutes ago. You better put on our show. You probably got it on the wrong channel."

He would get up in a huff and spin the dial so quickly through the channels, they were a blur. Then he would turn back to the game. "See, it's Channel 2. How many times do I have to tell you they keep stopping the clock. When the clock stops, that means time stops."

"You can't stop no time! How two minutes last five minutes? You trying to cheat us out our show. Mama, make him turn on our show."

"He told you it ain't on yet, Connie. Michael, turn the dial slow so they can see," Mama would say.

My sisters and I were incredulous. Our show wasn't on. We mushed our cookies into our ice cream and ate it while those giant men we hated violated the laws of time.

Though I grew to love football enough to get cable so I can watch the late, late Sunday night games, then I didn't care for it much, and my brother and I would play basketball as a late game wound down.

With a winter glove for a ball, preferably one of Michael's because it had more weight to it, we would shoot into our "hoop." Our hoop was the curtain rod on the kitchen door. For about fifteen minutes, we would battle it out, driving to the hoop, doing lay-ups, bank shots, bombing away from the outside—the kitchen table. We played quietly, so our parents wouldn't hear us. It did not matter if Michael stepped on my foot, or boxed me out with an elbow to the ribs, or hip-checked me to the floor, I bore the fouls in silence, and kept on playing. I seldom won, but winning was not the thing. Playing the game with him was. Into late fall we kept on playing, bending the rod, dirtying the curtains while snow piled up outside the door.

Our dad would send Michael out to shovel it. Our father was disabled, at this point in his life weighing well over three hundred pounds. Growing up during the Depression, he had quit school in the sixth grade to help support his family. He was someone who had worked just about all his life and felt that work was something good for everyone. All of us kids had chores, dishes and dusting, sweeping and vacuuming. Michael's was putting out the trash and shoveling.

Even while it was still snowing, an inch an hour, two inches, out Michael went with a big, heavy steel shovel. I would watch him through the door, clearing off patches of glass that my breath clouded up. His hat and coat would crust with snow, and to me, it seemed like a miracle that when I opened the door to give him rock salt for the sidewalk, it would already be covered in white again. I don't think our father had ever heard the story of Sisyphus and was quite unaware that every time it snowed, he sent my brother outside to act out a variation of his story.

I liked the snow. It meant that Christmas was coming. Santa Claus was coming straight to the ghetto.

I am amazed that our parents were able to do as much as they did for us at Christmas. There are black-and-white pictures of my oldest brothers standing before a real tree draped in tinsel. They are wearing corduroy pants and flannel shirts, shooting toy guns at the camera. Behind them is a floor full of toys.

Our younger family had an aluminum tree. I thought it

was beautiful. It was silver, and there was a flood light that shone on it. Before the light was a four-paneled disk, red, green, blue, yellow, that revolved. Best of all, the whole tree revolved. My sisters and I would lie under it and watch our faces reflected in the red ornaments that spun slowly like stars above our heads, dreaming about what would be under the tree on Christmas morning. Already we had each claimed pages of booty from the Sears wish book.

Michael didn't join in our wishing. He was in high school and too busy with homework and his paper route. By the time we arrived home from school, he had folded his papers and loaded them on his Flexible Flyer. Off he would go into the snowy, darkening afternoon, pulling the heavy sled. I thought it must be fun. If I delivered the papers, and my sled was empty at the end of the route, I thought, I'd come coasting home belly down in the moonlight. But I knew from his complaints that delivering wasn't fun. Customers didn't pay on time, dogs chased him.

Once a week Michael had to balance his account. He would get out his coin changer. Sometimes he would let me spit out the coins onto the living-room table. I thought he was rich, and that it wouldn't be so bad if I took one penny. You could buy something with a penny then—a Squirrel Nut, three Peach Stones, two chocolate Kisses. But I knew I couldn't have even a penny. Michael owed that money to the *Buffalo Evening News*. If he was short, he had to pay the difference.

But at Christmas, things were better. Michael's customers tipped him, gave him gifts. What I liked best was that some of them gave him cookies. He brought home boxes of them from the Italian, German, and Polish women who lived in the houses near our projects. He shared them with us—cookies dusted with powdered sugar, shaped like snowflakes and crescent moons, seasoned with spices we never had tasted before; mace, anise, cardamom. I was proud of my brother, that his customers thought enough of him to give him gifts, and that he thought enough of us to share with us. I felt they knew how special he was. So did my mother.

Our father provided for us. He knew it took money to make a Christmas. He made sure that money was always there, especially when we were teenagers, when we would get practical gifts like a coat or new pair of boots and money for us to buy whatever else we wanted. But our mother knew that Christmas was more. It was a time for a new outfit to wear to Sunday school and give our speeches in. She would stay up night after night feeding yards of velvet and ribbon and lace through the sewing machine. She spent hours baking homemade bread, cinnamon rolls and cookies, hams and turkeys, making sweet potato pies. Somehow she also found time to get us something special, personal, in addition to the toys, in addition to the money and clothes.

*O*ne Christmas, my sisters and I woke at three in the morning and attempted to sneak downstairs past our father, only to be sent back to bed until a decent hour — 5:00 A.M. In the darkness, our feet bare, we burst downstairs and flipped on the light, to see what looked like an explosion in a toy factory. There were coloring books and crayons, an Etch-A-Sketch, an Easy Bake oven, Barbies, toy pots and pans and dishes, and, parked in the middle of everything, two pink bicycles. One for me and one for my next oldest sister. With high-rise handlebars, white banana seats, and white flowered baskets, they were going to be the best bikes on the block when we could take them out in five or six months.

Michael didn't come down until nearly noon. I didn't understand how he could sleep so late on Christmas. I felt bad that there were no toys for him, felt bad that he was going to get some boring clothes and money. He did have a special gift from Mama, in a small wrapped box. A pair of gloves. At first I thought, "Great, two new basketballs!" But when I touched them, I knew they could never be used for our game.

They were beautiful, made of soft brown leather and lined in rabbit fur. The leather smelled like something I thought a rich person would have. I put my hands inside to feel the sleek fur and rolled back the tops to feel it on my face. Michael liked the gloves, too, and our father gave him a chance to try them out. He sent Michael out to shovel.

I watched Michael, hunched over as he shoveled. Of course, it was still snowing. The snow even made the garbage bins overflowing with garbage look beautiful. Those bins were filled with toy boxes. From the look of things, it seemed that Santa Claus had spent the entire night in the ghetto.

After Michael had come in from shoveling, our mother rolled out the dough for bread and cinnamon rolls while he, my sisters, and I jostled with one another, grabbing scraps of sweet dough she left behind on the table. When our mother got sick of us shoving and passing licks, she slapped at our hands with a spoon and sent us into the living room to straighten it up.

We put the stereo on real low on the soul station to listen to the Christmas music. (Our father had bought the family a stereo, but never wanted it played loud.) After The Jackson Five sang "I Saw Mommy Kissing Santa Claus" and the Temptations, "Silent Night," James Brown came on singing my song. I knew he was singing about me. He was singing about us. He was telling a story about our unstoried lives. James Brown was singing about our home. He was proving to himself something I was to discover years later. You *can* go home again, even when that home is not yours anymore, even when some other family has moved inside its tiny box that held your lives like gifts waiting to be opened on Christmas.

I am hoping that this year Michael can join us at my house for Christmas, because no matter how much music may move us, no matter how James Brown may take me home, I don't want to make the trip alone. I hope Michael will be there, and we will tell the story of one night when he and my sisters and I were home and our parents went out.

We got in a fight, screaming and scratching, kicking and shoving and slapping, that somehow led to the heavy glass butter dish being thrown through a lamp in the living room. I still don't remember who went to the kitchen to get it, or why one of us thought to take aim at the rest with that heavy dish. The dish didn't break, but it knocked a hole in the lamp's base, startling us. We stopped fighting then and united to clean up the living room and kitchen, and carefully arrange the lamp to hide the hole in its base. When our parents came home, we had all bathed and were quietly watching television. Not one of us had a story to tell about what happened while they were out.

It is another story in our unstoried lives that we sealed our lips to, that needs to be told again, that needs to be chanted while Michael sits with us this time, while James Brown sings, and our nieces and nephews giggle and eat by candlelight, their faces glowing, their lives opening before us like gifts.

Brothers Are . . .

Kiini Ibura Ya Salaam

Brothers are beings who feign indifference but willingly drive you and your belongings nine hundred miles across the country when you want to relocate. Brothers are creatures who have no moral qualms about using their black-belt expertise to kick your ass during childhood, then refuse to hurt others for fear of karmic retribution as an adult. Souls who only grant you a pause when you return home after a year abroad. "You don't look no different" is their welcome-home statement, as they turn back to their Nintendo game. At least *my* brothers are these types of concoctions.

When my two brothers frequently referred to me as a freak, I smiled, confident it was they who were the anomalies. We female siblings often wondered from whence my brothers sprang. Yes, they too were born of my father's sperm and my mother's egg, but what else was thrown in the mix? There must have been some odd shifting occurring during their incubation period. My mother must have been force-fed a piece of pork, and the fat bubbles must have gotten imbedded in their brains and lodged in their hearts. That must be it, I would convince myself, that must be why they're so strange.

Distance affords the mind interesting perspective. More and more of my mental space is used for pride and bragging rather than disgust and confusion where my brothers are concerned. Yes, they are different from me and my sisters, but I'm now seeing new patterns in their lives. These patterns suggest that my original disdain for their behavior is misguided. My brothers' lives explain them as logical offspring of my parents' union. They are as loyal to their upbringing as my sisters and I are, no matter how false the lives they lead may make that seem. Distance has made me admit that my brothers are my parents' children too.

I write this from New York, where I've been living for a year now. Yet I could have penned this at any moment in the past six years that I've lived away from New Orleans. "I just realized I don't know my brothers." This I am muttering to my father during a phone call from London. It is a cry echoed by my little sister during her first trip abroad. It's true that absence makes the heart grow fonder. It doesn't make the times spent with my brothers any sweeter, it just makes me long for more of them.

Growing up in an Africa-centered, revolution-based, ancestor-focused household can do a number on you. Being the child of two community leaders can make you a little strange. It can make you think crazy, convince you the world is yours. It can make you think you can fly. For years I thought my brothers feared the wings our parents nurtured in us. Hadn't they stayed home while my sisters and I flew around the globe? Hadn't they shunned college for the work world and everyday survival? Hadn't they abandoned any interest in the arts or any personal pursuit of a passion in life? Hadn't they chosen partners and confined themselves to family at ridiculously young ages? Ain't they still in New Orleans?

Even while dismissing my brothers in this way, I had never

ceased to consider them geniuses. My brothers are big-brained men who enjoy verbal sparring and mental challenges. My younger brother Tuta speaks fluent ghetto Latin and puts together five- and ten-thousand-piece puzzles as fast as an eyeblink. My older brother Mtume is a relentless questioner, who learned all the two-letter words in the dictionary for better dominance in Scrabble. I never understood, however, why my brothers confined their genius to kicking ass in Pitty Pat and in video games. I guess I was caught in the external landscape because when I examine their personal lives, I find they have carefully carved a freedom-space for themselves in what could otherwise be an oppressive existence. They have quietly used their upbringing to shun the world and make some phenomenal achievements at extremely young ages.

My siblings and I always joke that we were the ultimate experiment in parenting. No TV, no sugar, no perms, no candy, no pop music, no meat, no white people, no processed food, down with America, up with Afrika, the revolution is here and we are living it. Our parents and their peers achieved total isolation from the larger society by establishing an organization called Ahidiana. Ahidiana created a private school, which taught awareness, history, and self-sufficiency to Black children in the community. The land on which the school stood was six blocks from our house. During our formative years, my brothers, sisters, cousins, and friends socialized at school, at Kwanzaa events, at political and social events, and at each other's homes, which were all in the same impoverished New Orleans ghetto. A network of like-minded adults sheltered us and closely monitored our isolation.

But the adults nurturing us couldn't protect us forever. When we were eight or nine, we were released into the world and integrated into the public schools. To call the result of this integration culture shock would be a gross understatement. The children we encountered on the streets hadn't been informed that a cultural revolution had shaken America's consciousness. They were adamantly unaware that Black was now beautiful. The late eighties was a hellified time to sport African print and Afros. The power of the jheri curl coaxed criticisms and confusion wherever my siblings and I happened to wander. In the lunchroom, our food was strange. In the classroom, our names were strange. On the street, our looks were strange. In reaction, it seemed to me, my brothers desperately strove for normality.

If we were to gather for a family portrait, in the photographer's eye our differences in physical adornment would be astounding. Locks adorn the sisters' heads, silver bracelets circle their wrists. Among them would be some African print (probably wrapped around the waist of the youngest), and a number of ankhs. Glasses shield the brothers' eyes, expensive watches adorn the wrists. A tight haircut with a precise trim on the younger brother, a neat Afro on the older. Sagging pants drip off the waist of the younger brother, maybe one pants leg is pulled up high and hugging his left calf. The latest kicks cover his feet. The older brother is belted, tucked in, and vehemently against all patterns, let alone African ones.

If my younger brother Tuta was passionate about anything, it was about being average. He didn't want to stand out among the other young men in the ninth ward. He let his pants sag and dreamed of one day driving a huge, gas-guzzling player's hooptie. When he was old enough to make his own choices, he left juice behind in favor of all drinks carbonated, left vegetables behind in favor of all foods packaged. In terms of musical taste, Tuta defiantly refused to follow in our father's footsteps. Instead of collecting a wide range of music, Tuta committed himself to gangsta posturing early on. If it wasn't bass, he wasn't having it. If there were no curse words embedded in the lyrics, the music was too soft. In his refusal to assert his unique-

ness, he regularly allowed his teachers and classmates to mispro-
nounce his name. "Tutashinda nchi na Salaam" was a mouthful
for anyone to pronounce, but "Tuta," the shortened version of
his names, was by no means difficult.

My older brother Mtume seemed to be chasing the Black
Republican image. He had a dizzying array of thoughts and
ideas that supported his objections to our Black-only lifestyle.
Mtume's strong work ethic allowed him to surround himself
with the material objects that made his life comfortable. During
childhood, his room was a maze of comic books and records. A
constant philosopher, Mtume always had the blueprint for everything. Well-groomed, intelligent, self-sufficient, and conservative, his solution to life seemed to be to discreetly and quietly collect the kudos he needed to get where he wanted to go.
His wrestling with normality seemed to happen within, whereas
Tuta's seemed to happen in his outside world.

However they chose to integrate their renegade upbringing
into the mainstream world, both my brothers followed eerily
similar paths to similar ends. Because of Ahidiana's powerful
educational success, Tuta was three years ahead of his classmates, and Mtume was two years ahead of his. We were all
painfully conscious of their relentless intelligence, yet they refused to display it in school. Bored beyond belief, both preferred
to belittle the school system rather than participate in it. It
seemed the punishments my parents devised for bad grades
were made for my brothers. Every time report cards arrived, my
brothers received some new punishment for the oft-recurring
Cs, Ds, and Fs.

Summer punishments eventually earned laughter from my
brothers as they expressed nothing but disdain for their education. Tuta and Mtume's classroom mischief exasperated their
teachers, who always described them as intelligent, charming
students who were not working up to their full potential. De-

spite dismal grades, Tuta and Mtume constantly scored remarkably high on standardized exams. A testament to the control my brothers exerted on their lives was the sudden turnaround in their grades as soon as they perceived high marks to be pertinent to their lives. This sudden improvement in grades occurred during their last two years of high school, allowing both to gain entrance into good colleges, from which both dropped out.

Mtume left Loyola University in New Orleans after his first semester. Tuta returned home from Georgia Institute of Technology after his fifth trimester. Characteristically, Mtume's flight from college was relatively quiet. He had a good job at Tower Records, where he was pursuing a career in the music industry. To outward appearances at least, Mtume was leaving school to pursue other interests. Before attending Georgia Tech, Tuta had proudly proclaimed he was pursuing a career in engineering for the paycheck that would undoubtedly be attached. My uncle tried to convince Tuta otherwise. Our upbringing prepared us to live meaningful lives that would contribute something to our community. It was my uncle's contention that Tuta wouldn't be able to build his life on the pursuit of money because he wasn't raised to be a slave to money. Tuta, in his obstinacy and self-assurance, insisted he could.

After enduring semesters of homesickness and frustration at his $10-per-hour engineering internship, Tuta decided it just wasn't worth it. Never one to mince words, Tuta simply stated that he was "tired of working with white people" and that he was coming home. Tuta communicated his decision at the Kwanzaa celebrations. All five of us Salaam siblings showed constant reluctance and embarrassment in the face of our annual Kwanzaa gatherings. When we were younger, our discomfort was expressed with giggles and mutual jokes. As he got older, Mtume began to make himself unavailable on those mornings during which we had to light the Kwanzaa candles. Eventually he moved out, assuring his freedom from such rituals. Tuta, on the other hand, was too young to leave, and so came slouching. He sat when everyone else was standing and mumbled when he was supposed to read.

On the morning of Tuta's announcement, just he, my mother, and I were in the house. He showed uncharacteristic participation in the entire ritual, even volunteering to light the candles. When we were discussing what self-determination meant to us, for it was Kujichagulia, the second day of Kwanzaa, Tuta explained the importance of determining his own life and ended his discussion with "and so I've decided not to go back to school next semester."

My jaw dropped open.

His respect for my mother was clear. He wished not to hurt her but to make her understand his motives in her own terms. He used the self-governing principles we had been taught to explain his dissent from the preconceived track. His loyalty to his upbringing was not immediately clear to us. There were many bitter comments and much confusion. Many family members clearly felt he was ruining his life. What kind of job could he get without a college degree? Eventually, though, his decision became a source of comfort for me. It proved his mind had been open during his formative years. It was evidence that he had soaked up the same fierce, uncompromising training my sisters and I were so proud of. His decision showed strength of character, as he threw off the role everyone had placed on his shoulders and followed his own plans.

Kwanzaa is not something that will ever be celebrated in either of my brothers' homes. They have an inexplicable distaste for the conventions of the lifestyle that reared them. I remember Mtume haughtily proclaiming "there's more to life than not eating hamburgers" when I expressed surprise at his choice of meat from a dinner menu. Even as a high school student he had rejected the constrictions of our staunch pro-Black, vegetarian lifestyle. Before he developed his pro-human perspective, he befriended a white person on a deeper level than any of us ever had. He had that friend come to our house in the ghetto to spend the weekend. My little sister and I were seized by a savage attack of the giggles, so tickled were we at the prospect of a white person coming to our poverty-ridden neighborhood. My brother had to keep his friend outside upon arrival, throwing a football around, while my mother quieted us down. Now Mtume has fully developed his humanist theories and tenets. Those beliefs cause him to reject one of my projects, an independent magazine called *Red Clay Magazine*, as too Black and lacking in class consciousness. When we are pressed in discussion, though, Mtume and I find we share more theoretical common ground than it appears.

Understanding our common ground has helped me grasp a fundamental fact of my brothers' resistance. Where their desires and actions seemed the very antithesis of the values my parents taught us, they have dutifully absorbed the principles of self-respect, self-discipline, and independence. What they have rejected is the Afrocentric, vegetarian wrapping in which those principles were delivered. They peeled away at the African print that covered our upbringing and swallowed the essence of our lessons' life-giving Vitamin C. It is this essence that informs their lives today.

The seriousness of our upbringing influenced them to eschew dating and womanizing and to make important love selections, marrying and settling down at early ages. Mtume Ya Salaam, which means "prophet of peace," is a record representative for Warner Brothers and Atlantic. At twenty-five years old, he has been happily married for three years. Our upbringing allowed my brothers to become homeowners during their early twenties.

Tutashinda nchi na Salaam means "we will win land and peace." He is a driver for the New Orleans airport shuttle. At twenty-one years old, he is the proud father of a three-year-old daughter, a homeowner, and a husband. The emphasis my parents placed on responsibility made Tuta claim his space as an equal partner in the rearing of his daughter without hesitation.

The irony of my negative reaction to the "strange" beings I think my brothers have developed into is that Mtume and Tuta have become the bedrock of my family. Now, when we sisters go back to New Orleans, our childhood home no longer welcomes us. It houses another family with other dreams and other lives. My father lives in a house across the river which my family never crosses, on the west bank of New Orleans with his significant other. My mother lives in a dorm in Baton Rouge at Louisiana State University, where she is pursuing a master's degree. Consequently, when we visit home, we go to our brothers' homes. Mtume and Tuta juggle my sisters and my mother in their guest bedrooms, bearing the responsibility for our shelter. Their choice of stability is essential to our flight. It is Mtume and Tuta's seemingly incongruent choices that make it possible for us to make the impossible leaps our upbringing encouraged us to take. They also uncompromisingly chose their own paths, no matter how Black or African our upbringing prepared them to be, no matter how middle-class our intellectual level bred them to be, they chose homes, families, and New Orleans.

Homecoming

Gloria Wade-Gayles

They talked about him, the uncle I had never seen. The gifted son and brother who went wrong. Who disappeared. Without a good-bye note, they said. Without a ritual of farewell. No hugs and kisses and tears. "Just—whoosh! Left home. Just like that!" they said.

They knew he was alive. Occasionally he called or sent postcards written in near calligraphy, bearing different postmarks and the same message. He was well. He promised to come back. For a visit. They took comfort in his promise. But there were times during Friday night fish dinners when their conversation about him belied their trust. They wanted him home.

In his absence, he was larger than life. An artist who worked magic with charcoal and paints. Who could have become a real artist only if. They had proof. Where Grandmama kept them, I never knew, but I remember her showing them to me. The drawings. The paintings. The proof. I was impressed. This man, this artist, surely couldn't be related to me. I could not draw a straight line or even a curve, which they say draws itself.

I was impressed, most of all by the stories that proved my uncle was special, different, gifted. A genius. "That's why he didn't stay in school," Mama would tell my sister and me. "He was bored. Just plain bored." An artist and a genius who loved poetry. Poetry? But men don't like poetry. Surely they were exaggerating. Creating a brother and a son so wonderful they couldn't hate him for leaving home. Without a ritual of farewell. Without hugs and kisses and tears.

I created stories about him, which gave me status with my friends. He was my phantom uncle, but when I talked about him, he was real. "I have an uncle who can draw anything and make it look real." I was telling the truth. I had seen the proof. "And he is smarter than anybody." That's what my mother said, and she never lied about anything. "He's been all over the world." More than one place away from the South was all over the world. Sometimes my friends would laugh at his name: "Prince Albert." It was a funny name, but my grandmother said he wore it well.

In my secret fantasies, I saw him returning home dressed like a prince and carrying colorful boxes just for me. Presents from all the places he had been. We would be the best of buddies. He would be the brother I had always wanted, and I would be his princess. We would live in a world all our own of poetry and laughter and secrets bearing our names.

I remember awakening earlier than usual one Saturday morning and going downstairs to open the thick inside door and latch the screen door. It was hot, unseasonably hot, even for the South. Our small two-bedroom apartment needed what Mama called "a little breeze of fresh air." I spread my silver jacks on the porch and threw up the small red ball. It was then that I saw him.

He was a thin man, the color of light caramel. His hair was

red and naturally curly. He was unkempt, and he swaggered a little when he walked. The kind of stranger I was taught to avoid, run from if necessary. Boldly he approached our immaculate porch. Immediately I ran inside. Seconds later, he was at the door.

"Bertha Lee!" I heard him call. "Bertha Lee!" I thought to myself that he was one of Mama's close friends because only friends and family dared use her middle name. I will never forget how quickly my mother, who was not thin by anyone's definition, made her way from the kitchen to the front door. Without seeing the stranger, she knew who he was. She ran, screaming, "ThankyouJesus! ThankyouJesus!" Her brother was home.

He had finally arrived, but without the gifts and the majesty I had expected. The man my mother would not release from her embrace was not the uncle I had heard about for years. I wondered if they too had made up stories about him.

In a short time, everyone in my small family was present in our apartment: my uncle, who had become a preacher since Prince's departure; my aunt, her husband, and her daughter; my grandmother; and of course, Mama and Faye and me. They were thankful to God that he had come home. He hadn't changed, they said. He looked good, they said. They loved him, they said. The questions began.

Where had he been all those years? Traveling. Hoboing his way across the country. Living here and there, with this one and that one. How did he make it? Working at odd jobs. Doing this and that. Did he miss us? Always. He'd wanted to come home but dreaded returning to the South he hated, the South that suffocated him, took the genius in him and threw it into a junkpile of lost dreams. Was he tired? Of course. He had been traveling for days. Hopping freights and thumbing rides. He needed to rest.

While he slept in the bed my sister and I shared, they went

shopping for the celebration—for food, for gifts, for clothes. Mama prepared a feast fit for a prince. A king, really. She cooked collard greens (his favorite), boiled okra (his favorite), cornbread (his favorite), and roast beef with gravy (also his favorite). Everything was for him. The prodigal son had returned home. They were excited. I was confused. And disappointed. My feelings changed when he came downstairs later that day after his long nap. He was clean shaven and dressed in the princely outfit my aunt had purchased for him. He was lovable, colorful, entertaining, and so incredibly warm that I wanted to cuddle up in his arms. They had told the truth. My uncle possessed a magic that made him special and different. A genius.

He regaled us with stories about his travels, describing places and people so vividly I felt as if I had been with him in all of the experiences he shared. Our kitchen (which is where we gathered) became a theatre that echoed with my applauding laughter. I was quiet only when he was quiet, and that was only when he drew. My sister and I stood on either side, looking over his shoulders, and watched the pencil move in his thin fingers. Lines and circles became people, places, objects, even feelings. For me, a young girl of eight who had never known an artist, the pictures were miracles.

His magic continued when he recited poems from a repertoire which, I would learn over the coming months, was large. My mother and my aunt requested two of their favorites, "My Last Duchess" and "The Face on the Barroom Floor." As if on stage, with the proper scenery and a large audience leaning forward to hear every syllable, my uncle changed his voice, he moved his hands, he walked around, he cried, and he fell lifeless on the kitchen floor. I had not yet been introduced to dramatic poems, adult poems that required you to think and to feel, but I sat in rapt attention as my uncle, made for teaching (which is, in a way, performance) taught us. My love for poetry was born in those family gatherings.

For weeks after that night, we gathered in the kitchen to savor the joy of his homecoming, and after each gathering, he became more special to me. I spread the word among my friends that my uncle was home, and they came in small groups to watch him perform as I requested. "Draw her, Uncle Prince," I would say, and he would comply, missing nothing in his representation of the face that, like mine, smiled in awe of his masterful hand. "Tell them about the time you hoboed from Illinois to Indiana," I would request, and he would comply, adding hyperbole, I am now certain, for our enjoyment. He recited poems and the latest songs comically. I was proud of him. He was my poet–uncle. My artist–uncle. My friend. My prince.

The family lost no time helping my uncle put his life back together. They bought him a full wardrobe: suits, colorful ties, dress shoes, and a Stetson hat. They made a home for him in all of the places where each one stayed. He could have stayed with my aunt and her husband, or my grandmother and his brother, but he chose to stay with Mama, Faye, and me. That is where he was supposed to stay, I believed. We were supposed to share the same space because my dreams about him were what had brought him home.

My family had not lied about my uncle. Nor had they told the whole truth: my uncle was an alcoholic. For four years, I saw and heard, but I chose denial. I was still young, and besides, his drinking did not alter my world one bit. If anything, it made him more charming and magical. When he drank, he danced around the women in the family, calling them "Pretty Mama." When he knew Mama or Aunt Mae was angry with him, he sang, tipping an imaginary hat, "Hey, Pretty Mama. How come you treat me so bad?" I thought he was the most beautiful then and wished my friends could see him. He was my funny uncle, and I loved him.

Mama and Aunt Mae could not stay angry with my uncle for long. He was gentle. Humble. Loving. Easily forgiven. "He has a heart of gold," Aunt Mae would say. Sober or intoxicated, he couldn't hurt anyone. When he fell asleep on the living-room sofa, fully dressed because he had one drink too many, I would cover him with a blanket and sometimes, when no one was looking, kiss him on his forehead. When he came home very late at night and yelled for us to open the door, I would rush downstairs to let him in. As young as I was, I knew that his drinking was related to the stories I had heard him tell and to the world I was slowly beginning to see with new eyes.

It might have been the collective consciousness of the race that gave me understanding of racial pain, but I think it was the message I read in Uncle Prince's eyes when he recalled the difficult times my mother's family had had growing up. During the first two decades of the twentieth century, they had lived in Clarksdale, Mississippi. Later they moved to Memphis, "as bad as any Mississippi town," my uncle would often say. Theirs was a reality of racial violence. My uncle just didn't "have the stomach" for it, Mama often said. It was devastating for someone as sensitive as he. When my grandmother "pinched and scrimped," as she said, to buy him a bicycle to encourage him to return to the classroom where he had handed out papers and run errands for the teacher, he took a hammer and bent the bicycle into metal even a scrap yard would not want. That was his rage. I understood him and told myself, "He has a right to drink!"

Many years after, I would read Toni Morrison's *Sula* and think about my uncle. Sula had no outlets for her creativity. A frustrated artist without clay or paint, she became destructive and self-destructive as well. My uncle, an artist, had only the pencils available to him in my grandmother's kitchen and nowhere to display his art. In addition to experiencing the harsh reality of racial violence in the South, my uncle, hungry for knowledge, attended schools that had no programs for gifted children. And so he grew bored, pained, angry, was suffocated and destroyed. He usually had what Mama called "spending change" or, when she was angry with him, "drinking money." He earned it by working with the Italian market man who had a monopoly in the Black community on the south side of Memphis. Sometimes my uncle would announce the market man's coming with a song, but his job was to bag the vegetables people selected from the wagon and carry them to their doorsteps. When the weather was warm, he earned additional money— "light change"—by "shaking the red card" on Beale Street. Mama called it gambling; I called it magic. My uncle would lay three playing cards, two black clubs and one red ace, face up on the sidewalk and then turn them face down as he demonstrated for onlookers what he was going to do. He would move the cards fast, but not too fast because, in the trial run, they were supposed to win. Once they were hooked and bet money on being able to find the only red card in the trio, my uncle's magic began. He would "shake" the cards faster than before, sliding them fast to the right and fast to the left, very fast over and under one another. The bettors would watch every move, closely, but my uncle's slim hands were too fast for their eyes, so fast that he was nicknamed "Beale Street Red."

I understood why Mama wanted him to make a decent living for himself. After all, he was an adult. A man. But I had mixed feelings about his holding down a job. Steady employment would cut into his time with me and, worse, demean him. He was too different, too gifted to work at menial jobs, and those were the only ones available to a Black male without an education and without skills. I remember feeling sad and angry

when, at my family's insistence, he took a job as an orderly at
John Gaston Hospital.

In retrospect, I realize that the job wasn't the problem.
Rather, it was the place itself. If you were Black, you didn't
need to be an adult or a researcher to know about racism at
John Gaston. Regardless of the medical emergency, if you were
Black, you were not seen until all white patients had been
treated, and dismissed with a smile and the promise of recovery.
Horror stories about racism at John Gaston were rife in the
Black community. "I knew a man who went there with a simple
wound in his foot," went one story, "and he had to go home and
come back so many days, waiting 'til all the white folks been
seen, that he got gangrene. They cut off his foot, but he still
died. The waiting, that's what killed him." I just didn't want my
uncle to work at John Gaston.

Two days after being hired, he came home well past midnight wearing old clothes instead of the good ones that the family had purchased for him and loafers that slipped easily off his
thin heels. He was very intoxicated, and yet very clear about
what he had done, and why.

"They think I'm some kind of fool," he said to my mother.
"I might be a drunk, but I'm no fool. I'm not a damned
fool."

At other times when he had disappointed the family, my
uncle would say he was sorry and promise to do better. But this
time, he had no apologies.

"Not me, Bertha," he told my mother. "You won't find me
pouring out other people's piss with a white man looking over
my shoulder. Not me!"

It might not make sense to say that an alcoholic has dignity, but in my uncle's case it makes all the sense in the world. I
was convinced that it was his dignity that made him drink, and
his dignity that made him unemployed. "I ain't working for

white folks," he would say with conviction. Unfortunately, they were the only people for whom he could have worked.

His unemployment was somewhat of a benefit to my sister and me, and perhaps Mama as well: he became the housemother of the family. Mama worked, and Uncle Prince stayed home cleaning and washing and cooking. When my sister and I came home from school, he would be waiting for us, smiling "like a Cheshire cat" over the work we showed him. He pushed us to be serious about the very experience he had rejected. There was little we were studying that he did not know something about. History. He knew the names of all the presidents, knew the Preamble, the Bill of Rights, and the Emancipation Proclamation, knew about wars this country had been engaged in, and knew something about the lives of so-called leaders. He had read the books. Geography. He had traveled all over the States and could draw a map better than any in our books. Math. He knew that, too. Literature. He was our talking, performing anthology. And politics. That he knew in a painful way. I was not embarrassed by his drinking because he was so smart, so artistic, so supportive, so very maternal.

As the years passed, my uncle remained the same, but I changed. I grew into a young lady who worried Mama about "fixing" my hair in different styles, knowing that her Woolworth tin curling irons could only do so much. I wanted to wear makeup and, in spite of my skinny legs, stockings and high-heeled shoes. In relationships with boys, I wanted to trade kisses rather than marbles. I entered puberty and a world of romantic fantasies. My uncle became a problem for me. He seemed to choose the worst times to become intoxicated. When I was walking home from high school with a boy I hoped would like me, he was there. When I came home from a date, he was there. He was never ugly, never obtrusive, never profane—just intoxicated. That was enough to open a chasm between us. My sister, who was always saner than I about everything, was tolerant, if not also understanding. She accepted him; I attacked him.

"Why don't you do something with your life?" I would ask, looking at him in disgust. "All you do is hang around and get drunk."

He rebuffed my harsh words by dancing and singing. When he was intoxicated, that is. He would sing, "Hey, Pretty Mama," or sometimes the refrain from a popular song about a stubborn Black woman named Caldonia. "Caldonia! Caldonia!" he sang. "What makes your big head so hard. Bam. But I love you . . ."

"Don't try that on me. It won't work anymore," I would say, interrupting him before he began his dance. "I'm not blind anymore. I see you for what you are."

"Glory Jean. Glory Jean." He would chant. "Glory Jean. Glor*ee* Jean." Affectionately.

"That's not my name," I would say, rejecting what had once been a term of endearment for me. "My name is Gloria. Glo Ree Ah. Gloria Jean. Not Glory Jean."

"I know you, but *you* don't know you."

"And what is that supposed to mean?"

"Just keep on living," he would say. "Just keep on living."

Years earlier when he would say those very words, offering them as words of wisdom about the uncertainty of life, I accepted them as profound, even prophetic. But now they began to sound like nonsense. And I would mimic him.

"Just keep on living. Just keep on living," I would say, poking my tongue. "That's not saying anything. Everybody is going to keep on living until they die."

"That's just the point," he would answer, his mood changing, becoming serious. "Just keep on living and you'll see. You know where you've been, but you don't know where you're going."

He could have said ugly things to me; he knew my vulner-abilities. He knew that I had a complex about my size; the children said I was so skinny they could whisper in my direction and I would be gone with the winds. But he never responded to me in kind. He took my harsh words and swallowed them the way he swallowed cheap wine. Like wine, they burned inside. But they did not lift him to temporary euphoria. They wounded him. I could see the pain in his eyes when I ended our arguments with the same phrase: "I wish you would leave. Go back where you were. I wish you had never come back." I wounded him.

The family was in conflict over what to do about my uncle's drinking. Depending on the day of the week or the incident under discussion, someone was always reprimanded for indulging him. Enabling him. My mother reprimanded my grandmother for babying him, not turning away when he came by drunk. Grandmama would respond: "I can't do that, Bertha. He's your brother, but he's my son." I would hear a similar response from Mama when I reprimanded her for letting him destroy our lives. "He's your uncle," she would say, "but he's my brother. I taught him how to walk. I can't throw him away."

We tried what today would be called "tough love." We took away his key and refused to open the door when he came home intoxicated. Inebriated. Drunk. We would let him sleep outside. But if there were rain, just a light drizzle, or if the temperature dropped, just slightly, Mama would open the door and lay out linen for the living-room sofa.

After a major binge, he would promise not to drink again. To get a job and stay sober. I remember one time in particular that we deluded ourselves into believing he could cure himself. He placed his hands on the family Bible and swore that he had heard God speaking to him. He wept. He lay there prostrate on the floor, praying and thanking God for the revelation. He would become a new man. A miracle was what we always knew would be needed to change him. We were exuberant. Grateful. Expectant. He left home, a new man in search of a job. He returned later that night unchanged.

In the face of a problem one cannot solve, anything that is not a problem becomes a blessing. Something to celebrate. That is how it was with my family's reading of Uncle Prince. "All he does is drink," the family would say. And they were correct. He was impeccably clean about his person and about our small apartment. He was compassionate. I remember how he felt for my sister and me when we would get monthly cramps. I remember his efforts to meet the needs before they occurred. And he was honest. For alcoholics, we were told, honesty is rare. Many are known to steal from their loved ones in order to feed their habit. We kept an open jar of coins and small bills in the kitchen cabinet. My uncle never touched it. He was generous. Out of the little he had, he was willing to give much. Had I not been angry with him, he would have been what we called in the project "a dollar uncle." Not a "nickel uncle" or a "quarter uncle." When he had money, he shared. The only liquids in our small refrigerator were milk, juices, and soft drinks. My uncle never drank at home.

I remember the routine of his life. He worked with the market man from dawn until two in the afternoon. He was with his drinking buddies by four, and by midnight he was inebriated. At least twice a month, sometimes more frequently, he was in a cell in a downtown precinct. My mother or my grandmother would take the bus downtown, pay the $11 fine, and return home with my uncle.

Stories about his incarceration afforded us laughter when we would agree to give him an audience. And sometimes pain. Although his offense was drunkenness—nothing else—he was sometimes beaten at the precinct. Not enough to bruise badly, but enough for him to experience real pain. His mouth, he would tell us, not his drinking, was the problem. He never went easily into the police car or into the cell. It all depended on who was on duty, he would explain. Two white policemen who had arrested him many times took a liking to him (perhaps he shook the red card for them), called him "Red," and protected him from abuse. Even in jail, my uncle had the audacity to be charming and defiant.

The frequent arrests and beatings did not change him. He continued to drink, and I began to see him as a visitor who had stayed too long. Who had filled my life with his pain. That was the source of my anger. His pain, which was always with me. I could feel it and smell it. Hear it pleading for my understanding. Angered by my own helplessness, I refused to acknowledge his existence. When he spoke to me, always with affection, I would not answer. When he entered a room, I would leave. Once, in a fit of rage, and pain, I pounded on his chest with my fists. I wanted him to leave. Become my phantom uncle. Larger than life. Perfect. I wanted him to leave. I wanted to love him again.

It was a Friday night in my junior year in high school. I know it was Friday because the family was at our house on Fridays and at my grandmother's on Saturdays. I know that it was my junior year because when my uncle and I only a week earlier had argued, he had said to me, "You know where you've been, but you don't know where you're going. Glory Jean. Miss Smart Ass Junior."

We were sitting in the kitchen talking. My uncle was in the living room, or so we thought. Suddenly, he walked into the kitchen and in a clear voice said something about our not having to bother with him anymore. Trying "tough love," we ignored him. This time, he said, he meant it. We wouldn't have to be bothered with him anymore. We ignored him. He put a bottle to his mouth and began drinking. Another one of his performances, we said to one another with our eyes. Someone said that he had emptied out whatever was in the bottle and filled it with water. We ignored him. He finished drinking and walked out of the kitchen. Minutes passed. How many I don't know. He returned to the kitchen. We ignored him. Suddenly, he collapsed.

I remember the sound of the ambulance siren as it searched for our apartment and the countless hours my sister and I stayed at home alone waiting for some word from the hospital. I remember praying, "Please don't let him die. Lord, please don't let him die. Please. Please. Please. I'll love him when he comes back. Just please let him come back. Please let him come home."

The phone rang early in the morning. We picked it up before there was a full ring. Mama was on the other end. My sister and I were screaming. "Stop crying," Mama said. "Stop crying, he's going to be okay. They pumped his stomach. We got him here in time. He's going to be all right."

There was no big feast for this homecoming; my uncle could eat very little. But there was a celebration more special than the first one. We sat around the living room, not the kitchen, the entire family, entertaining him, performing for him. He knew he was loved. He knew he was loved. When he became tired, we helped him up the iron steps to the room my sister and I shared. He would sleep there until he was strong again. I pulled the covers around his thin body and kissed him on the forehead as I had done when I was younger. "I love you, Uncle Prince," I said softly. He squeezed my hand gently and said, "Glory Jean."

Even if he had not attempted suicide, my uncle would have returned to his special place in my life. As I matured, I would have learned how to handle the difficult combination of helplessness and love. I would have become woman enough to do what counselors call "reality therapy," which makes it possible for us to accept what we cannot change without anger, without guilt. That change in me began when I entered college. There I learned from books much of what my uncle had learned all his painful life. Growing racial awareness brought us closer than we had been in earlier years. He was no longer my toy. My performer. He became my confidant and my teacher.

I began college in the early fifties, when all across the South Black people were becoming intolerant of Jim Crowism. I was my uncle's "child." I was angry and impatient. I wanted to organize a boycott of Memphis buses like the one that was taking place in Montgomery, Alabama. My mother was concerned about my safety because I had begun "talking back" to white people and refusing to sit on the back of the bus. "Just walk everywhere, Gloria," she told me. "Walk everywhere." I remember a new surge of anger when Nat King Cole, whom my mother loved, was attacked by a white mob in Birmingham. I remember that a group of us at LeMoyne, among them Marion Barry, who would later become mayor of Washington, D.C., challenged the racial position of the board of trustees of the college, creating somewhat of an uproar in Memphis. I wore my racial anger like a badge. My uncle understood. In his own way, he had nurtured the anger, but in a strange way, his presence in my life prevented me from letting the anger become consuming rage. When we were pushed back to strength, we were also pushed into pain, his defeat, his regret. He never spoke of regret, but I saw it in his eyes, and I felt it in the hugs he gave me when I did well in school. I heard it when he encouraged Faye and me to be "smart girls in school," offering his own life as an example of the failure we should avoid. I understood what could happen to any Black person who responded to racism with consuming rage. Mama said rage was a corrosive emotion: "If you give in to it, you never win." I wanted to win—for my uncle. For all of them.

My uncle's racial memory became mine, and my struggles in the movement his. I am convinced that had there been a movement when he was growing up in a vicious and cruel South, he would have been involved as a leader giving moving speeches, an artist drawing compelling posters, a thinker shaping strategy. But it was the tragedy of the time that there was no channel for his rage and no channel for his genius. During all of my experiences in the movement, many of them more frightening than my uncle could have imagined, I thought about him. He was in my mind and in my heart in every demonstration and in every cell block. In my own way, I was seeking revenge, a nonviolent one, but revenge nevertheless against the system that had stolen his life.

Uncle Prince lived to see the beginning of the new South. Signs designating places where only whites could drink or eat were removed reluctantly, but they were removed, even in Birmingham. We thought the opportunities and security and freedom to live in dignity that he had never experienced were imminent for Blacks in Memphis. My uncle was happy about the changes that were taking place in the city, but he saw them as minor alterations. They were mere cosmetics concealing a deadly backlash against the movement, one which would long victimize Blacks in the city, among them my uncle.

I did not know about the tragic incident that crippled my uncle for the remainder of his life until my husband Joe and I went to Memphis three days after Christmas in 1969, following a holiday celebration with his parents and two brothers in Birmingham. Christmas at home was always wonderful. It would be especially so this year because we were bearing gifts for the family: our son Jonathan, and daughter Monica, an infant of two months. Mama had not yet told me about what had happened to Uncle Prince because I had been in my ninth month with Monica when it occurred. With a composure that did not succeed in concealing her rage and her pain, she now told us the heartbreaking story.

When he did not return home and the family did not receive a call from the downtown precinct, no one was overly concerned. Sometimes he spent the night incarcerated, sleeping off the alcohol. They were concerned the second night, but not in a state of panic. By the third night, though, they knew something was wrong. My mother called every precinct in the city and in outlying areas. There was no record of his arrest. She called John Gaston, the only hospital in the city that admitted poor people, Blacks and whites, and hospitals in West Memphis, Arkansas, across the bridge, where he sometimes went with drinking buddies. There was no admission record for a Prince Albert Reese. The family never thought he had left home again. In their souls, they knew something was wrong. Terribly wrong. "It is that way with love," my mother would say when she talked about that night. They feared for his life.

On the fourth night, my family made the calls again, and this time, John Gaston had a record of his admission. He had been in the hospital for three days, transferred there from the workhouse where he had been taken after his arrest for drunkenness and vagrancy. The police had not informed us of his arrest. They had concealed his whereabouts. En route to the hospital, my family feared the worst because the authorities — white people — had kept him from us for three days.

He lay unconscious, hooked up to wires, in the Black section of the hospital. My mother said she became a madwoman, wanting answers. Insisting on them at the risk of being arrested for disorderly conduct. A police sergeant came. He was careful with his words. My uncle was arrested. Taken to the workhouse. He became sick there. Very sick with seizures. So they transferred him to the hospital. No one explained why my uncle was unable to talk coherently.

I heard the tragic story that Christmas with disbelief. Extreme sadness. Grief. Wrenching pain. Rage. Guilt. I wished I had been home when he needed me most. Rationally, I knew I could have done nothing to protect him, but I had never been rational about my uncle.

Once the family's best performer, my uncle became a spectator to our performances of love. A man of silence, speaking only with his eyes. He moved slowly, with effort, fearful of losing his footing and falling as he had done so many times on Beale Street sidewalks. He would sit in one place for hours, looking straight ahead and responding to questions in half-sentences. Sometimes struggling for words that never came. Even our names he could not pronounce. "Who am I?" we would ask him, hoping that some miracle had occurred since the last time we asked the question. He would point to us, smile, and say only, "You know." To me, it meant "Glory Jean." I was twice-over a woman, but still his "Glory Jean."

He could not hold my toddler son and my infant daughter in his arms, but he studied them with eyes that were remarkable because they smiled. Mama pointed to Monica. "Who is this, Prince?" My uncle said, "You know," meaning that she was, as everyone in the family agreed, the spitting image of my grandmother. As an infant, my son was a mixture of his father and his paternal grandfather, but he was not a child anyone in our family had "spat" out. When asked who Jonathan was, my uncle only smiled.

In the spring of the following year, my uncle was admitted once again to John Gaston Hospital and, while there, he suffered first-degree burns. He was smoking in bed when the sheets caught on fire. A nurse was called only when another patient saw the flames. My uncle, unable to speak, could not call for help.

When we went home for Christmas in 1972, he was moving more slowly and with stiffness because of the skin grafting. Genius. Artist. A gentle man who didn't hurt anyone. My uncle deserved more from life. "How are you, Uncle Prince?" I asked. He would answer, "You know."

With each year, the children's faces changed. In 1973, at the age of three, Monica was beginning to look more like me and like her paternal grandmother. Jonathan, at the age of five, had become a number of faces—his father's most definitely, mine somewhat, and increasingly my uncle's. When we were home for Christmas that year, my uncle could not keep his eyes off of our son.

"Who is this, Prince?" Mama asked. "Who is this? Do you know who this is?"

My uncle smiled. He pointed to himself.

That was the last time we saw him. My Uncle Prince died June 4, 1974.

Through the years I have preached, literally preached, to my children about the dangers of alcohol. My sermon is not unlike my mother's sermon: "You got it in your family. Don't ever drink." The sermon worked for my sister and me; it also worked for my children. Both of them are very conscious about what they eat (making efforts to be vegetarians), and neither one touches alcohol. Their good habits, I tell them, are gifts from my Uncle Prince. They remember him only vaguely, but they know who he was and what he meant to me. Because of the stories—his and the real ones I share about my life with him.

My daughter, at twenty-two, still resembles my grandmother, but each day she becomes more the spitting image of her father and me. My son, at twenty-three, wears my uncle's face. Like my uncle, he has a winning personality. He performs for the family—singing, dancing, delivering speeches, telling jokes, reciting poems. He loves and even writes poetry. He draws and paints. He talks race and change. My uncle was a renegade; my son is a revolutionary. I think that my Uncle Prince has had his final homecoming in my son. I see each man in photographs of the other. The only difference is in the hat. My uncle wears a Stetson; my son, an African *kufu*.

Part III

Sons
and
Grandsons

My Special Agent

Lillian G. Allen

I am eighty-seven years old. Spent most of my life working in some white woman's kitchen, cooking and cleaning and doing somebody's laundry. My husband left me and my daughter, Carolyn, when she was three years old, so I cleaned and saved enough until I could open my own beauty salon. All the years of working, and the best job I ever did was raising my grandson, Reese.

I see him infrequently now. When I do, I remember the mischievous little boy he once was. Speeding around my beauty salon on his tricycle, causing my patrons to hastily draw in their feet. One customer stopped coming. Said she loved my work but couldn't stand that boy, that dog, that bicycle, and that noise.

His parents were high-school sweethearts. She was sixteen. Cute and petite, with an engaging smile and a reticent manner. I scrimped and saved and sent her away to Palmer Memorial. In those days it was a boarding school for children from good Negro families, down in North Carolina. I wanted to get her away from the neighborhood kids, who I considered unsuitable. Several of them had been arrested for shoplifting and always seemed to be in trouble. Possibly because of my long working hours, we had very little time together and we seldom had the mother–daughter talks I wanted to encourage. After her first year at Palmer she begged me not to be sent away again. She assured me that every parent had high aspirations to get their kids out of the shadow of bad influences, but the students at Palmer were no better than the ones in the Pittsburgh public schools. She convinced me that many of them at Palmer had already acquired some bad habits. They just hid them well from the faculty.

I remember Ronald, the little boyfriend she had all summer. He was seventeen. A shy boy wearing thick-rimmed glasses. My old Aunt Sally, who lived with me, tried to watch her but she was too old to keep up with a sixteen-year-old. Carolyn hid her pregnancy well. I sent her to a doctor when I first became suspicious. I learned later that she had begged him not to tell me. She knew she was too young. She knew I would insist on an abortion.

I wasn't going to stand for it. There was no way I was going to allow my grandchild to be born out of wedlock. Talking time was over, but I wanted to yell at somebody. Before the Schenley High School teachers were aware of it, I marched my daughter into the principal's office and told him of her pregnancy. I then called the boy's mother, and told her there had to be a wedding. I said I would pick her up, and we would go to the license bureau together, since they were underage. The poor lady was very upset. She was also a beautician, but she worked out of her home. She had customers, she said. Told me she couldn't possibly go at the hour I had arranged.

I was in no mood for arbitration. "Lady! My only child is pregnant by your son. They are going to be married! Now I will pick you up in one half-hour. You be ready! Your customers can wait a few minutes. We will be there when the courthouse office opens, it won't take long. Now I mean be ready!"

Being a beautician at holiday time, I was very busy, but I threw a coat over my uniform and hurried out to meet her. She was standing on the curb when I drove up. We were both single mothers. She was widowed. I was divorced. We were both upset by the situation so we had little to say to each other.

The little ceremony was held in the parsonage. The house was all decorated since it was Christmas Eve. The minister warned me not to throw rice on his new carpet. Said his wife would be mad.

"Are you kidding?" I said. "If I throw anything, it would be a brick!"

I went back to the shop to work. My daughter went home to a cold supper. Her husband went home with his mother.

My grandson arrived on January 31, 1965. A day so cold that the locks froze on my car. His delivery was rough. My daughter screamed and squeezed my hand so hard, my wedding ring cut into my finger. We christened him "Maurese." His father wanted to name him "Maurese" after his best friend. We thought it sounded too arty, so we dubbed him "Reese," a name only family members and close friends use.

Carolyn's mother-in-law took care of her and the baby for a month. I was very grateful, then I informed her that she should continue to take care of her own son and I would take care of my family. He could visit, but he could not live with us.

My daughter and I had our first serious mother–daughter talk to decide what she would do. Going to college was out. She would go to a trade or technical school after she finished high school to learn a skill. She chose to finish at Fifth Avenue High instead of going back to Schenley. She was too embarrassed. Her class had already graduated. She decided to attend a computer training school, which helped her get a good job—which was a good thing. When her husband got out of school, he tried to provide a home for them, but the marriage didn't work; they were too young. Their interests were too different. He had a love for big cars and gambling. She wanted to travel and learn more about the world. She got a job as a reservation clerk with USAir. She was excited when she got company passes to tour the Hawaiian Islands. He wanted to drive his new Cadillac to Virginia Beach. He refused to go with her. She moved back home.

It was hard every day getting the baby to a sitter, me to work, and my daughter off to school. I sold my house in Highland Park and rented a building in the Oakland district, where we lived in an apartment over my beauty salon. That way I was able to take care of my grandson while I worked. I loved him from the first minute I saw him. It was so wonderful to have a baby in the house again. I only had had one child and wanted more, so Reese became more special to me with each and every day.

Carlow Catholic College is nearby. It had a kindergarten and primary grades, so we enrolled Reese there. I would walk him over every morning and leave him with the sisters. His mother would pick him up every evening. Things worked out fine, except for Ronald, Reese's father. Carolyn and he stopped speaking when he wouldn't give her child support or help pay the fees to keep Reese at the Catholic school. He said public school was good enough for him, it was good enough for his son. He kept coming around for a while, but they lost touch. Carolyn got a divorce and met somebody else.

Reese was about six when Sister Agnes, one of his teachers, called me to say he was wearing a watch that belonged to a classmate. When questioned, Reese said he had found it. The teacher said the owner of the watch had placed it under a radiator while swimming. Reese's mother took off from work the next day and went up to the school with him. In front of the whole class she made him return the watch and admit that he had picked it up. He never stole again.

Reese was a happy, inquisitive child, always asking questions until it would tire me out. At four or five, he would tell his playmates, "Ask my Grandma, she knows everything!" Around thirteen he changed his mind about all that. Then he would say, "Don't ask my Grandma. She'll send you to the dictionary." He had a quick wit and a great sense of humor. I looked forward to his hearty laugh when I related an amusing incident, like the time his uncle came into the beauty shop wearing his Sunday best, smelling like a bakery. He had sprayed on some vanilla flavoring he had purchased on the street, thinking it was cologne.

Reese was around seven when an older white boy started pushing him around. My daughter went to the boy's home and told his mother that if she didn't make her boy leave Reese alone, that she would be back to take on the mother. That was the end of that. There is something about an angry Black woman that commands attention.

We decided it was time Reese learned to defend himself. He entered karate school. His teacher, Curtis Smith, was a great influence in his life. He became Reese's mentor, the big brother, the kind of man he needed in his life. With the right kind of attention, Reese became a prize pupil. Audiences enjoyed seeing this little 120-pound boy tossing a 200-pound big man around. I was so proud of all the medals he won in the competitions. Curtis is still on the security staff at the University of Pittsburgh, and he still volunteers to train young bodies in karate.

In high school, Reese started to goof off. I called this behavior his smart-alecky days. He wanted to hang out with kids whose parents could afford to get them out of little escapades.

His grades were not up to his potential until he realized that he might not get into college. I sat him down one day and gave him a good talking to. Made sure he understood we did not want him getting into any trouble with the law and the wrong kind. I got his karate teacher to talk to him and work with him to stay out of trouble.

Karate and playing football seemed to take up his time and give him enough to keep him busy and out of trouble. Football got him a partial scholarship to Montana Technical College in Butte, Montana, specializing in engineering. It was the first time he ever went away from home. I worried about him being so far away, but I prayed that he would be okay. To please his mother, he studied engineering, since that was the scholarship he could get. It was a five-year course. Reese feared that he would get failing grades with his rigorous football schedule, so he signed up for twelve credits instead of fifteen. That way it took him six years to get his degree.

The partial scholarship and what little money we could send paid his room and board. Reese tried to get extra work at the college and in the town. Once he called and excitedly told me that he and a classmate were now disc jockeys for all the college dances. They did that because none of the white girls would dance with them. I tried to explain racism to him but couldn't. Nobody else could either. He learned about racism in other ways, no matter how subtle.

Another time, Reese and Rick, a Puerto Rican classmate who had two black belts in karate, wanted to earn extra money and decided to start a class for the men at the local sheriff's department, about self-defense without guns. They pooled their pennies and printed flyers and rented a hall one Saturday to do a demonstration. No one came. He was so hurt and forlorn when he called and told me how they had sat there for hours with their materials and their refreshments. They were completely boycotted. Again, I found it painful to tell him about racism. He found it hard to accept.

"Honey, you're in the Northwest. It's a small town. They know you're Black. Some of those people think they're superior to us. They don't think we can teach them anything. Don't feel bad. It's their loss. You and Rick could have taught them plenty about self-defense." I tried to speak calmly, but I was seething inside.

In college, he took a police test and passed it but he was only nineteen and too young to join the force. He worked nights as a security guard for the Three Rivers Stadium, where he was permitted to carry a gun. His pay was $4.50 an hour. Asked why he worked for such low wages with his qualifications, he replied, "It's better than nothing!" That's when he decided that he preferred criminal justice work.

After college, Reese took the test for the FBI. He failed by two points. He was told he could take it again. After graduation, he studied for the test. It was the same test he had taken before. He took the test and was told that he had failed. He knew he had passed, but the organization was battling a suit for discrimination against minorities. We were glad he hadn't been accepted.

His next attempt was for the Treasury Department. His examiner told the agent who sponsored him that he failed because of body fat. He was fifteen pounds overweight. Just under six feet, Reese is sort of chunky but he is two hundred pounds of hard muscle. This was not told to Reese. He had simply failed, that was that. His sponsor asked if he couldn't lose a few pounds. Two weeks later, Reese showed up twelve pounds lighter. They had to accept him.

The training school for the Treasury Department was in Georgia. Reese had never been South. A part of his training was surveillance of a white woman. He related, "I stood on a corner near a bus stop, reading a newspaper, waiting for her to come out of a drugstore. I was doing everything by the book when my instructor came up and told me I was busted. Naturally I wanted to know what I had done wrong. He told me that no Black man stands around on a street corner reading a newspaper in a white section of Georgia." We had a good laugh when he related his experiences.

We were all invited to his graduation including his father, who had finally showed up again and had helped him out during his last two years in college. There were thirty white agents and four Blacks.

When he graduated from Treasury training and got his position as a Secret Service special agent I felt compelled to write to that sheriff's department back in Montana and tell them of his achievement.

When I told Reese what I had done he was appalled. "Grandma! You didn't!"

"Oh, yes, I did! What they did to you has rankled in my craw all these years!"

"What did you write? I hope you didn't mention names!"

"No, I didn't, but I'm sure after my letter they will look you up! I told them that you were now a special agent, that your duties were to guard the President and other visiting dignitaries. That they might read about you in the papers, but never see you again unless your route passed through their hick town. That you two could have taught them maneuvers that could possibly save their lives without the use of a gun.

"I also told them that they were a bunch of small-minded bigots that they didn't realize that intelligence comes in all races. I felt real good after writing that letter. I signed it, 'A Proud Grandmother.'" He was so shocked he didn't talk to me for hours, but from the smile on his face, I think he was happy I did it for him.

• • •

*I*n college, Reese would call me on a regular basis and tell me about the different kinds of people he met in his classes. The Mormons. The Native Americans. He said he loved learning about the differences but he respected them all. He said he could relate to something in all religions and cultures.

He was popular with all his classmates, so they often invited him home on school breaks. One of his Montana classmates took him to his home on a short holiday because Reese didn't have money to come home for Thanksgiving. That's where he met his classmate's sister, Laurie. She took one look and decided that this was the man she wanted to marry. She pursued him for over a year and agreed to live with him until he was ready for marriage.

His mother and I were not happy about it at all. We had hoped so much that he would marry a Black girl. Someone to really appreciate who he was. When Reese decided to bring her home to meet us, Carolyn was so angry she refused to meet her. Instead she took some vacation time and went to Nassau for two weeks. We had preached against racism but never expected that he would choose a white wife. Her family accepted him much more graciously than we did her. Her parents came and brought her all the way to Pittsburgh and helped them set up an apartment, and they weren't even married. I couldn't have done what they did.

When they decided that they would get married, his mother did not want to go to the wedding but we both did. We had to accept the fact that all we really wanted was someone who truly appreciated him. After a while we had to see that love is color-blind. Reese had finally taught me something then. About my own racism.

• • •

A few months after graduation, Reese called me to say he was assigned to guard King Hussein of Jordan. I was excited because I had seen the king in Morocco in 1976 when I took advantage of a tour my daughter had arranged through USAir. She has worked there since they employed Blacks after the death of Martin Luther King, Jr.

"Ask him if he remembers the parade the king held for him in Morocco," I joked. "Tell him your grandmother was there."

One night during the trip, Reese said, he finally got to talk to the king of Jordan. He related it thus. "My grandmother says she met you in 1976 when you visited the king of Morocco. Do you remember?"

He said the king was thoughtful for a minute, then said to Reese in his impeccable English, "Regrettably, I do not recall meeting your grandmother, but I'm sure it was a beautiful occasion."

I was floored. I couldn't believe that Reese thought I had actually met the king. "Reese, I was standing in a crowd of thousands, trying to get a look at the king!"

Reese grinned sheepishly. "Grandma, knowing you, I thought you had met him." I was happy he thought so highly of me, but I told him, "Honey, get real!"

His stepfather loves Reese as if he was his own son. Says he admires his elevator mentality. I asked for an explanation.

"I mean that he adjusts mentally to whatever group he is in. He can talk to the high and mighty dignitaries at his job or he can talk to the ghetto kids he grew up with."

"Don't you think maybe that was the reason he was hired?" I suggested.

Reese calls regularly to let us know how and where he is.

When I look at television now and the President is on, I try to see if I can get a glimpse of the Secret Service men, to see if I can find Reese in the crowd. He's my special agent.

*A*ll in all, Reese has turned out to be a good boy. To my knowledge, he never experimented with drugs. He learned early that participation in sports meant having respect for his body. Being a Black man, to get ahead he had to have a good education. Having attended Catholic schools, Reese believes devoutly in God, but he does not attend church on a regular basis. If he ever joins a church, it will be his admiration for the minister rather than for a particular denomination. I have seen him go to mass and watched him smile while listening to one of Minister Farrakhan's lectures. I tried to instill in him all the traits I hoped to find in a man, but never did. Someone loving, intelligent, considerate, and a good provider. I take pleasure in seeing the way he defers to his wife on important decisions.

*M*y only regret is that I did not teach him to clean up after himself. He is not neat. His wife says it annoys her when she trips over a misplaced shoe, or has to hang up a suit, but she adds that his untidiness is minor compared to his other qualities. Like surprising her with flowers for no special reason, making dinner first if he gets home early, or picking up a little something sweet on the way home, or going out of his way to rearrange his schedule for them to go to a movie or the gym together. She says she has no regrets. That assures me that my daughter and I did a good job. In this age of violence and anger in young Black men, I am blessed to have him for a grandson.

Saving Our Sons

Marita Golden

Michael is an Aquarius child, born on Valentine's Day, like his maternal grandmother, who died seven years before his birth. At fifteen, he is five feet eight, nearly as tall as his father, towering six inches over me. Caramel-colored, he possesses his father's small ears and high forehead. Yet everyone has said I "spat him out," he looks so much like me. I see it too, in the cheeks, the curve of his lips. Thumbing through the photo album that charted his growth and mine, I see as well what is his alone. There is the smile, radiant, aggressive, always ready for the camera. There is no holding back, no shyness or hesitation. That is not me, always a bit uneasy before the camera, unsure whether to pose or be myself. I have resisted the camera, my son embraces it with unexpected mugging just before the flash, and an ease that says, "Of course you want a picture of me."

One summer when Michael was six, I traveled to Belgium to visit friends I had made the year before during a trip to Senegal. Michael remained behind with a friend for three weeks and then flew alone to join me. When I met him at Charles de Gaulle Airport, the stewardess told me, grinning and shaking her head in amazement, "He was seated next to a businessman from Chicago; they talked nonstop almost the whole flight."

Maybe it is his ability to talk that is my endowment. I play with, shape, and transform words on paper. Michael is enamored of their sound, their music and rhythm manifested through speech. He loves to tell jokes, make puns; and to my dismay, year after year in school he earned distinction as the class clown. At eight he started reading the sports page daily and over dinner produced a new multisyllable word two or three times a week.

Burdened with talents and gifts, Michael drew well early and naturally, impressing the teachers in the Saturday afternoon classes at the Corcoran Art School. He had a flair for cooking, was an agile, enthusiastic athlete, and, when interested, could master a subject quickly.

The years before his adolescence now seem to have been an extended, auspicious gardening, the planting of the seed, the quiet, sometimes breathless tending, the praying for rain and hoping for sun. Then comes the breaking of the sod and soil. You wake up one morning and there it is, a seedling; there he is, an adult, a man.

That spring when I was searching for the souls, examining the lives, of young Black males, I was learning, often against my will, clumsily but insistently, to let go. And this feeling of letting my son go was as heady and intoxicating as holding him tight in my arms, tucked beneath my breast. We had spent our lives together traveling toward the moments that awaited us, moments when he would turn his back on my beliefs, reject and then reclaim a value I had told him to honor; years when he would discover, abuse, and master free will, revel in his independence, yet thank God he could always come home if he had to.

What if he was like me in the end, restless, searching, remaking myself like clockwork every few years by a new set of fantasies and goals. What if he ever said what I said to my mother when I was nineteen, brazen and so emboldened by the gospel of Black Power that I stood before her, hands on hips, and prophesied, "We won't make any progress until your generation dies off."

In the car one afternoon after Michael and I left a bookstore where I had had a friendly conversation with the owner about my newest book, a conversation during which I playfully lapsed into a fake Southern accent, Michael observed moodily as we drove off, "Why do you do that?"

"Do what?"

"Act different around white people. You and Joe. I've seen you. It's like you're tomming with them or something, it's like with them you're somebody else." The words doused me with surprise, and an embarrassment I couldn't explain.

Angrily clutching the steering wheel tighter, I said, "Nobody's tomming. What you call tomming is being friendly, that's all."

"Oh sure." My son's voice was derisive, surprisingly bitter. "You both act like they're something special. You're just normal in a Black store or restaurant. You're not fake there, why?"

How was I to tell him that despite our dinner table conversations about African history, capital punishment, war in Europe, economic crisis in America, of which he is routinely a part—conversations in which intelligence and compassion make the morass manageable—the world is not black-and-white but often fuzzy, muted, and out of focus. I didn't tell him that when Joe receives an inquiry about the rooms in the rental property we own, if the prospective tenant is a woman, Joe insists that I come to the interview with him. As his wife I have a vested interest in this business matter too. But my presence, with a ring on the fourth finger of my left hand, also defuses some of what makes white women afraid and Black women suspicious, the fact that Joe is a Black man. Was I to tell Michael, that day in the car, that the world feared him? Maybe he already knew.

And so I said instead, "Michael, you don't know what you're talking about."

"Yes I do," he insisted defiantly.

"Being decent, even friendly, to whites isn't tomming, Michael, and I sure hope you don't think it is."

This anger, as fervent as a small brushfire beside me, represented my son's battle with the burden that in America his race has become. Perennially intractable, race as limit and as boundary had tied my son metaphorically in knots. This was how he would know one day that he was an adult. I had told him that he could be anything in a world where whites control everything political and material that matters. I had told him to respect himself, but my lectures about racism had perhaps instilled the suspicion that whites didn't deserve the respect he extended to himself. And, increasingly, I was lecturing him to be as careful around young boys who looked just like him as in the presence of white people who didn't. "Ambivalence" and "compromise" were words my son at fifteen could spell, perhaps even define. But they were words that had not yet tested his resolve or courage.

I was still dazed, flushed by the emotions Michael's accusation had unearthed. And as we turned onto our street, I heard him mutter again through clenched teeth, "When I grow up I'll never be a tom."

I said nothing more, for I was letting go of him and it was messy and scary. He was letting go of me and I wondered how that felt.

*O*nce, we talked about everything. Now it seemed so hard. Was it because my son was a teenage Black male and so, as a result, so much of what I felt compelled to say other than "I love you" was warning, caution, and critique? For Michael, the line of demarcation between child and adulthood was not a border but a precipice. There was so much to tell and so much he had to know, so little time and so few situations within which to frame the conversation.

Michael has the soul of a bear in winter, for at night he sinks not merely into sleep but into a hibernation that defies alarm clocks, my screams up the stairs to get up, even sometimes the smell of pancakes in the kitchen. Meeting my teenaged son in the hall at 7 A.M. was like running into a man with evil on his mind in a dark alley.

When he took up residence in the bathroom, his ever-deepening voice, resonating like a talking drum, filled the hall-way with the latest hot rap lyrics, uttered so quickly in a bat-tered staccato that they whizzed by like bullets ricocheting off the walls.

Allegedly awake, walking as slowly through the house as if each step had been choreographed for special effect, he would enter the kitchen wearing a shirt two sizes too big (he was in style), jeans, unlaced sneakers, a jacket inappropriate for the weather outside. Looking into the refrigerator (his favorite pas-time), he'd grab a Sprite. "Not in this house," I'd say, lifting the soda from his hand and placing a glass of orange juice there instead. Apparently, breakfast was uncool, for it required five minutes of debate to get him to eat a slice of toast.

No time to talk now. I would hustle him out the door, fuming as I watched him walk, as though on a picnic in the woods, not as though already late, toward the subway and school.

After school, when homework was done, he'd go outside, talk to boys on the block. I was cooking dinner once when he trooped in with two friends, Leonard and Calvin. No video games on school nights, no TV until after dinner, so the three boys sat in the living room trading baseball cards. While I moved between kitchen and dining room, it was Michael's voice I heard most as he regaled his two friends with anecdotes, statistics about players and games. With Michael's edgy yet playful laughter filling the house, he stood up before the other two to imitate a play, sprawled over the couch one minute, edged closer to Leonard the next to sell him a card. With his peers he was natural, easy, and soon all three were laughing, joking. Michael was ringmaster of the event.

And yet he was comfortable being alone. Saturday afternoons he might spend in his room drawing, reading magazines, playing video games, and staunchly resist the call of friends to join them. As an only child, he learned to entertain himself, feeling perhaps that his thoughts possessed more integrity than the lure of tales others might weave. Of all the traits my son possesses, I admire most in him this independence. More than anything, I would wish for him a fierce loyalty to being who he is, who he wants to be—if need be, by himself.

Over dinner, finally there was time to talk. But not always of the most important things. Skillful mastery of the mundane, I had learned, was part of parenting too. With Joe teaching math three nights a week at Armstrong Adult Education Center, Michael and I could be alone. We talked about the news, school, family, friends. There were still times, even now, when we flashed back to an intimacy that I missed and he had not yet completely forsaken.

Many of our most memorable conversations took place in the car, driving to karate lessons, art classes, or on weekends when the three of us often headed to the mall for a movie. The car was where we talked about sex. I'd found a condom on the floor of Michael's bathroom the day before. The unused yellowish device, limp and harmless in my palm, symbolized all the "official" lectures about sex that Michael had endured. In the fifth grade he brought home a form from school for me to sign, giving permission for him to take the sex education class. I had bought a human anatomy book for children for him when he was five. In eighth grade there were lectures on sexually transmitted diseases in health class. He was vaguely aware, I suspected, of the nuts and bolts, the mechanics of intercourse from all this, which equated the act with dissecting a frog or building a chair.

A few minutes into our drive—this day, to the dentist— and after mentally sifting through the two dozen ways I had considered broaching the topic, I finally asked, "Where'd the condom come from?" I strove to balance nonchalance and concern, so as not to tip the always precarious balance we now seemed to maintain against full disclosure. Michael said he'd been given the condom during a lecture about AIDS prevention at the all-male after-school program he attended. During the lecture the boys had practiced putting a condom on a banana. I was not certain, however, that this meant they would put it on themselves.

"Who'd you say gave the AIDS lecture?" I asked, stopping at a red light. I wondered if I sounded as wired to Michael as I did to myself.

"Some lady from the city health department."

"Oh." Uncomfortable pause. "You probably knew a lot of what she talked about, I guess, huh?" I said, wondering how much he really knew, realizing that we'd had a couple of brief conversations about sex, hit-and-miss, hit-and-run efforts, but nothing like the in-depth cozy dialogues with your child the manuals advise.

"I knew some of it." He shrugged, opening the glove compartment and reaching for a stick of gum. The sound of the gum wrapper being squashed by his fingers was the only sound in the car. I turned on the radio for support, and asked, "What didn't you know?"

"Well, like about the different kind of condoms, the best

ones to use, and how even when you do other stuff you can get AIDS."

"Other stuff?" I turned to look at Michael and he was gazing out his window, taking refuge in the sight of familiar streets.

"What other stuff? You mean like drug use?"

"I knew that," he said to the window, his voice nearly muffled.

"Well, what other stuff?"

"Like oral sex." Michael turned to face me now, his gaze gauging the effect of his words.

"Oooooooooohhhhhhh, oral sex," I said, as though I had never heard the words before in my life. Hoping to regain control, I said, "So much of what everyone tells you about sex, Michael, is clinical and it's easy to lose the real meaning of it." I was back on solid ground, entrenched in the touchy-feely, slightly intellectual mode I handle best. But was he listening?

"I mean, what sex is really about is two people who respect and care for each other, and sex is an expression of that. You shouldn't, for example, have sex to prove anything. And there are so many emotions involved in having sex. Your body may feel ready but you may not in fact be prepared, mentally I mean."

"A lot of my friends say they've had sex."

"A lot?"

"Sure. But I know they haven't. I can tell. When we're together they say stuff like 'Yeah man, it was so good. She didn't want me to stop. I was killing her.' "

I sat imagining the young boys who entered our house to play video games and bicycle down to the mall talking like this. I nearly hit a pedestrian crossing the street.

"Does that make you want to have sex?"

"No. Not just because they did."

"Have you had sex?"

There, I've said it, I thought. Suddenly I felt lighter. I could even breathe again.

"No, I didn't have sex yet," he said calmly, but clearly anguished, angry, and embarrassed that I had asked.

"Well, don't rush into it. Don't do it with just anybody. You've got plenty of time."

"Okay, mom. Okay."

"Your body isn't something you share with just anybody. It's special, remember that."

"Okay, mom. Okay."

I was breathlessly issuing orders, pleading for sanity and safety. Relieved he hadn't had sex yet, still scared knowing one day he would, so I added, "And when you do use a condom."

"Okay, mom. Okay," he said gently, placing a hand on my arm as we arrived at our destination.

I turned to look at him, imagining an AIDS-emaciated face staring back at me, recalling the article I'd read that chronicled the increase in AIDS among Black youth, citing it as a close second to homicides in some cities as the leading cause of death.

"If you don't ever want me to have sex, just say so." Michael grinned, brazenly sarcastic.

"Michael, I just want you to be careful," I told him, smiling as I attempted to be less grim. In the wake of this assurance I thought, as I do every day, although I did not say it, "And I just want you to live."

*I*t was in Africa that I became a mother. I had married into a large Yoruba extended family whose members included my U.S.-educated husband, Femi, and other similarly educated cousins and brothers and sisters, as well as family members who were barely literate. The Ajayis were a clan of strivers and upwardly mobile achievers. My husband's great-great-great-grandfather had been a member of the royal court of a Yoruba king, and the entire family wore this genealogical inheritance like a cherished mantle.

My son was named, as custom allowed, by his grandmother: Akintunde Babatope and, at my insistence, Michael. His first name means "The spirit of the father returns"; all the male names in the family carry "Akin" as a prefix. Babatope means "Praise be to God."

In my husband's culture, when a woman gave birth to a child, she gave up her name to be called "Mama [name of child]." It was a society in which fertility was worshiped, fecundity prized. So as a male, my son was not just welcomed but treasured. His gender bestowed honor and legitimacy on me, status on his father. My first child had also been a boy, but he had died three days after his premature birth at seven months. And so Michael held within him some part as well of the brother who had preceded him.

To celebrate the birth of our son, friends and family gave us monetary gifts totaling the equivalent of fifteen hundred dollars, and we held an elaborate naming ceremony, which began with an old family friend acting as a priest, addressing everyone gathered. He poured a libation, sprinkling gin onto the floor to honor the Ajayi ancestors, believed always to be present. My son was officially named as child of us all, belonging not just to his father, Femi, and me but to all the Ajayi clan. Then the priest reached into several bowls, placed on a nearby table, and dabbed a bit of each ingredient (honey so life would be sweet, water so he would be great like the sea, salt so he would know that life is difficult) onto my son's tongue and mine and Femi's, and the bowls were passed around the room for all who had gathered to share. Later that evening one of Femi's older brothers sat with me and celebrated the birth of my son by telling me the history of the Ajayi clan, acting as griot and charging me to tell the story to Akintunde one day too.

I had wanted family and it was family that I now had. But I had come to Nigeria a feminist and was confronted again and again by the regressive roles and treatment of women in my adopted country and what they portended for me and for my son. My mother-in-law, a feisty, quick-witted, intelligent woman, had worked long hours on her husband's rubber plantation, had sold foodstuffs in the market, and had borne three sons, two of whom she helped send to study abroad. My sister-in-law helped my husband's brother work his way through school in London. She was a kind of human dynamo, running her household and her stall in the local market with breathtaking efficiency. Both these women, and others like them, were valued among the Yorubas because they worked hard and bore sons. Among the Yorubas a woman was encouraged to be financially independent and to have a trade of her own.

But the journalism classes I taught at the University of Lagos were overwhelmingly male because it was considered a waste to send a girl to college. I knew that female children were still subjected to clitorectomies, a form of genital mutilation that no one I asked seemed willing or able to explain. Polygamy still flourished, was respected and practiced widely. The few single Nigerian women I had met could not imagine themselves remaining single. One woman, a reporter for the country's most respected newspaper, told me, "There would be no place for me in my society as a single woman. I would not count, would not even exist in the minds of my family and friends."

Here was a country that was one of the largest, most populous, and most influential in Africa. My son was, by birth, the member of a tribe whose culture was deep, rich, and complex. We lived in a nation where the head of state was Black, where when I boarded a plane the pilot was Black, and where all the women possessed my hue, or some variation of it, and my broad hips. I saw some resonant, primal part of myself everywhere I looked. And I wanted this racial inheritance for my son.

But what was the inheritance really? Corruption in Nigeria was rampant, the oil wealth was being wasted, and I knew that a group of men could meet around a wood-paneled table in a bank in Luxembourg or London and, with a show of hands or their signatures on a piece of paper, cripple or completely destroy the economy of the country. Nigeria was large and populous, but like every country in the third world, it was a nation of paupers. Its popular culture was schizoid, with young people using bleaching creams on their skin, listening to American music, and visiting juju men in moments of doubt. Half the population was still illiterate, and every attempt at democracy had been sabotaged by the military. What really was my son a part of? His heritage and inheritance here were as conflicted and bittersweet as the ones he would have had if born in America.

When I left my husband four years after I had arrived in Nigeria and a year after my son's birth, my departure had more to do with emotional incompatibility than with politics. Yet the expectations Femi and I brought to our union had been shaped by how we had seen men and women love one another in the cultures that had produced us. Culture and mythology are political. Nigeria taught me that.

Our separation and subsequent divorce were bitter, recriminatory, and for me launched a long period of paranoia and fear that Femi would attempt to take him from me forever (a fear stoked by threats made repeatedly in the heat of anger and by my knowledge that in the Nigerian context my son, no matter what a court in the United States said, "belonged" to his father). The decision to restrict Michael's access to his father and, for long periods of time, not to allow his father to know where we lived was a painful, difficult one. It was made, however, based on my knowledge of how Femi handled anger and frustration. He had never trusted me, really, with his deepest feelings. How could I trust him with our son?

Black fathers, actually and legendarily, have often been the psychological missing link in the African-American community. But I had known and loved my father; he was present in my life, a commanding, impossible-to-ignore influence, even after my mother left him. The specter of the shiftless-can't-be-trusted-never-around-when-you-need-him-can't-or-won't-respect-or-protect-his-woman Black man harnesses and corrupts so many Black women's expectations of the men who are their fathers, husbands, lovers, friends, and sons.

And so the absence of my son's father in his life was not merely my own private tragedy. It was, in my eyes, a failure of community as well. For my divorce, and my estrangement from my son's father, pushed Michael and me closer to the starting line of a race we would have to run already crippled. I had witnessed my parents after their separation forge forgiveness and respect from the remains of a passionate, difficult union. But I wanted to give my son the ideal family even though I knew it did not exist. I wanted him to have a father in his life, despite the statistics that informed me there were eighty-nine Black men for every one hundred Black women. Was that why I married an African? Maybe, I thought in moments of greatest doubt, we can't escape history. But still, I tried. Many days I did. I never would have imagined myself as a mother who will-fully denied a child of mine his father.

The decision I made, out of fear, brought order to my life but little peace of mind. The prayers I mouthed each night, prayers that my son never heard, asked to know when I could reach out to a man I had once loved and now did not trust. When the answer came, it was my son who showed me the way.

My "Do-Over" American Son

Elizabeth Nunez

My son made his presence known from the moment he was conceived, and from that moment on I loved him in a way I had never known myself to love. In the fifth month of my pregnancy, when I had perfected the sway-back walk, the dramatic style of easing myself into a chair with my left leg bent, my right leg stuck out stiffly in front of me—ways of walking and sitting not at all warranted by my still fairly small stomach—a woman who had never cared much for me said to my face that I was acting as if I were the first woman in the world to have a baby. She was right. But I was not acting. The miracle of life growing inside of me had filled me with such awe and astonishment that reason was not enough to dissuade my imagination otherwise. I felt, believed, and acted like no one before me had experienced this miracle. It had been created for me alone.

It was not that my pregnancy was an easy one. My son did not occupy my womb; he invaded it, causing such disruption inside of me that, long after those dreaded early weeks of morning sickness were supposed to be over, I threw up my insides after every meal, sometimes merely at the odor of food. Of course, those who loved me had their theories. My marriage seemed headed for the rocks at the time. My husband was having an affair, which he justified, I think, by a distorted conviction that I'd planned this baby to ruin our carefree fun. (Fun was what he said he wanted at that time. Later he said it was money. The loss of both, I suppose, was what he feared a baby would cost him.)

I discovered many years since that my husband was not unusual in this reasoning. Many men have affairs during their mates' pregnancies. A feral response to competition for their mates' attention? Perhaps. Or perhaps (this is what I've been told) merely acting out a genetic coding that programs them to hunt the fecund female. Since with my pregnancy I had achieved the pinnacle of fecundity, I was no longer worth the hunt, no longer of interest. An unsubstantiated testosterone theory perhaps, yet it has allowed me not to take my husband's betrayal personally. On reflection, I hope he has found some analogous mythology to forgive my seemingly total absorption in the life growing inside of me.

Not that I had a chance not to be so absorbed. It may have been a random turn on the cosmic wheel that shot my son into our terrestrial plane (I tell him he was always an idea in the mind of God waiting to be manifested), but once here, he wanted to make his presence known in the world. Since the only world he knew was my womb, that was where he announced his arrival and his intention to stay. So my friends' theories of my marital woes notwithstanding, I blame my unremitting nausea and my irresistible urge to eat *tous qui bouge* ("everything that moves," as the Martiniquans say, their equivalent for the English expression "leave no stone unturned") on my son's impatience to grow arms and legs and other body parts fast enough and strong enough for him to get out and join the rest of us. The consequence, of course, was that I blew up like a hippopotamus, exceeding my normal weight by over seventy pounds, but then, by the time he was born, my son was already the size of a one-month-old baby, and now at twenty, he is a full twelve inches taller than I.

Jason, or so I unimaginatively named my child, not thinking then of the scourge of Medea, came into this world hungry for life, not wanting to miss a moment of it. When he was an infant, it would take me hours to get him to fall asleep. With the exception of a rare colic, he was not a cranky baby, but he refused to shut his eyes, following every sound and movement around him as if he could never get enough. I'd watch him struggle against the pull of exhaustion, forcing his eyelids open each time they threatened to shut on him. When he was eleven, he told me he wanted to remain eleven forever. He said the same when he was twelve and again when he was thirteen. I understood that it wasn't because he did not want to grow up and become a man like his father and uncles, but rather because he was acutely aware even then, when most children are consumed with play in the present, that every day in the future was a day closer to taking him away from the life he loved. "Mom," he would ask me, "how does it feel to be so old? How does it feel to be so close to the end of your life?" I was thirty-four then.

Jason was not a depressed child. He was not morbidly obsessed with death—just conscious that it was inevitable and aging brought us closer to that inevitable day when we would permanently leave the world. He was born with an instinct for joy and a defiance of mortality, as I was for long suffering and acceptance of the transience of our existence. Perhaps this is a harsh thing that I say about myself. And perhaps I say it because I am still reeling from the bitter words my ex-husband lashed out at me in the months before our divorce. "You are genetically unhappy," he said. "If happiness came your way, you would not recognize it." Perhaps that was so. When you are one of eleven children born to parents obsessively unified in the single goal of liberating their children through education from the deceptively benign limitations of colonial rule, happiness is not a luxury you can afford. Success is your goal, and it comes through effort and hard work—the Sisyphian climb up a mountain pushing a boulder against the forces of gravity. Happiness, if the word is appropriate here, is in that brief moment of triumph when the boulder inches forward. Yet it is clouded always by an acute awareness that it is only through your intense vigilance that the boulder does not roll back and crush you. I understood that clearly the first time my nursery-school teacher put an end to my carefree scrawling and made me force my chalk, painfully wrapped by my fingers in her way, to shape the letter *A* on my slate board.

Not my American son. He was instinctive about his constitutional rights to life, liberty, and the pursuit of happiness from the moment he sucked in air on the planet he never wants to leave, and nothing and no one could make him do something he did not want to do until he wanted to do it. That included following Dr. Spock's instructions about when babies should sleep.

I tell myself sometimes that it couldn't be all instinct. In spite of my ex-husband's dismal conclusions, my son must have learned something about joy from me. My mother marvels at our closeness. She tells me that during her holidays at my home, she would listen from her bedroom to the early morning chatter between my son and me, a habit that we continued until my son left home for college and continue even now when he returns for vacation. Our intimacy seems miraculous to her. I understand why. Like mothers of her generation, she expressed her love for her children through stern discipline, convinced that a display of affection would keep us in a perpetual state of immaturity. She refused to "baby" us. Such was the expression then for the part mothers played in creating adults who were never quite able to support themselves. My mother was preparing her eleven children to face an unfair world, in which only the strong survive. She wanted us to succeed, but like many professional women of my generation, I judged her loving harshly. I assumed that I would have acquired the tenacity, focus, self-control, and skills that allow me to cope with the hurdles of living in a new and ravenous world in spite of her tough love. Now I am moved by the grief I hear in her voice when she speaks with admiration of the relationship I have with my son. I know that she still mourns the loss of an intimacy she could have had with her own children, if only the colonialism she knew had not made her so afraid for our future. But hers was the only way she knew to teach the ones she loved best the resilience they needed to succeed in the unjust world she experienced.

The world I was getting my son ready for was no less unjust. Indeed, it was more unjust than any world my mother could have imagined, as terrible as the colonial system was. My mother could not have imagined a world where her son would be on the list of endangered species, where every night she would fall asleep, as other Black mothers in America did, worried about the physical safety of her child. As an immigrant, believing as my mother must have that life held more possibilities, more hope, in a richer, more developed country, I was slow to accept the realities of America. By the time I understood the dangers in which I had placed my son by virtue of his birth here, the racist situations he had already encountered had taught him to protect himself.

Though we lived in a Black residential area, we were zoned in a school district where my son was either the only one or one of two Black children throughout elementary school. In the first grade, after a year of nursery school, he understood long before the truth penetrated my brain that the little white children in his class refused to hold his hand at school outings because he was Black. When he told me so, I dismissed his reasoning as infantile and ridiculous, and solicited the help of the parents of the other children to find a partner for my son. Yet even when they expressed their reluctance to do so ("We don't think it's right for parents to force friends on children"), I still didn't get the point. I had come from a country where discrimination more often revolved around issues of class rather than race, so it did not occur to me that my child, the son of two college professors, could be considered socially inferior to the children of parents who, I was certain, were less educated than we. My son by this time was adamantly refusing to go on any school outings that involved hand-holding. By the fourth grade he was acting out in class and, frustrated, I almost succumbed to the recommendation of the school psychologist that I put him on Ritalin before I discovered that the parents of little Black children in similar school situations were given the same recommendation.

Yet I am grateful for my ignorance. In this instance it served me well. Unburdened, as my mother was not, with fears for my son's future, I was free to lavish my love on him. I was free to hug and kiss him and tell him I love him. I was free to talk to him, not preach to him. I had not yet envisioned a future in which he would need to learn how to cope with unfair deprivation or how to survive hostile discrimination.

I will take some credit, then, for what I called my son's instinct for his constitutional rights to life, liberty, and the pursuit of happiness. I envy him for what in my ignorance I allowed myself to give him: the security of knowing he was loved *unconditionally*, and the confidence and self-esteem that result from that knowledge. Failure does not intimidate my son as it did me. He picks himself up and tries again. He believes that success is always there waiting for him.

Sometimes I also think that it is not I who helped him

acquire this fearless confidence, but rather this country. America, in spite of its many flaws, engenders an almost naive optimism in its citizens. Billy Crystal reminds his despairing friend in the otherwise unmemorable movie *City Slickers* that there was always a "Do-Over" when they played baseball as children, a second chance to get it right. It was the easy assumption of this option, as if it were a birthright, that yawned like a chasm between my son and me. Do-Over? In the island of my youth I learned early that there were no Do-Overs. By age twelve I had to prove I was university material, or from then on my education would be limited to learning a trade. If I were lucky enough to pass the qualifying exams at twelve, I had four years to prove my worth or I'd be whisked off to training school in some technical area that would not demand more of my brain than was determined it could deliver. If I lasted two years beyond that, there was the plum prize of a civil service job, or, for those who had distinguished themselves in exams set by Cambridge University in England, the rare opportunity to go to college. At each step Do-Overs were infrequent and required bribery of some sort. All middle-class adolescent girls knew that if they became pregnant, they had to get married. A Catholic, I knew that if I got married there would be no question of divorce.

No, I did not know about Do-Overs. I had learned only that I must do it right the first time or suffer the consequences of my failure. Such discipline and focus, my father taught me, built character. When my marriage became more and more troubled, I wrapped myself in my mantle of unhappiness and endured. It was my lot in life to have a bad marriage. I would accept it. At least I had character. But my Do-Over American son saw nothing admirable in my martyrdom. Life offered too many possibilities of joy for him. Not one moment was to be wasted.

I remember well the day I became a child in his fourteen-year-old hands as he sketched a metaphor on a drawing pad for me. Here, Mom, is this big rock, and it is standing in the way of the river. Now what should the river do? According to Billy Crystal the answer was obvious to any pre-school kid in America from his first introduction to the national pastime. However, I thought in terms of absolutes, and so although I knew that there was one thing the river could do and that was pass around the rock, my training had prepared me for warfare: victory or surrender with dignity. Patience and tenacity were key elements. So I began calculating things like river volume and speed. If the river bided its time, it seemed to me, it could easily crash over the rock in the rainy season during the storm.

My son was aghast. Why fight the rock, Mom, when you can move on in a different direction? And so my son, who adored his father, helped me find the courage to take the first step toward making a decision I had known for a long time I would have to make: Dad is that rock, Mom. Move on around him. Get past him. His pencil drew the river parting around the rock and coming together again wider and stronger.

Where did my son learn the confidence to say what I could barely imagine? Did he get so much love that he never felt the desperation too many of us know for just a little of it? How were his pubescent fingers so sure that once past the rock the river would get stronger? Had this country of his taught him this optimism? This America where the children of those it once enslaved faced mountains higher than Everest and moved on, moved on to take their place in every area that had been denied them? This son on whom I lavished the love I wished had been lavished on me taught me not only this lesson of faith and hope, but he taught me too what he so easily took for granted—that I, like he, deserved to be loved.

Jason had just turned nineteen when once again he became my teacher, I his student. He had fallen in love at a time I thought was most inconvenient for both him and me, for it had only been one year since he had shown any interest in his education. For years he and I had fought a bitter war over his lack of concern about his schoolwork, a war which I lost in spite of my best efforts: tutors, expensive private schools, bribery, tears, all of which were for naught. The results were the same. Every parent–teacher night I had to listen to the same litany about his poor performance; the same consolation that he was a bright child, that he could do better if he put his mind to it. But there was nothing I could do to put Jason's mind to it. There were too many things more interesting to him, things that captured his attention and imagination: music, model cars, wrestling, basketball, friends, family. He loved people, and they loved him back. He so charmed my late friend, the writer's writer DorisJean Austin, that she rarely spoke to me without asking about him. He's such a little gentleman, she would say, melting under the attention he poured on her. Above all, Jason loved family, and because mine was scattered throughout the Caribbean and the United States, I paid heavily in overseas and long-distance phone calls for his insistence on keeping in touch. When I worried about his schoolwork, DorisJean made excuses for him. He's too full of life for the dry world of textbooks, she would say.

But all that suddenly changed when he went to college. For the first time he became focused and involved in his studies. He wanted to know more. He told me that reading his biology books was not like studying. Why would someone not want to know about the parts of their body? he asked me. Or about the world around them? It was the point I had been trying to make to him for years. Yet, afraid that after merely one year it was too early to predict if he would keep this interest, I was nervous when he said he was in love. How this would distract him, I did not know. Jason had fallen in love with a girl from Africa who was equally interested in the subjects that intrigued him. She was also beautiful; like me, she was an immigrant; she believed in the values I believed in. It didn't take me long to hope she would be the daughter I had also wanted to have. For a whole summer Jason and I were in love, Jason with this girl with whom he envisioned an entire future replete with a house in suburbia, two kids, a dog, and a fulfilling career; I with the same girl, with whom I envisioned the mother–daughter relationship of my dreams, made even more magical when his girlfriend told me that she had been abandoned by her mother. My chance at last to rewrite my past!

On many a starlit night, the three of us would have dinner on the back deck of my townhouse: the adoring mom, the smitten son, the beautiful girl unabashedly basking in the attention we poured over her. She shared my love for classical music, good literature, and foreign films. She knew, understood, and had a keen appreciation for African art and culture. Before long, my son, who had resisted my attempts to acquaint him with the arts, was visiting museums, going to concerts, and avant garde movies, reading *Othello* in his spare time, and bombarding me with questions about Haile Selassie. And then, it all ended.

A month after he returned to college Jason called me and told me it was over. Finished. He and the girl had made an agreement at the end of the summer that they would write to each other twice a week and call once a week. In four weeks she had not written to him and had called once. He had kept his side of the agreement and more, he told me: I deserve better, Mom, he said. I deserve someone who loves me, who cares about my feelings.

In typical immigrant fashion, I put my will to work. It was my will that had brought the limited success I had achieved. It was my will I trusted. It was my will that made things happen for me. Without my son's knowledge, I called his girlfriend. She said she had been busy with the beginning of the school year, that she had written Jason a letter and planned to send another one. My level of need and desperation was such that I believed her, reminding my son that some of my letters to him had been lost in the school mail. No, he said, that wasn't good enough. He deserved better than that.

I saw my stoicism reflected in my son for a whole year but with a difference: While mine was bred of despair, his was bred of hope. Not believing I was worthy, I had been willing to sacrifice myself for some semblance of love, while my son, convinced of his worth, would accept no less or give no less than real love. I watched him with admiration, never succumbing to pity but bleeding all the same. He threw himself into his college work and his friends. By the end of the academic year he was on the Dean's List, he had made more friends, he was talking to me about putting off serious involvement with a girl until he had finished college.

How was he able to do what I, decades his senior, had never been able to do? Why didn't he panic, grovel, beg? How was he so sure that he would get his dream mate? "There'll be other girls, Mom," he said. The baseball Do-Over. The American pastime. Why was it so hard for me to see the possibility of a Do-Over? The easy answer is that my son was young, young enough to be optimistic. But I was young once too, and yet I never had that confidence and optimism, at least not so far as the heart was concerned. I could say it is because he is male. He is not bound by statistics of ten to one, by the law of supply and demand. But that does not adequately explain my desperation, nor his refusal to accept less than he deserves.

No, that he is young, that he is male, are inadequate explanations for his sense of confidence, his conviction of his self-worth, his faith in himself. I had believed that education was the key that would unlock doors for Jason. For years, unable to get him interested in his schoolwork, I despaired that he would be barred from the happiness life could offer him. Now I know that the unconditional love I showered on him was the most important gift I could have given him. There were times when others warned me that I was giving him too much love. I was spoiling Jason, they said. "Spare the rod, spoil the child," they said. But I had my own childhood to remember; my own desperate search for love as an adult to keep me believing that even too much love is not enough.

It was because I loved Jason so much that he loved himself too, that he believed he was worthy of being loved. If I, who he loved, loved him so much, then he must be deserving of love. I think it is this conviction that gave him the freedom and the confidence to explore his world, to trust his own timetable, to focus on what he wanted when he was ready for it, to survive a broken heart without damage to his self-esteem, to believe in himself and his future. To have the courage and the strength to pursue happiness.

In the end, I have received abundantly more than I have given. If I taught my son what I learned from my childhood, that is, the importance of setting goals, of sacrificing now for a better future, my son, unburdened by the anxieties of needing to prove his worth, taught me that the route to the goal was as important as the goal itself, and that no better future was worth the heavy mortgage of a present that comes only once and is never given back to us again. But most important of all, my son taught me about the American Do-Over. If something prevents me from reaching my goal—my own limitations, or obstacles beyond my control—Do-Over. Life is full of possibilities. Happiness is waiting for me. I only have to find the courage to pursue it.

My Foghorn

Patrice Wagner

The New York City subway system provided me with a rare experience last summer—the chance to see my son through the eyes of others. I got on the train at 157th Street, headed downtown on a Saturday afternoon with Ayinde, my sixteen-year-old son, and Arah, one of his best friends. Although the car was relatively empty, the boys chose to stand. I sat in a seat near the door and watched the reaction of everyone who got on the train to two young African-American males in sneakers, baggy pants, oversized shirts and caps, who stood legs apart, arms crossed, faces serious, revealing no feeling or emotion.

A lone white woman got on at 103rd Street. With her eyes fixed on them, she clutched her purse closer to her body, bowed her head, and moved, cowering and fearful, to the farthest end of the car. The boys were totally oblivious to her. She had nothing they wanted or needed.

I watched the response of the other people who got on the train, all the way down to Thirty-fourth Street. While white women appeared to be the most nervous, everyone looked at them suspiciously and moved away, whites and African-Americans alike. All they saw was what the media had taught them to see in young Black men—menace, thief, gangster, thug, Central Park rapist, a thing to be feared.

I was flooded with a range of emotions. I wanted to laugh, to cry, to fight. To laugh because they were the first thing on the mind of that woman, and she was the last thing on theirs. I wanted to cry because unless something extraordinary occurred in her life, she, like so many others, would forever look at young Black men with eyes that filtered out their humanity, their creativity, and their individuality.

I wanted to fight, to beat it into the heads of each of these people that my son and his friends were artists, intellectuals, musicians, activists, builders; gentle caring boys, loving sons; serious and committed young men with dreams, hopes, and plans.

I wanted to make them see Ayinde for what he was to me: a young man who has given me faith in the birth of a new and better world, the one person who has helped me to become a better self. He has been my savior and my beacon in what has often been a murky and foggy existence.

"*I* think I have cancer," I said to my significant other on a warm June morning in 1978 after jogging on Riverside Drive. The year before, a friend's aunt had died at twenty-six of bone cancer. For some reason, I was certain I was next. I felt as if a tumor was sapping my strength, my life's blood, my *chi*. A week earlier I had been young, active, and vibrant, but at twenty-eight years old everything had suddenly become an effort. Someone had pulled my plug. I postponed the inevitable. I didn't go to the doctor because I didn't want evidence of the obvious.

Two weeks later, walking down Park Avenue at lunchtime, I had a revelation. Even though my period wasn't late yet, I realized I was carrying life. I was filled with an overwhelming sensation of ecstasy and elation. Minor symptoms began to appear—sore breasts, vague feelings of nausea, and no period — not a minor symptom. Two tests confirmed what I knew.

Soon I couldn't button my pants without feeling as if a knife were digging into me. I felt continually bloated. My physical feelings and emotions were no longer my own. The most trivial comments sent me on long crying jags. Even though I envisioned a parasite, sucking all of my energy, strength, and nourishment from me, I was more than willing to give it all I had. It was the first lesson my son taught me—the lesson of selflessness.

Six months later, I sat on my bed one evening, mindlessly watching the news. Half dozing, I didn't hear the beginning of the story. When I looked up, I saw four people being shot by a faceless, nameless gunman. I assumed that this was in Beirut, where young people were always being shot in the streets. But it wasn't Beirut or Palestine. It was Durham, North Carolina, where four Black political activists were killed in the streets by members of the Ku Klux Klan.

Three minutes later, the anchor reported that the body of a twelve-year-old Black boy had been found hanging from a pipe in the basement of an apartment building in the Bronx. The only mark on him was a deep gash in his wrist, where all of the blood had drained from his body. The workings of a cult, they said, a ritual sacrifice, they suspected. I was suffused with horror and fear. How could I bring life into a world where life was so wantonly taken? How could I give birth in a place so full of destruction? Perhaps I was making a terrible mistake, but it was too late.

● ● ●

*M*arch 1979. I was lying in a hospital permeated with pain that battered me like relentless waves, stunning me to speechlessness. I couldn't remember how to breathe or why I was there.

Perhaps I will die, I thought. I viewed death as my only salvation. From deep within me came an "Oh, God."

"No moaning, no groaning."

Who was that? Why was I here?

"It won't be long now." What won't be long?

I couldn't see anything around me. Everything was black, a tunnel to an apparently imminent death. I started to scream, but in the part of my brain where a modicum of consciousness remained, I remembered that screaming made it worse. Another deep moan slipped out of me.

"Come now, it won't be long," said the faceless voice. "Soon you're going to have a brand-new baby."

A baby. That was it. I was in a birthing room at St. Luke's Roosevelt Hospital. But if I were having a baby, what was this specter of death that hung over my bed? This wasn't at all the way it was described in the innumerable books his father and I had read. This wasn't the peaceful, serene, spiritual experience my partner and I had anticipated.

This was something the old women I had known forgot to tell me. Deceitful bitches, all of them, to know and not tell. Another of their many secrets. I didn't care, I would tell everything. I would refuse to go along with the conspiracy.

"It's time for third-stage breathing," someone said. What the hell was that?

"Do you want to hear some music?" It was the voice of my child's father, Khalid. Music? Why would anyone want to hear music at a time like this? The pregnancy books had suggested music to facilitate the birthing process. Who were the people who wrote those damn books? The tape had sounded so wonderful when we had made it last month—Nina Simone, Sweet

Honey in the Rock, John Coltrane, and Ravi Shankar. Now it was the last thing I wanted to hear.

"Okay," the voice said, "Push, push."

My insides were coming out, my kidneys, my lungs, my intestines, there was nothing left for me to push!

"Open your eyes, Mother," said my midwife.

When I looked down, only his head was out, his back to mine, so he was looking right up at me with his eyes wide open. My midwife pulled him out and put him in my arms.

"You have a brand new baby boy." A beautiful baby boy it was, a pale tan tiny thing with shiny black hair, long, delicate fingers, and two big black stars in his face where his eyes should have been.

*T*he apex of some days was his laughter, a chortle from deep in the middle of his stomach that seemed too big for someone who only weighed eleven pounds. Some days, it was his smile, that made the stars in his eyes brighter or deepened the dimples in his cheeks. Watching his delight at the shine of a piece of aluminum foil or his trying to grab bright rods of sunshine out of the air became my delight. He needed no toys; his intense curiosity brought out the fascination in the most inconsequential things — a piece of paper, a penny, the gentle wave of a leaf in the wind. He savored each characteristic, each variation, and always tried to put it into his mouth.

One day he discovered glass. He looked from one side to the other, looking and touching it, amazed that this hard thing was something you could see through. You could see the wonder in his face. My child taught me virtues long forgotten — curiosity, awe, and amazement. He gave me the gift that only infants and toddlers can give, the ability to see the world through new eyes.

Years later he would grab for toys that no longer worked or toys that were inaccessible and expensive. Like the $60 laser tag that my father had searched for one Christmas Eve, only to find that he had to make a two-hour drive to another toy store because all the laser tags within a 120-mile radius were sold out. By the following Christmas my son wouldn't remember where it was, and laser tags would be marked down to $10 at a corner store.

When Ayinde was four months old, I noticed a poster on the subway while riding downtown one day. It was the face of six-year-old Etan Patz. His mother had decided to let him walk to the school bus by himself one morning. Perhaps he had told her he was a big boy, and she wanted to encourage his independence. It was not far, and she had watched him go as far as she could see him, to the corner. He had stopped at the corner before he turned, and they had waved good-bye to each other. She never saw him again. He was abducted.

I was a new mother, and her pain was unfathomable to me. I put it out of my mind that this could ever happen — that he could ever be taken away from me. When Ayinde was a year old and walking, it hit me more acutely. I arranged his life so that he was never alone and someone was always there to protect him. I thought of Etan Patz and his mother again the first time we were in a restaurant and my son went to the men's room alone. If he went to visit classmates or to a movie without an adult, I worried. I met each departure with fear and nagging questions. Khalid was, and is, a very important part of Ayinde's life, but we separated and Khalid chose to move to New Orleans. The day-in, day-out decisions and traumas became mine alone.

My son was going to be the "new man." He would be unencumbered by the trappings and perils of mass culture. I would shield him from the worship of imaginary idols and false ideals. He wouldn't be a slave to Disneyland and "Sesame

Street." I wouldn't buy him guns for toys. He would be antimilitarist and nonsexist.

It worked only as long as the confines of his world were his home and immediate family. When he came home from the baby-sitter at eighteen months old singing "I wanna be a macho man," I got a glimmer of what I was up against—television, comic books, advertisements, all telling him the opposite of what I was telling him. When he was three he told me he wanted to marry Princess Leia in *Star Wars* because she carried a gun. At five, every picture he drew and every object he played with was his imaginary gun. I pondered the consequences of denial. I rethought my position and bought him a toy rifle for Christmas that year.

I, who thought I knew so much, encountered his many questions and found that I had no answers: What is suffering? Why do people who struggle have to die? Who made the sky? Who made the trees? What is politics? What is sex? I began to wonder if I was cut out for parenting, when I didn't know the answers or whether I was doing the right thing. When do I compromise and when do I hold on? How much freedom is too much? How do I not stifle his spirit, make him fearful? What is humiliation?

From kindergarten to fourth grade Ayinde was driven back and forth to school each day by the same bus service. That spring, the van driver announced his retirement. Ayinde would have to take public transportation. He was ready and eager. I was terrified. I could no longer hold him to me or keep him forever in my sight so I could be sure he was safe.

I was in the midst of a battle for his life and his soul. I had expected a battle. They say there are no atheists in the trenches. And there are no atheists among Black mothers whose children travel city streets each day, navigating through the constant barrage of possible violence and random threats that come their way. I began to pray. I had prayed as a child because my mother had made me say my prayers, but for years I didn't pray because I didn't know what I believed. When I became a mother, I realized it didn't matter what I believed. I knew no other way to protect my son from a world I hadn't made. Prayer was the only medicine I knew, the only magic, the only power. It was all that I had. My son's presence in my heart brought me back to God in a way I never expected. I prayed not only to protect him but also to give thanks.

When he was seven, we looked for a living role model for him to write about for Black History Month. The teacher had told them not to write about Jesse Jackson—she didn't want to read thirty rewrites of news articles about Jesse Jackson. I didn't want him to write about an athlete or an entertainer. He had grown up surrounded by books, pictures, and posters of African-American leaders and people I wanted him to emulate, those who had attempted to create a better world for us. Patrice Lumumba, Kwame Nkrumah, Samora Machel, Agostino Neto, Maurice Bishop, Steven Biko, Thomas Sankaro. Great African leaders and theoreticians. Malcolm, Martin, Medgar, George Jackson, men who loved their people more than themselves, exemplary men, men who thought well and deeply about the plight of African people. Men who were murdered in the line of duty. Most of them would only now be approaching the prime of their lives.

"I want to write about someone who is alive," he said. "Is Frederick Douglass alive? Is Malcolm X alive? Is Martin Luther King alive? Is Marcus Garvey alive? Is Harriet Tubman alive? Is Steven Biko alive?" How could I tell him why there are so few living revolutionaries? When I answered "No" to each question, the questions stopped.

"Write about whoever you want to write about. It doesn't matter. I don't care."

He looked at me quizzically. He couldn't understand my change of heart.

"You're fickle."

"Yes, I am."

My black-and-white world burst, suddenly, into a million gradations of gray, interspersed now and then with bright splotches of color. I was forced to rethink everything, to see another viewpoint. I thought the questions had been hard before. He wanted to know the purpose of education, and when I work, who is it that I really work for? If I don't like my job, why do I keep doing it? If I say I want to do one thing, why do I do something else? What is politics, and what does the government really do? What is the purpose of life, and why are we here? Why is the sky blue? Who is God? Where is God? What is God? Do you know Jesus?

These were times that I felt I had given birth to a monster. We spent years in battle, arguing and disagreeing. I wanted him to learn the lessons the way I had learned them, to see life as I saw it. That's how we spent most of his puberty. Finally, weary of battle and recognizing that I was up against a formidable foe, I began to accept that his life was his own. That no matter what I wanted for him or how badly I wanted it, he would always get what he wanted for himself. I could not shape his thoughts, his values, his opinions. I can teach him what I feel is important, but his beliefs are his own.

At thirteen, I had encouraged him to apply to A Better Chance, a nationwide program that connects talented and gifted children of color with prestigious private boarding and day schools across the country. Ayinde received a full scholarship to Deerfield Academy and was accepted to Northfield Mount Hermon School, both boarding schools in Massachusetts. A separate letter congratulated me for the support I had given him and reassured me of what I already knew; my son was brilliant, talented, and unique. Along with the letter came a mailing tube, which held a poster of gothic buildings shrouded in fog.

"It looks scary," Ayinde remarked, and I agreed. And then he said, "I'm not the boarding-school type."

The four pale, laughing children on the poster did little to dispel the aura of mystery and gloom. They symbolized the fear and trepidation, the doubt and ambivalence that tainted the pride and joy of his acceptance.

"Why did they pick me?" he asked. He did not understand why he was being congratulated, that there were people who would give an arm or leg to be accepted to these schools. He did not understand his value, his beauty, his worth.

I thought back to the years of veiled insults and put-downs from teachers who had denigrated his intellect and identity. When his second-grade Cuban teacher told me "He speaks such good standard English," I was taken aback. What else would he speak? He had two educated parents and was probably speaking English before she was.

"Your son is arrogant," I was often told. He was raised to love himself, so his pride was often mistaken for arrogance. He challenged and questioned his teachers, just as he challenged and questioned me. Many of his teachers had a difficult time dealing with a Black male child who was confident in his intellect. They felt threatened.

"They picked you because you're smart, you're a leader, you're artistic, and on top of everything else . . . you're a homeboy." I hugged him and gave him the high five sign. But behind my pride, I was afraid. I didn't want to send him anywhere if he couldn't be himself and love himself. I wanted him to feel safe and special and understood.

What did the people at these schools know about my son's life, his history, and his culture? Had they ever been in a place where their music, their clothes, their language were misunderstood, denigrated, and disrespected?

But the public schools he had attended for ten years had not been right for him. At parent-teacher meetings, teachers had criticized him for being "arrogant," "too self-confident." "He wants to do what he wants to do when he wants to do it." "He isn't cooperative." "His academics are fine but he has a problem with his attitude." His worst grades had always been in conduct.

I never quite knew how to take these remarks. I had taught him to question everything. Was I supposed to tell him to be more docile, more conciliatory, to give in, to keep his opinions to himself?

We chose Northfield and he went reluctantly; both of us full of ambivalence. I cried the day he left. Each step he took from that point on in his life would carry him further away from me, into situations where his decisions and plans would become more and more his own. Even though I conceived him, gave birth to him, worried over him for the years that I diapered and fed him, he was becoming less of my son and more of his own man. Soon he would no longer belong to me.

The Urban League recently published an article on the state of Black men in America. They are reaching the status of the bald eagle, the rain forest, the dinosaur. I experienced a knot in my stomach when I read it. The report said that, statistically, the odds are that my son will never reach manhood, let alone grow to a ripe old age. I felt weak. Not only could I not protect him, I could not even keep him alive. I prayed and tried to surrender him to God's grace, like every Black mother does.

I cannot think of anything I could have done, except become a nun or a mystic, that would have taught me what I learned from being a mother to my son: selflessness, self-sacrifice, curiosity, awe, tolerance, responsibility, discipline, forgiveness, spirituality, love of nature, and the rare chance to experience true intimacy and true love.

One of the most difficult lessons of parenthood has been to love and to let go. Every lesson provides an equivalent or greater reward. My son is becoming my friend, someone I can talk to, someone whose values and spirit I respect. I become annoyed and irritated, but he keeps me real and he keeps me honest. He helps me to be my best self. It is not just that he criticizes my procrastination, my lethargy, my immobility. I want to be my best self for him.

*O*ne day when he came home for spring break, I was feeling particularly out of sorts. I was walking around in circles, aimless and unfocused.

"What's wrong, Ma?" Ayinde asked.

"I feel as if I'm in a fog."

"Well, I'm here, Ma, I'll be your foghorn," he said. And he is.

When he was young I used to tell him never to forget what is real and what is important in life, and now, when I forget, he reminds me. He nudges at the edges of my complacency and passivity as I slouch toward middle class and middle age.

My son taught me that all men are boys at heart, who sometimes, only get tall. I learned more about men from my son than I learned from any man I had ever been with. The boy never dies. He is forced to go underground, to hide, to sometimes cower and crouch for protection. But the boy, that spirit of freedom, that sense of freeness is always there. I pray that the world in which he grows into manhood will allow him to fulfill his dreams, to always be both man and child.

He works to keep me alive and healthy and young. I quit smoking because I could not smoke in peace around him. "You're going to die, Mommy. You're going to catch 'empasema.'" He forces me to recycle, to turn off the water. He encourages me to exercise, to do the things that are important to me, to eat healthy food, to turn off the television, to write my books.

Parenting is exaltation and crucifixion, an experience that brought out the best and worst in me. I would never have known who I really was had I not become a parent. Parenting saved me from my worst self. My temperament and nature seemed to me, at times, antithetical to the demands of motherhood. I had always been essentially a solitary person. I loved to read, to stay up late, to sit and contemplate. I hated to cook and clean, to do laundry and wash dishes. My mother, after all, had not raised a domestic. I hated doing the same thing every day or doing something because it had to be done. I did not like the idea of imposing rules on somebody else. I did not want to be responsible for anyone else's life. I was having a hard enough time being responsible for my own.

They say that children choose their parents. I do not know why my son chose me, but I am glad that he did. I tell him that although I was born on my birthday, on his birthday I was born again. For years I thought that I was saving him, only to wake up one morning to discover that he had, in fact, saved me.

Part IV

Husbands
and
Lovers

It's Ten O'Clock and I Worry About Where My Husband Is

Rosemary Bray

He phoned more than an hour ago to say he was on his way home, but I have yet to hear the scrape of the iron gate, the rattling keys, so I worry.

Most married women fret about a tardy husband; young women like myself worry more. For most people in New York—truth be told—the urban bogeyman is a young Black man in sneakers. But we live in central Harlem, where every young man is Black and wears sneakers, so we learn to look into the eyes of young males and discern the difference between youthful bravado and the true danger of the streets. No, I have other fears. I fear white men in police uniforms; white teenagers driving by in a car with Jersey plates; thin, panicky, middle-aged white men on the subway. Most of all, I fear that their path and my husband's will cross one night as he makes his way home.

Bob is tall, five feet ten or so, dark, with thick hair and wire-rimmed glasses. He carries a knapsack stuffed with papers from the office, old crossword puzzles, Philip Glass tapes, *Ebony Man* and *People* magazines. When it rains, he carries his good shoes in the bag and wears his Reebok sneakers. He cracks his knuckles a lot and wears a peculiar grimace when his mind is elsewhere. He looks dear and gentle to me, but then, I have looked into his eyes for a long time.

I worry that some white person will see that grim, focused look of concentration and will see the intent to victimize. I fear some white person will look at him and see only his or her nightmare—another Black man in sneakers. In fact, my husband *is* another Black man in sneakers. He's also a writer, an amateur cyclist, a lousy basketball player, his parents' son, my life's companion. When I put aside the book I'm reading to peek out the window, the visions in my head are those of blind white panic at my husband's Black presence, visions of a flashing gun, a gleaming knife: I see myself a sudden, horrified widow at thirty-four.

Once upon a time, I was vaguely ashamed of my paranoia about his safety in the world outside our home. After all, he is a grown man. But he is a grown Black man on the streets alone, a menace to white New Yorkers—even the nice sympathetic liberal ones who smile at us when we're together. And I am reminded, over and over, how dangerous white people still can be, how their fears are a hazard to our health. When white people are ruled by their fears of everything Black, every Black woman, an addict, a whore, every Black man is a rapist—even a murderer.

Charles Stuart understood this fear enough to manipulate an entire nation. When he said a Black man in Boston's Mission Hill district put a bullet through the head of his pregnant wife, who could doubt him? So a city's police force moved through the neighborhood, stopping and strip searching Black men at random, looking for the apocryphal Black savage who, it turned out, existed only in Boston's collective imagination. Yet an innocent African-American man, William Bennett, was paraded before the nation for weeks, until Stuart's brother had an attack of conscience and went to the police.

The Stuart case was shameful, but it could have been worse. After all, William Bennett is still alive. When whites' fear of Black people is allowed its free reign, Black people can die. Wasn't Michael Griffith a bum out to make trouble when a teenage posse in Howard Beach chased him onto the Shore Parkway and into the path of a car? Wasn't Yusef Hawkins a thug coming to beat up a white man in Bensonhurst when he was surrounded by a gang of teenagers and shot? It doesn't seem to matter that Michael Griffith was a construction worker, that Yusef Hawkins was a student looking for a used car. Someone looked at those two men and saw danger, and so they are dead. And the women who waited for them—who peeked out the front windows and listened for their footsteps on the stairs—waited in vain.

So, when it's ten o'clock and he's not home yet, my thoughts can't help but wander to other Black men—husbands, fathers, sons, brothers—who never do make it home and to other Black women whose fingers no longer rest at a curtain's edge. Even after I hear the scrape of our iron gate, the key in the lock, even after I hear that old knapsack hit the floor of the downstairs hallway and Bob's voice calling to me, my thoughts return to them.

A Femme Kind of Love

Mali Michelle Fleming

I never really liked skirts until I wrapped a *lapa* neatly around my ample backside and thighs, securing it gently at my waist. In those two yards of African fabric, there was an automatic freedom to explore the femme in me, to feel the subtleties of being a woman.

And I'd never felt like a woman in love until I loved an African man.

Yes, I'd been in love before. I'd dated brothers from Latin America, the West Indies, and the United States. With my first serious affair, I unconsciously set the tone for subsequent relationships with men. At eighteen, I fell in love with Paul. Eight years my senior, street-wise, and witty, he was my learning experience in the womanizing, worldly ways of New York men. He'd been around the world—twice—and was on the ten-year plan for putting himself through college.

Next was Niles, a charming twenty-six-year-old Trinidadian journalist, an adoring friend and steady workout buddy who became my lover. The drama of our relationship swung like a heavy pendulum from emotionally draining episodes of making up and breaking up to cycling, swimming, and lifting weights together or hanging out in New York. After nearly five years of him telling me what was wrong with me, I finally decided that there was something missing in him. After all the ups and downs of that alliance, I concluded that any man who was to be my lover would also have to be my best friend and be faithful.

With these and other men, I was an androgynous partner in an androgynous kind of love. There were no clear-cut roles in the relationship; we just made up the rules as the drama unfolded. Our roles became very evident, however, when we got that love jones. Whenever it was time to get busy, the "me man, you woman" thing would surface. We both knew what time it was, and it was then that I was reminded of what it meant to be a woman.

Although I cared for these brothers—some more than others, of course—I knew that there was more to this male-female thing. I knew that there was more to being a woman than opening up my heart and my legs for lovemaking. I knew that there was more to a relationship with a man than being a partner in love and a woman in bed.

But what was it? As far as I was concerned, I had it going on. Hell, I was an accomplished African woman. As a professional journalist and African dancer, I had academic credentials, a job with a decent salary, a car, a cute apartment, and a lover. I had a good life.

Emotionally, I'd been drop-kicked into womanhood after my first love affair as a young adult in college. Like most other sisters, I'd survived and lived to tell about that fiasco. For all the bruises that relationship left, I knew those scars would vanish with enough introspection, leaving a stronger, wiser woman standing with healed, not festering, wounds.

As a culturally conscious sister, I'd crossed the bridge to

Africa a long time ago, sporting all kinds of natural do's, from the tiniest Afro to locks. My adornment was cowrie, my dress was accented with mud cloth and kente, and my talk was of the Motherland. Politically, I viewed myself as a nationalist, and socially, I identified with sisters and brothers from the African diaspora. My lineage as an African woman was very clear in my mind.

But instinctively, I knew that something very important and special was missing for me as an African woman. I didn't quite know what it was until the moment Akoja and I laid eyes on each other. The minute our spirits were reunited—yes, we'd *definitely* met before—I was filled. That nagging emptiness that I'd felt with other men was suddenly gone. I was about to understand this man–woman thing a whole lot more, his eyes told me.

I actually felt his presence before I saw him that Friday night at Kilimanjaro. The sweet sound of *soukous* music rolled from the club's speakers around the bar, as a largely African crowd mingled, dancing and nursing drinks. I sensed him circling me, silently appraising me as I stood talking to a sister-friend. I spotted a buddy from Guinea-Bissau leaning on the bar, so I went over to chat. We had started reminiscing about our days at my alma mater, Columbia University, when I realized that suddenly the two of us had become three.

His voice was deep and resonant, with a British West African accent. As he told cosmopolitan stories of his life and travels, the nostrils on his broad nose flared, his full lips danced, his slanted, delicate eyes burned into my soul. Dressed in the flyest new European gear, with a wide bald head that guided a strong, wiry frame of milk chocolate, he oozed "me man–you woman"— and he hadn't even touched me yet!

We spent that first evening politely feeling each other out. We danced together once, and when I saw how effortlessly our bodies moved in unison, I knew that I had to get to know this man from Sierra Leone. After a restless night dreaming about Akoja, I went back to the club the following evening. I had no idea what had come over me. My lover was in the West Indies visiting his family, and all I could think about was Akoja. I knew that I wanted to be near him. What I didn't know was that our mating dance had begun.

Akoja was regal, ambitious, and almost arrogant. Like most African men born in the Motherland that I've met, he was extremely proud. At our very first meeting, I knew that I was his and he was mine, just as it was always meant to be.

When we finally made love, he reminded me with every caress and movement that I was indeed his. He possessed me with a confidence that I'd never experienced before from a man. I belonged to him as he belonged to me, physically, emotionally, and for the first time in my life, *spiritually*. He made me understand what Aretha was talking about when she sang "Natural Woman," because my soul was certainly in the lost and found until Akoja claimed it.

With facile agility he wore masculine energy, and it was with a natural ease that I began to tap into my feminine spirit. The changes were subtle at first. I put down the baggy pants that I'd been wearing and started donning more dresses. When he called, my voice, once cool and aloof, purred niceties for his ears alone.

When we went out, he was intent on protecting me and providing for me. Akoja made certain that whenever we were on the town that I was always accounted for. If he couldn't be around me, he made sure that one of his "brothers" (close friends) was by my side. As long as he was in my life, no harm was ever going to come my way if he or his brothers could help it.

Instead of paying my way as I usually did when I went out

with a brother, I allowed Akoja to take care of the tab. Otherwise, there was an argument—from him. "Hell, I am a man," he'd say, ego all bent out of shape. "I'm an independent woman, and I don't need for you to pay all the time," I'd counter. But it was his place to pay whenever he and his lady went out! As a man, it was his *job* to provide for his woman, he'd assert, incredulous of my whole point of view. What was with this feminist bullshit about going dutch anyway? My African lover just wasn't having it. After a few more of these go-arounds, neither was I.

My friends noticed the changes. That understated toughness that I'd built up after years of living in my native Washington, D.C., and New York City slowly dissolved in his presence. With Akoja, the hardened edges I'd developed became only crystallized sugar that melted into a river of syrupy sweet love, all for him.

My African lover made me feel that being a Black woman was a source of infinite power and strength. No longer were we the mules of the world. He spoke cryptically of African women's secret female societies in his country, who were so strong spiritually that they were both feared and respected by men. He let me know through words and deeds that he was one of those brothers who'd grown in his lifetime to respect the power of the feminine spirit. With Akoja, there was never a question of my strength as a woman; it was simply a given, a birthright. My feminine spirit was different, and potentially greater, than his male one.

There was no tension over who was supposed to be doing what in our relationship. We instinctively fell into natural roles. He was a Westernized African brother, and I am an Africanized sister born in America. He was not one of those African men who tries to keep a woman down and in her place. No, my lover supported any endeavor that I wanted to take on. There were no restrictions on what I could do as a woman; in his eyes, the skies weren't even the limit. On the domestic scene, he often cooked and cleaned more than I did. He could do it all, if necessary. What was most important was that we shared our time, space, and energies.

In loving him, I realized a softness that I'd almost pronounced dead. There was no need to be a butch in love, a superwoman who only needs a man for lovemaking. I could finally be a femme in love and explore all sides of my womanhood because I knew that he had my back. I kissed androgynous love good-bye and found space in my heart and spirit for a man.

Initially, I felt totally off balance. For one thing, I was already in a steady relationship with a kind brother from the Caribbean. After meeting Akoja, however, my whole purpose for being a woman in love was up for grabs. Was having a nice brother, talking of children, and living a comfortable lifestyle all there was to this man–woman union? My spirit guided the rest of me reluctantly to my African lover for a precious life lesson, assuring me that with him a new worldview would be revealed based on old-world truths.

But before I finally gave in to all the feelings Akoja had unleashed inside of me, I planned a revolt. I'd just returned from a four-day sojourn in Antigua, where I'd spent my twenty-fifth birthday alone. Walking on the powdery beach, listening to the roll of the ocean, and being quiet had been just the kind of soul food I needed: time to separate myself from the love triangle I'd been drawn into. By the time I got on the plane to come back to New York, I knew what I had to do. I had to cut Akoja loose. He was making my life too complicated, and I'd decided to stay in the relationship that I was already in.

We met in the pouring rain the very next day at my favorite health-food restaurant in his neighborhood, across from Columbia University. As we ran inside, dripping wet, I could tell that he was puzzled. He'd offered his apartment for this impromptu rendezvous, but I'd turned him down. He knew something was up, but as always, he was a gentleman. He took my soaking umbrella and shook it. I headed upstairs and sat at a secluded table in the rear of the balcony.

Waiting for Akoja to join me, I clasped my hands and stared at the table in front of me as I recited my speech again in my head: "Akoja, I can't see you anymore. I care about you a great deal, but I want to work on the relationship that I'm already in. I'm sorry if I've led you on, but we can't go on with this any further. The only thing we can be is friends."

Just as I finished my mini-monologue, I glanced at Akoja climbing the stairs. His beige rain jacket was hugging his wet body. As he sat down, he wiped his moist face and neck with a handkerchief and said, "So what's up?"

I took a deep breath and said, "I have something to tell you."

"And you couldn't tell me at home? This must be something good," he said, rolling his eyes at me with a half-smile on his face.

I looked him straight in the eyes and braced myself. I took another deep breath and carefully recited my speech, this time out loud. When I finished, I bit the inside of my mouth nervously and waited for the bomb I'd just dropped to crush his heart.

And wait I did. Akoja took his sweet time digesting my words. I searched his countenance and lean body for clues to what he was thinking, but I found none. I'd never seen this man who'd crept so effortlessly into my world angry, and I wondered if I was about to experience his wrath now in public. Maybe meeting him here was a bad move. Maybe I should have just written him a "Dear John" letter instead. But it was too late now to rewrite this scene.

I looked down at my still-clasped hands and saw his coming toward them. He encircled my hands with his and cradled them. Our eyes met as he gently squeezed my hands, and the silence was finally pierced with his resolute response.

"I won't let you go," Akoja said coolly.

His confidence sent me into an emotional tizzy. Didn't I just diss this brother for another man? Hadn't I just told him that we *cannot* be together? And *he* wasn't gonna let *me* go? What part of my little speech didn't he get? His native tongue was English, so I knew that he had understood me. I shook my head in disbelief, and he repeated his words, as if he'd read my incredulous mind.

"You can do what you want to do, but I'm not letting you go," he repeated in such a polite voice that it sounded like he was paying me an unexpected compliment.

I laughed nervously because I could tell that Akoja was very serious. He meant what he said, and deep down inside, I knew it. He'd called my bluff before I even realized that it was one. His poker face said it all. No matter what you throw my way, I can handle it, no problem. We were destined to be together. End of story.

In two weeks' time, we tumbled right back into his bed. From that point on, I never questioned the boundaries of our union. I allowed our story to unfold naturally and savored every moment that I could steal to be with this man, who felt I belonged to him.

Slowly, and sometimes painfully, Akoja and I became one. Our union was based on the complementary combination of our energies—masculine and feminine—as we sought to find equilibrium of the spirit. As I became more comfortable with my feminine energy, a balance of power began to emerge, and Akoja and I realized the wonderment of being soulmates.

In Akoja's presence, I began to revel in the ultimate gift of womanhood—the ability to create. The scope of my feminine power blossomed in his rich African soil, and he watered and cultivated the budding petals of my spirit with the utmost of care. I stopped trying to do the things that men did, stepping out of the heavy armor of the superwoman and slipping into the lightness and comfort of my lapa. I savored the goddess in me and tapped into my intuition for guidance. Inner seeing, inner hearing, and inner knowing became my guiding lights.

Before I met Akoja, I'd been experiencing *hambre del alma*, or "song of the starved soul," as Dr. Clarissa Pinkola Estes calls it in *Women Who Run with the Wolves*. I was one of the many sisters who'd lost what Estes calls their "soulfooting."

As African women, many of us have been so busy ensuring the survival of the race, assuming woman-warrior stances, that we haven't had the time or the wherewithal to cultivate our softer sides. Estes writes about both wildlife and wild women being endangered species, but all we hear about in the media is that our young brothers are at risk, killing themselves and each other in droves. However, we've also suffered a collective death as sisters, not only because we continue to lose our lovers, husbands, brothers, fathers, and sons. We've also lost touch with our feminine spirits.

Our womanhood was besieged and forced into unnatural rhythms from the day that we hit these shores. The feminine spirit of Black women was pillaged and bullied into a stoic submission, but the natural resilience of our spirits as African women would not allow Massa to have the last word. So as our men were emasculated, we were defeminized. Is it any wonder that in the wake of not being able to marry our men or take care of our own families if we were allowed to stay with them, and being maids and wet nurses to Miss Sally's kids, that we tried to become irascible superwomen? We *had* to, out of necessity; our men weren't allowed to protect or provide for us, a shame that still weighs on their weary shoulders. Lacking any real measure of autonomy over our lives, we donned the armor and continue to battle for our lives today. Were it not for Black women's warrior spirits in the face of such dire circumstances, our race probably would be a footnote in American history books today.

Since history is drawn to encore performances, it's no surprise that African sisters are still acting like superwomen, calling on their superpowers to try to save ourselves and the men we love. Our brothers aren't being lynched or hunted down like animals by Massa anymore; it's a different homeboy and his posse that are putting the finishing touches on the annihilation of Black men.

After nearly four hundred years of missing our men, we've assumed the roles of both men and women to survive America. As women, we've been so busy taking care of the business of our jobs and often single-parent households, that we can't even hear our feminine spirit calling anymore. When we do, the possibility of getting played by a brother—or any man, for that matter— scares the hell out of us. So we strap that metal-plated bustier back into place to protect our hearts and our backs.

And our men, still reeling from the nihilistic energy of America, try to be more sensitive like we sisters say we want them to be. Often they're left scratching their heads, trying to figure out where they really fit into the lives of these African heroines who seem to have it all together. The end result is a bunch of androgynous characters wondering what the hell is going on with our people, and how the hell we got so far off track.

Some sisters might think I'm retrograde, and I confess that I am. I had to look back to hear my feminine spirit calling my name. I needed to find a balance in the womanhood that I'm learning to wear now into the future. Once I tapped into that life-giving energy, I knew that I'd been initiated into the essence of my African womanhood.

Looking back, it seems that Akoja disappeared from my life just as he'd appeared: quickly and intensely. After we spent nearly two years together, he was inspired to return to Africa following a coup in Sierra Leone. His dreams of trying to rebuild his country could finally be realized, and he had to leave me to do that.

I wasn't surprised. He'd always made it very clear that his stay in the United States was temporary; Sierra Leone was his home. But somehow, I thought we would be reunited and would spend the rest of our lives living happily ever after. It really didn't matter to me where we lived, as long as we were together.

Akoja was a man on a mission, however. The few phone calls that I received with cautious excitement in the first year after his return evaporated over time. I scoured the papers for tidbits of information on Sierra Leone and wondered constantly if he was dead or alive.

I haven't spoken with Akoja in over two years. In that time, I have come to the conclusion that our love was one to be experienced, not one to build a foundation on. We were meant to share some very special moments together for only a short period of time.

Since he left in 1992, I have dated sporadically. Yet it has taken me four years of intense soul-searching and closure to finally open up and get ready to receive another serious lover in my life. While I know that a potential mate must still fulfill the requirement of being my close friend, I also know that the brother must speak to all parts of my womanhood—the physical, the mental, and the spiritual.

I have finally moved on, but the gift Akoja gave me continues to transform my life. I'm blessed that he came into my heart and spirit to guide me back home, so that I could finally experience a femme kind of love.

His Story

Donna Wise

I had no choice. It was Friday night, and I was blessed with a hairdo that only occurs once in a lifetime when the stars are aligned. This could not have been planned. My appointment was moved up because my hairdresser had to leave town for a funeral. I told her I'd wait until she got back, but, strangely, she insisted I have it done that day. I resisted because it would be harder to keep it looking good until Monday, and I didn't want to waste it on a weekend spent curled up with a book.

Hearing an unusual urgency in her voice, I agreed. By 8 P.M., everyone in the salon was staring at me in awe. They complimented her on her masterpiece, and she had to admit that she had outdone herself.

"Girl, you got to go try that out. Where you going tonight?"

"Home."

"Uh-uh, girl. You got to play that for all it's worth. You lookin' good!" Everyone seemed to be in agreement, more so than in the usual salon camaraderie. Tickets to a fundraising dinner downtown were suddenly thrust into my hands by I know not whom. I headed out the door to look for some adventure.

After looking for a parking space for half an hour, I realized that what I was doing was ridiculous. After all, I wasn't desperate. Men weren't lining up at my door, but I was satisfied with my acquaintances. They were intelligent, charming, handsome, romantic, generous, gentle, and confident. So what if all these characteristics didn't happen to be displayed by the same individual at the same time? No one said they were perfect.

I abandoned my search and returned home to find my roommate still sitting on the couch. "I thought you were going to your Alcoholics Anonymous party?"

She frowned. "I changed my mind since you didn't want to come along."

"I told you, I'm not going to try to party with a bunch of weirdos (present company excluded), but you should go. You were looking forward to it."

"The truth is, I need a ride," she admitted. Just as she completed her sentence, I turned to the mirror in the hall and was amazed to find that the magic coif still had its effect and had transformed me into someone else for the evening. With renewed courage bestowed by this new identity, I agreed to take her to the party.

It was held at an upscale clubhouse. I was impressed that all the party-goers actually looked normal. Always supportive of my roommate's commitment to staying sober, I nevertheless viewed her world as something so totally foreign that I didn't even want to know how it worked.

"Hello, my name is George, and I have been sober for one year," said the first to approach with a gleaming smile.

"I'm happy for you." Maybe this was a mistake, I thought. But eventually, after juice and cookies, good music, and meeting a few more recent converts, I was able to relax. It had been a while since I had felt so comfortable at a party. No pretenses here, no facades. Everyone was proud to have been able to achieve what they had, and to maintain it, one day at a time.

Then the cookie crumbled. In walked a group of eight guys who looked like they had just stepped off the prisoner bus, rough and ready. They entered with an untamed arrogance, haughtily searching the crowd for their first victims. Astute as I am, I quickly made my way to the opposite end of the room and buried my face in a bowl of potato chips. My magic hairdo began to draw the wrong kind of action. The least attractive and shortest of the posse found me in my corner and asked me to dance. Since Funky Cold Medina was on the box, I couldn't resist. Just as I thought I could safely enjoy the dance and ignore him, he spoke.

"So, like uh, whus yo' name?" This was odd. He was the first one that evening who didn't immediately share his AA credentials. I told him my name and quickly gave the signal all girls learn, which says, "I'm not interested in you, I just want to dance."

As soon as the song was over, I retreated to the ladies' room. This new crew was obviously crashing the party, probably on their way to the nearest bar. I decided I would find my roommate and soon we would be gone.

Before my eyes could seek her out, another from the crew approached me. This one was dark and tall in tight jeans, cowboy boots, and brimmed hat. Trouble nonetheless, I assured myself. I was ready to say something rude to discourage further conversation, but he flashed the brightest, most beautiful smile I had ever seen, and said, "Hi, my name is Tommy, and I've been clean for four and a half months."

Up close, I could see he wasn't as arrogant as the rest had seemed. There was something very positive and trustworthy in his demeanor.

"What about you?" he asked.

"Oh, I'm just visiting!" I said, louder than usual. I wanted him to know I was not a member of the fellowship who wanted to share support. Before I knew it, he had invited me to sit down. A certain intensity in his glance and an infectious smile made me stay.

I learned that his group was different. They were all members of Narcotics Anonymous who had heard about the AA party and decided to check it out. All, of course, except for the first one who had asked me to dance. He said they were working on trying to get him to go into treatment . . . again. We talked for what seemed like hours about "his story." That's what they call an addict's history in the program. Tommy was honest about his struggles with alcohol, cocaine, uppers, and even crack. He shared with me the pain of losing his family's trust, his self-respect, and his desire to keep on living.

"Do you know what it's like to hit rock bottom? To live for nothing more than a roller coaster of highs and lows and always end up on the downswing?" I knew he didn't want an answer, only a good listener. His thoughts then took him to someplace inside that he wouldn't share. "I did some terrible things while I was using. You just can't imagine."

I set the record straight. "On the contrary. I may not be an addict, but I grew up in North Philly where many of my friends were strung out by the time they reached eighth grade: alcohol, pills, heroin. None of them had a happy ending. Except for my relatives, most of the men I knew were gangsters." What I didn't tell him was that even though my family had monitored my moves, I had been crazy enough to have had a crush on some of these untouchables, caught up in the schoolgirl belief that my love could change them, heal them, save them. But he was right. I didn't know the trials and tribulations that had knocked him on his butt and brought him to where he was sick and tired of being sick and tired.

"Would you mind escorting me to the door?" I followed along, like a faithful puppy. Then I spotted the cigarette.

"Disgusting habit, isn't it?"

"Filthy, vile, and stupid," I agreed. I'd never been able to tolerate smokers for long, especially after watching two relatives perish from lung cancer. He must have read my mind.

"You know, this is the next mountain I have to climb," he continued as he held up the burning stick and blew smoke slowly away from my direction and stared out into the night.

"After what you've been through, that should be a piece of cake for you," I offered.

The program, I learned, teaches that honesty is salvation. No secrets are allowed, so everyone used the familiar confessional-type introduction. (My roommate had never explained this to me.) He was straight with me about the hospital treatment program he had just completed, and his experience with withdrawal and detoxification, spiritual reflection and peer support. The sincere note in his voice made me believe that he was truly beyond it all, satisfied with what he had accomplished for himself, and really trying to move on and rediscover what else life had to offer him. I lost all track of time as I listened because I knew that what I had before me was a miracle. "But I have been going on and on about me. Let's talk about you," he offered.

Miracle of miracles, Flashlight came on the box and I had to get up and move.

"Well, I like to dance," I shared. So we danced, and there was a chemistry that was totally innocent, a harmony of movement without an agenda. By then my hair was a total sweaty mess, but he didn't seem to notice. I felt he truly wanted to know the real me. It was not a superficial attraction. I was ready to settle down and talk for another few hours when he looked at his watch and quietly said, "Uh-oh, I'm afraid I'm going to turn into a pumpkin."

"I beg your pardon?" I found myself ready to spout all the tired clichés and phrases that a man usually hands a woman that he wants to hold on to. How can you go now? The night is young! But we just met!

Without explaining, he continued, "Would you walk me to the door? I have to head home." Until that point, I hadn't realized my attachment. I felt that in knowing "his story," I somehow had rights to his future, or at least a reason to continue the present. "We have a curfew at the halfway house. We have to be in by midnight."

Halfway house?! What the hell am I thinking? Slapped back to reality, I realized I would probably be better off if I never saw him again. We were from two different worlds. I was inspired by his story, but it didn't fit with mine. Having changed his "profession," he was about to embark on a major search for a "real" job. With no degree, no experience, and a drug treatment on his record, I thought his prospects were bleak. I, on the other hand, had two degrees from a major university and a successful ten-year track record in a good profession in corporate America, great benefits, and a 401(k) plan. All I needed was an equally "successful" husband, preferably one with a big heart and an even bigger bank account.

"I'd like to keep in touch, may I have your number?" No way. He was cute, but I didn't need his instability in my life right now. As we parted, though, I felt I should give him some glimmer of support.

"I'll tell you what, you give me your number and I'll call to check on you from time to time," I lied, "to see how you're doing, climbing that mountain."

In the absence of paper, he wrote his number on my five-dollar bill. I have always believed that things happen for a reason. If I had to spend the money, it would mean that I needed to forget about him. He asked me for a hug, which by then I had learned was an AA thing to do, so I obliged. There was nothing sexual about the embrace, only an honest warmth and genuine tell-all release of self. I hadn't felt that with a man in a long time.

Giving in to economic pressure, though, I spent the five-dollar bill a week later and accepted that I would never know the outcome of the miracle beginning to unfold. But as inauspiciously as my hair appointment, I found myself agreeing to drop my roommate off at another AA party two weeks later. What were the chances that his NA house crew would hear about this one and decide to crash it also? I understood the Anonymous movement to be an elaborate underground comprised of hundreds, if not thousands, of devotees. It was a large city. But just in case, I decided to wear something that I thought he would like. I went through the closet three times, pulled out six different outfits, changed clothes twice. Too casual? Too sexy? Too businesslike? Too laid back? I asked my roommate twice how I looked. This time I didn't fuss with the hair. If I did see him, he would see the everyday me. I imagined him busting into the party again with his posse. I would see some red eyes, maybe smell the tobacco on his breath, and that would make it easier for me to say, "Hello, and so long."

I searched the crowd for the "prisoner group," was disappointed when they didn't show up. It took about ten minutes for me to see him, alone, sitting meditatively on the stairs. He was looking for me. I felt my stomach lurch like a schoolgirl's. I had butterflies in my stomach and a tingling down my spine. We picked up right where we had left off the last time, danced up a sweat, laughed, and talked until curfew time.

Caution was the word for our first date. Go easy. Check him out. I decided that lunch at an ice cream and sandwich place a block from my office would be the perfect barrier; time constraints, a public place, a professional atmosphere. He showed up with a single pink rose, smiled, pulled out my chair, and told me to order anything. I knew he was broke and insisted on dutch treat. We talked non-stop, about my family, music, his job search, my career, and his enthusiasm for a new life. I was intrigued by his honesty. He admitted his shortcomings. When I rudely asked why he spoke so slowly, he explained that the drugs still had his brain a little clouded, but he was confident that his head would clear up soon enough. I could say that the food at the ice cream shop had never tasted so good, but I don't remember what I ate. I was two hours late getting back to work. Talking had never felt so intimate. There was no kissing, no hand-holding, just talking. We gradually got to know each other over lunches, movies, and picnics. I even went to his twelve-step meetings with him.

"Hi, my name is Tommy and I'm a junkie and a drunk." In unison, they responded, "Hi, Tommy, and welcome." My blood chilled when I heard him say it. Later, I admonished him.

"You shouldn't say that! You're not a junkie and a drunk. Not anymore." He just smiled and explained why the program used the strategy of constantly being aware of addictions.

Much of Tommy's character was revealed to me at those meetings. Many who remembered him from his time on the streets painted a gruesome picture of him for me. They also said that even while he was struggling with detox, he was an inspiration to others. Tommy usually shared last at the meetings. Instead of whining about his problems or bragging about his accomplishments, he used his time on the floor to offer advice and encouragement to those who shared with him.

Over time, I learned the difference between the cultures of Narcotics Anonymous, Alcoholics Anonymous, Cocaine Anonymous, and related programs such as Overeaters Anonymous, Gamblers Anonymous, Shoppers Anonymous, and Emotions Anonymous. My perspective as an outsider, nonaddict, ran the gamut from thinking they were all crazy and needed serious professional psychiatric attention to understanding how pervasive addictive diseases are among all types of people. Tommy patiently confided in me that some of the regulars were doctors, lawyers, business owners, schoolteachers, and professionals just like me. After a few weeks, I began to share at the meetings about the ups and downs of my new friendship with an addict.

I learned that all kinds of people are susceptible to addiction and that it is an illness which can be arrested. Tommy was more dedicated to his recovery than I have known anyone to be dedicated to anything. Not only did he religiously attend regular meetings, but he unselfishly performed service work. We might be out on a Sunday drive when he would pull the car over, excuse himself, and go rap to a group of kids on a street corner, giving them his number and offering an ear.

Soon, the 185-pound, six-foot-two, chain-smoking, red-eyed man I had met on a good hair night began to get the drugs out of his system. His eyes cleared up, he began to lift weights, and the hesitation in his speech gave way to more clear, fluid expression. He moved out of the halfway house, cut down on his smoking, and got his life back on track. Within a few months he had gone back to school, started a job training program, and begun to clean up his credit. He was like a flower that had blossomed before my eyes, and he had only one commitment as important as his recovery—me.

Our differences were still stark in my eyes. I dressed conservatively, he sported any outfit that would best show off his bulging thigh, chest, and buttock muscles. I had a master's degree in film and broadcast, he had fled from his college campus to keep ahead of the law. A prized athlete, he was often excused from classes; his actual credits amounted to less than one full year's study. I was from the heart of Philadelphia, he was from a small town in the South. I was from a small family, and used to some individual attention. He was from a huge family, where you had to shout to be heard. I was Lutheran. He was Baptist. I loved to read, he loved to watch sports. His motto was "Don't worry, be happy. Everything's gonna work out." My motto was "Don't put off 'til tomorrow . . . Plan ahead." I ignored all of these differences and kept looking at something more important than commonalities: our willingness to accept and appreciate each other.

None of my closest friends would have dated Tommy. I didn't share him with them right away, but there was something about him that felt right to me. Still, I was unsure. The friendship continued to develop, without sexual involvement. I constantly reminded myself of my own philosophy—no man is perfect—but I began to search for skeletons. Tommy didn't talk much about his family, so I decided to get to know them. I kept asking questions; I imagined abject poverty, parental abuse, extreme neglect, some dark dysfunctional environment which would always haunt him, pulling him back into the mire. I kept pushing until he took me to Alabama.

"My baby is home!" His mother bubbled, and hugged him. One by one, his father and each of his seven sisters and brothers held him in their arms, talked about how much they had prayed for him and how proud they were that he had finally kicked his bad habits. His warmly supportive middle-class family had little to do with the mistakes he had made, except perhaps giving him too much freedom. They told me as we pored over pictures and newspaper clippings about Tommy's rise to fame as a high-school track star followed by his track scholarship to a major Southern university and his many broken records. As is so often the case with our athletes, the perceived power, glory, and cash that accompanied his new position got the better of him. Thus, in addition to becoming "the jock," he became "the connection." He developed an obsession which overpowered the sport, his studies, and all the warnings from the family . . . you know the drill.

Eight months after I met him, I knew it was time to bring him home to meet my folks. I was sold, but I needed clan approval. If there was anything I had missed, they would surround him, shine an inquisitive light in his face, question him to death, and grill him until he broke. I knew Tommy could charm them, but I was scared. Being the honest spirit I am, I had told them all about my new boyfriend. Everything from his days robbing and shooting folks and getting shot, to the night he hit bottom and prepared to jump off a bridge. Knowing how far he had come only endeared him to me that much more. I was proud of what he had accomplished and honored to share his one-year recovery birthday celebration with his home group of recovering addicts. I cried along with his family, who came to be with him that night.

No one else was quite as convinced as I. My mother was concerned for my safety. "What if he relapses and goes into a rage?" My father was concerned for my future. "The problem with diamonds in the rough is that after you pick them up and dust them off, they often forget where they came from."

We planned to drive to Philadelphia for Thanksgiving week, stopping in D.C. to visit my sister and her family. For some odd reason, Tommy decided that this was the week to stop smoking, knowing how my family hated smokers. I had no doubt he could do it, but why go through the cold-turkey withdrawal of bad moods and nervous ticks now? I begged him to wait until we got back to Atlanta.

"No," he insisted calmly, "now is the time because I'll be away from my rituals and everyday habits. Being with new people, yeah, that's the best way." He was the expert. I prayed he was right.

My sister, who was always on target in the character assessment department, said, "There is much more to this man than meets the eye." Tommy was okay until we got to Philly. When we arrived at my parents' house, it was a nightmare: he was restless, jumpy and irritable. In between strained pleasant-ries, he paced back and forth, often going outside to get some air. My folks thought he might be going out for something else. I begged him to smoke a cigarette, just one to take the edge off this frantic behavior. I explained to my family that he wasn't normally this testy and why he was doing this now. My father, normally a loose cannon, looked at both of us for a long mo-ment. He walked up to Tommy, stood close to him in one of those man-to-man moments that women can't enter, and stared him grimly in the eye. Everyone, especially me, held their breath. This relatively unaffectionate man, a habitual cigar smoker himself, reached out and hugged my new beau: "I re-spect a man who is more concerned with his principles and sticking to his ultimate goals than he is with trying to put on his best behavior." We left the two of them alone for several hours, and even now, neither of them has ever told me more of what was said.

Though I had no problem ignoring the doomsayers, I was unable to settle comfortably into this new relationship. I felt that things were going too smoothly. I had no fears that Tommy would relapse. His commitment to recovery was solid, but, in my mind, the laws of nature were such that something else had to be gravely deficient in this apparent saint. I waited for the other shoe to drop, continuously looking for his past to catch up with him, or to find out he was a wanted con artist with ten kids by some woman he had forgotten to mention.

One day it finally came. "There is something I need to tell you." I knew it. As I always say, they are only human, not perfect. It had been nice while it lasted. I prepared myself to be cool and to accept the news gracefully. After much deliberation and agonizing over which words to use, he finally got it out.

"You know my whole story, but there is one thing I was too ashamed to tell you." Whatever it was, I would probably not share this information so freely with my support network.

"I did something terrible, something awful in my attempt to raise money for my habit." Spit it out, for Christ's sake. I can't take the suspense.

"I sold myself . . . you know, for money."

"You mean, like a gigolo?" I asked.

He lowered then nodded his head in shame.

I couldn't help it. It started as a relieved smile, spread across my face, then progressed to a chuckle, and eventually became an all-out, uncontrollable giggle. Tommy looked at me like I was crazy.

"I'm telling you, I took advantage of vulnerable women, older lonely women mostly, with money. And you laugh?"

To put things into perspective, we had not yet consummated our newfound love. If this was the other shoe, the skeleton in the closet, the worst thing about him I had to accept, I was home free—or would be after getting the results of the AIDS test. All I could think was that if he was good enough to support a $100-a-day crack habit making women happy in bed, then I was luckier than I thought. At that point, I accepted the blessing, relaxed, and thanked God.

Exactly one year after our first meeting, we moved in together. We made an agreement that within one year, we would make a decision or move on. When the word got out, my friends were just plain worried. "Girl, what are you thinking? Gettin' involved with a crack-head, and blue collar at that? We thought you had more sense than that." They felt that I had lowered my otherwise respectable standards. As they dealt with issues like womanizing, drinking, joblessness, egomania, or mere lack of affection, all my friends were smugly secure that they had not hooked up with a crack addict. That is, if they were hooked up at all. They didn't hear me when I told them that he was everything I had always said was impossible to get in one package: honest, dependable, romantic, patient, sexy. And get this: his favorite saying was that "a real man is not afraid of change."

Fifteen months after we set up housekeeping together, we decided to get married. Along the way, we had made several other agreements. If he relapses, I kick him out. And if he cooks, I wash dishes. Everything about our union had been unconventional, and so was the wedding. "You are cordially invited to a Pre-Wedding BBQ Reception at 7:30 P.M. on the 4th of July," read the invitation. We barbecued and partied until 3 A.M. At 9 A.M. we were married in a small church we had joined three months before, surrounded by seventy-five loved ones. Still dressed in our wedding duds, we went straight from the church to the airport on our way to the Bahamas.

We celebrated our fifth wedding anniversary last year, and all my friends are disgusted by our honeymoon-like state. I still get flowers, just because he wants to give them to me. He hates to see me work too hard, so he does all the heavy housecleaning and always carries my briefcase. He sings in the kitchen while he cooks, because he enjoys it, and believe me, there is nothing I find more sexy than a good-looking man in an apron baking biscuits—in my kitchen. He still goes to NA meetings and counsels a group of young addicts each week. And he is always looking for new ways to improve our relationship. Don't get me wrong. He's not perfect. But neither am I.

While the doomsayers now acknowledge my insight and come to me for advice (which they take much more seriously these days), they still wait around for their perfect Black knights in shining armor. They dismiss every man they meet, as they go through their mental checklists of the requirements and credentials necessary before they can go out on a date. He must drive a Benz, earn six figures, be six feet four, have an M.B.A., Ph.D., or any of the other respectable initials after his name. One wants someone who has no kids, another seeks a mate who has perfectly manicured nails, still another has a thing for married men, thinking that they are easier to manipulate. Generosity with the ducats, flowers, and compliments are seen as measures of self-worth. Religious or political profiles are examined to ensure the right ideology. Sometimes women prefer to be alone. Sometimes they spend their Saturday evenings at my house, having dinner, watching TV, and laughing with Tommy and me. If only they would remember that a man is not perfect, only a man.

Part V

Friends
and
Mentors

The Men in My Life

DorisJean Austin

During the rest periods between those "ideal" sexual-spiritual unions (during which one prays for brevity), I seldom utilized my freedom and always dwelled on my limitation. I once thought all changes in romantic relationships (if it wasn't from single to married) marked The End. But I've since learned not to throw away people when relationships change. I've learned to savor the three men in my life: Earl, Ed, and Donald.

Let's start with Earl (ex-lover, present friend, and confidant). I'm always free to call him for a date—if he doesn't call me first. Earl's sharp wit and constant sense of humor lift the spirits of even a chronic depressive like me. His comic, lewd banter reminds me that I'm a desirable woman. He's a big man, which makes me feel small in his bear hugs. And, yes, I need and love to feel feminine and perfectly harbored in arms.

We have long dinners and brunches that are better for my head than therapy. And we've used each other's shoulders in some of our more tragicomic love affairs: He once called me at three in the morning to suggest I take a cab ride to another city to descend upon his latest love, for a confrontation about suspected betrayal that was straight out of a soap opera. I talked him into taking two aspirins, going to bed, and calling me in the morning. In that same year he reciprocated by counseling me in the ways of Ed (more about Ed later).

Earl has volunteered financial aid with no strings attached on occasions when the "starving artist" syndrome hovered too long at my door. We kiss and hug a lot (at least as much as we scream and fight), and we've never ruled out the possibility of a night of mutual sexual comfort on some cheerless winter evening. We don't have the responsibility of being one thing or all things at all times to each other; thus, our friendship thrives.

And then there's Ed, my ideal man. He's sophisticated, attractive, professional, divorced, and single—the kind of man my mama wanted me to marry. Ed and I have been dating sporadically almost two years, without much romance, and (bite my tongue) without sex. He wines and dines me with panache. He's at home in all situations—well, almost all. We talk into the wee hours at his apartment or mine, or in tiny bistros or swank restaurants, or just on the phone—local or long-distance. He calls when I'm out of town or he is. I love his company, his sense of humor, his politics; we agree on most things that matter to us. We've made a joke of his extreme macho attitudes, and we disagree well.

So what's wrong with this picture? Well, mostly I find myself resisting the urge to scream my demands for him to declare his intentions, propose, marry, and live "happily ever after." I've resisted these impulses so far. (Will he read this? Ah well, no risk, no gain!) The one thing I know for sure about the two of us: I enjoy it when it's happening. But later, at home alone, I regress. I call Earl.

Finally, there's Donald, who by stretching the imagination just a touch could be considered young enough to be my son. (The man, however, is thirty years old.) Don is a young writer spending occasional apprenticeship time with me (which I adore), showing up on Saturday mornings to type, proofread, and do other odds and ends. Our little "dates," I tell myself, are a part of the job. Once he bravely suggested that ours would be a wise marriage. Do I love this young man? You bet I do. And I admit I've had some dangerous dreams about him. So far he's safe; I'm not too sure I am. But I have fun when we are together because he so obviously enjoys spending time with me.

These are the men in my life (and in and out of my apartment with regularity) with whom I could, with a little push, fall in love—or fall in love with again. There was a time when I would have felt morally impelled to drop or neglect them and keep my life swept clean to await *him*. No more.

But I do have one *constant* lover: me. I've always loved my own company. (As a writer, I spend most of my time alone.) There are still occasions when my solitude invites "heartache by numbers," but I can't afford more than a few hours for that kind of dedicated suffering. I'm just too grown for the melodrama and, I thank the gods that be, too busy.

To Mr. Scriber, and Other Black Knights in Shining Armor
Evelyn Coleman

Men are a dime a dozen, but I'd give a whole lot more than a dime for the man in my life now, my husband, Talib Din. He's one of those men you can't write about because somebody would swear you're lying. I've known a lot of different kinds of men, good men, slow men, run-like-a-dog-after-women men, smart men, crazy-as-hell men, confused men, but never a bad-to-the-rotten-core man. I know they're out there, but I haven't had the bad luck to know 'em.

Of course, there was a brief time in my life when I thought if I'd had a gun I'd take it and blow the hell out of all men, starting with my first husband. It was when I'd decided I'd had enough of him, even if he was the father of my children.

He'd been catching hell from the world and resolved that he'd strike back at it through me. Now, some women, including me, can take a bunch of shit for a long time in the name of love and fatherhood, but one day fifteen little words whipped my "it's-not-his-fault" butt into shape. On that day I heard a Muslim minister say, "There are some men who will always have their happiness at the expense of others." I cannot tell you what chord in the strings of life those words played for me, but the tune I sang was "I'm getting the hell out of Dodge," known to me as North Carolina. And so I packed up my two small children and ran away as fast and far as I could from my beautiful new house, my good job, and my childhood sweetheart, who'd turned into Freddy Krueger on me.

In New Jersey, a friend and her husband took me in, but in less than a week she had to go into the hospital. Well, no self-respecting southern woman who'd had a husband that would chase the cheese from the moon would give another woman a minute's worry by staying in her house with her husband while she was laid up sick. Mind you, this woman's husband had never once stepped out of line with me and I never thought he would, but having been married to Casanova himself, staying just didn't seem right. So I only had one choice. After years of working every day, sometimes two jobs, I would have to resort to welfare, glamorously known today as public assistance.

I can tell you now if you're ever looking for a way to make somebody feel as low as a wart on the face of society just send them to a welfare office. After calling the office and finding out the only way they could help a woman with children who had no permanent address was for her to have "no address" at all, I packed my girls up and hit the street. From downtown Camden I called the welfare office and told them the honest-to-goodness truth: "I'm homeless, and all I have is ten bucks and two little girls, a suitcase full of clothes, a headache, and a borrowed phone booth that I don't think all three of us can sleep in tonight. Can you help me *now?*"

At the welfare office I was herded in by number, and the degradation and indignity they dished out was enough to make visions of slavery surface in your ancestral memory. My major regret was that these were Black people, and if they'd ever been in trouble I can assure you it didn't do a damn thing but make them mad as hell and pissed off at anybody who ever again darkened their door with the word "trouble." They didn't like trouble, and if you were in trouble that meant they didn't give a flying fuck about you.

So, when I finally got to speak to the man I had phoned, a Mr. Hal Scriber, I had only two prayers. Please let him not hate trouble, and let him be a white man, as his name implied to me (in my recollection of Black folks' names).

"Damn" is what I said when I saw him. Another prayer bit the dust. He was a Black man, much like the one I was fleeing. He was not old and not ugly, though, and he didn't seem very mean. The voice was gentle and patient, and he managed an occasional smile. Actually, he was cute for a man about ten years or more my senior. He looked like a thin Smokey Robinson. I was only twenty-five years old, and in those days anyone thirty-five or above reminded me of my own father. In other words, I was a young Moms Mabley. And an unlucky Moms at that, since he informed me that since I had showed up on the week of Labor Day, they could not find me an apartment. The only thing they could do was take me to a motel outside of the city where the welfare kept families who'd been burned out of their places. The last hotel I'd stayed in had been the Marriott at the Philadelphia airport, so this sounded great to me. It became clear that I knew nothing about slave quarters.

When we arrived, tears popped into my eyes. Trees and weeds grew out of the cracked swimming pool, if that helps you get the picture. The suite, which Mr. Scriber assured me was the best they had to offer, smelled like rotten apples on that hot day. The heat in the room made my nose trickle blood. The rug was so filthy and soiled that even though my girls were a healthy five and six years old, I lifted them both on my hips and carried them into the room, not wanting their feet to touch the floor. The rusty refrigerator might as well have been a petri dish, it had so much mold and fungus growing in it. Only the ocean floor could have held more.

"I need to go to the store, Mr. Scriber. If I must stay here I've got to clean up. Please," I pleaded. This motel with no name sat on a patch of overgrown land in the center of a busy four-lane highway in a township called Mapleshade. The name sounded a hell of a lot better than this motel looked. To get to the store you had to cross a hilly plot the size of three football fields or risk being smashed under the wheels of cars on the highway like the road kill you obviously were in the eyes of welfare.

Reluctantly he consented, once he understood that the only thing in my suitcase was clothes. I borrowed twenty bucks from him, which he assured me was against all the policies and could get him fired. At that moment, I wanted to feed my kids and his job didn't mean as much to me as it did to him, so I begged, pleaded, and cried to get that money. I spent much of it on cleaning stuff, and then I bought assorted cereals, plastic spoons, milk, bread, cheese, peanut butter, and a carton of eggs because my children loved eggs. That was before cholesterol warnings.

Back at the Hotel from Hell I thanked Mr. Scriber. Then I asked him, if he came back out there, would he loan me a frying pan and dishes?

"Well, Mrs. Dickerson, I don't know about that. You see, we're not supposed to get involved other than to find you placement. And I, well, I . . ."

After much hee-hawing about regulations, he finally agreed.

"Yes," he said, eyes glued to the floor. "I guess I can. But I don't know for sure what I have. I know my stuff doesn't match."

Was he for real? Did he really think I cared? It was then I

decided he was a nice honest man. My instincts were hardly ever wrong.

My stay there was my first taste of poverty and homelessness, and it is a choking kind of bile. I have no clue why it doesn't kill you if you have to endure it too long. After the first day there in 100-degree weather I heard my daughters yelling hysterically while outside playing. I raced to save them from whatever was causing their death screams, only to find that the other children had cornered a big fat rat and decided that somebody besides them needed to suffer. They were taking turns torturing the rat.

Later, I explained to my girls in tears that the cruelty they observed was not intentional but is what can happen if all you see in life is pain. I can tell you, even though those nights I cried myself to sleep on the red plastic ripped couch, while my children slept peacefully in the other room, I taught them some great lessons for living that summer, and they taught me some lessons, too. For one, the things I thought were important, like their swing set, playhouse, toys, and beautiful clothes didn't mean anything anymore. All they really cared about was having their mommy. So I capitalized on that. I showed them how to create games out of toilet paper, string, and macaroni. I helped them use their imaginations to manifest what they would need in life, by telling them that if they believed something would come to them, it would. Of course I didn't know for sure that was the truth, but it sounded good to them. I also learned that without them I probably would not have survived. They kept me going. They were making me more than a mother. Now I was the father, brother, and protector, too. In the African-American community you often hear people say that women are the backbone of our society. I say it's our children.

But on the last night I was there I had a foreboding. Suddenly, without warning fear crept into my gut and wouldn't let go. I piled all the furniture in the room up against the door, latched it, and sat watching the doorknob like the devil himself had promised to turn it. At 1:15 A.M. the knob turned. The door banged against the chain and the furniture wobbled but stayed put. The Spanish-accented voice of the manager demanded, "What are you doing? Open this damn door."

I didn't say a word but searched for a weapon. Anything. I determined by lifting them which chair would offer the most impact upside his head. Mind you, I'd never hit anyone. Never fought my husband when he'd hit me. Never even thought about it. But I'd believed that my husband would not hurt my girls no matter what. This man, I didn't know about. What I did know, though, is that if he came into the room he might decide to touch my girls, and he'd do that over my dead body. "Go away," I pleaded, "or I'll call the police."

There was no 911 in those days, and I had no clue where I was other than on an island in the middle of a highway, nor did I know which precinct to call.

He growled through the crack in the door. "Senorita. Don't give me no trouble, or I'll throw you out on your ass tonight. Now let me in. I've got a little present for you."

"I bet it is little," I said, always wittier under pressure and scared shitless. "You better go away, amigo."

"I'll give you money. You know you want money, don't you?"

"And you want a chair upside your head," I said, trying to control my terror, and at the same time not wake my daughters, thankful for the first time that they had some ways like their father's, as they slept like dead logs.

"Okay, bitch, don't let me in. Hold on. I'll be back."

Now the threat was real. I weighed what I could do, while my mind checked out how different "bitch" sounds with a Spanish accent. There was no way out the back. The small window in the other room had a rattling air conditioner in it. I could knock it out of the window. But I wasn't sure I could get my girls through the opening without hurting them. And there was no telling what lay outside that window, snakes, rats, other fools willing to hurt my children if I were dead.

Oh my God. Help me. The only number I knew was Mr. Scriber's. He'd jotted it down on a piece of paper, and it lay beside the phone. It was the number to his office, and under it was his home number with the added line FOR EMERGENCIES ONLY. This was as close to an emergency as I was going to have, so I dialed. My hand shook like a bad car motor while I counted the rings.

On the sixth ring he answered with a deep crockie voice, "Yes, Hal Scriber."

"Mr. Scriber, this man who runs this place is trying to break into my room."

"Where is he now?" he asked, and I could tell he'd come wide awake.

"He told me he'd be back. I don't know if he has a crowbar, a gun, or what but I'm scared," I cried into the phone. It was more like whimpering, since I was still trying not to wake my daughters but was slowly losing control emotionally and in the bladder, too.

"I'm going to call him. If he comes back before I get him on the phone tell him I'm on my way out there with the police. And I promise if he comes in that room he can kiss his job good-bye."

I waited, gripping the chair like it was a baseball bat, in case the manager already planned to quit and his bags were packed for Puerto Rico. He did not come back. Maybe an hour passed, then I heard Mr. Scriber at the door. I let him in.

"He's not going to bother you. I talked to him."

I fell into Mr. Scriber's arms, crying, thankful my daughters wouldn't have to know this had even happened, since they were still sound asleep.

He patted me on the shoulder for a second, and then gently shoved me away.

"I know," I said, smiling, "regulations."

He nodded yes. Then he said, "I can stay here until the morning if that will make you feel better. I found you a place, and I can take you there tomorrow."

Doubt hit me. His offer to stay was not what I'd expected from a man who seemed to cherish the rules.

He stood there, not looking at me but at his feet.

Suppose he's not so nice. Maybe he thinks you owe him for this trip out in the middle of the night. Clearly beyond the call of duty. Then I thought, Shit. Even if he raped me, it would be better than having Old Stink-breath do it. At least I didn't think he'd bother my girls, so I semi-lied. "Yes, I'd feel safer if you stayed the night."

In the other room, lying on the bed with my daughters, I thought about him. He was handsome, really, in an "I'm lonely and desperate" sort of way. I couldn't hear a sound from the other room, and a part of me wished he would snore, then I'd know if he were asleep or just looking up into the ceiling as I was doing. Maybe he did like me. So what? All men are dogs. I fell asleep with that thought.

The next morning Mr. Scriber left after asking me if I would like him to bring us some breakfast. I said no, because I wanted him to leave so I could wash up. And I wanted him to take care of his business so I could get out of there. He came back for us in a few hours. I didn't see the manager who'd tried to break into the room. I hugged the two women I'd made friends with there and left, happy to escape alive. My last wish was that I could take those two women and their children with us. Somehow I didn't think their fate was going to be a good one. They had not merely been burned out of their homes, but it seemed that the fiery interruption had canceled all their chances for a good life. I knew one day their children might corner more than a rat if something didn't change for them and that made me leave crying. I had more options than those women did, and I hated leaving them. Not that I wanted to stay, though. Hell, no. I felt guilty. But not that damn guilty.

Mr. Scriber took me to a set of old apartments, sturdy and well kept, in Pennsauken, New Jersey. Inside the floors were shiny hardwood, and the rooms were spotless. Sunlight burst through the big windows. Having just left the worst place I'd ever been in my life, this apartment made me want to sing. My daughters were thrilled; they could go outside again. There was no air conditioning, but I'd discovered there were worse things in life than being hot. Hell might not be so bad if the devil's not there.

Mr. Scriber gave me the $60 worth of food stamps that were to last me a month and that couldn't have fed Minnie Mouse. He also had a voucher for $310 that paid the month's rent. He wished me luck and opened the door to leave.

Sure, the place had refinished shiny hardwood floors, but hey, hardwood is just that, hard wood. "Hold it. What about furniture?" I asked him, incredulous. Could he or any other welfare person believe this could be called "help"?

"Sorry. They don't make provisions for furniture."

I couldn't hold it in any longer. I started crying. Thank God my girls had gone outside into the front yard.

"Listen," he said. "Don't cry."

I could see the frustration of all this on his face. He couldn't figure out what to do with his hands, so they flew through the air as he offered, "There's this church that sometimes helps people and gives them used furniture. I'll call them and see if they can't get you some beds. You can have the dishes and frying pan I loaned you. Okay. I'll check on you and your girls tomorrow." And he was gone, obviously not wanting to break any more rules in one day.

That evening I found the couple with two kids from the apartment next door sitting out under a tree in the yard. I didn't know them, but they were Black with southern accents and to me that meant it was okay to approach them. They agreed to let my children sleep over with their children. Their kids would sleep in one twin bed, and my girls could have the other. I could even sleep on their couch, but it didn't let out.

"No thanks, I'm fine," I lied. I walked around until I found a baby-sitter to watch my children, who agreed to take payment when I got a job. She was a white woman with one little girl. She let me have some sheets and a bedspread, and I slept on my shiny hardwood floors on a pallet that night. When I woke, I thought "hardwood" wasn't a fitting description after all. What about hard-cement-wood? The next morning, after dropping my children at the baby-sitter's, I headed out to look for a job.

When I didn't get the church furniture by the second day I phoned Mr. Scriber. He was sorry but they didn't have any beds when he'd called, but he'd check back with them. I told him how my job search was going, how I'd made a bargain with a baby-sitter and found some nice people to let my girls sleep over. I assured him that I'd be off this welfare gig in a month or kill myself.

He chuckled, then regrouped to his professional voice. "Are all of you all right? Really, I'm sorry we don't have a better system. I'll check on the beds for you. Okay?"

He sounded drained. I didn't realize then what a strain dealing with poverty can be, even if you're not the one who is poor.

The next day I called him and told him I'd gotten a job at a bank.

"Wow. That was fast. I've never had anybody who could get a job so fast. I'm happy for you and your kids."

He took me to one of those furniture stores where their sole intent is to price everything at hundreds more than it's worth and charge you thousands in interest for the pleasure of keeping it until you miss a few payments and they take it back. Nowadays they mostly call them furniture rental stores.

Anyway, the man said he'd give me credit, but he wanted $200 down for twin beds worth all of $50, and that didn't include the mattresses. I laughed. "I might be broke, sir, but I'm never stupid." Well, of course, I am often stupid, but he didn't need to know all my business.

Mr. Scriber was apologetic afterward, but I knew it wasn't his fault. It was the high price of poverty. I was beginning to like him better. He seemed shy and awkward at times, and I suppose he was terrified someone would discover him breaking the stringent rules about only offering minimum and inadequate help to those in need.

I went back planning to make three pallets until I could find some used beds and buy them outright.

The next day when I came home from my new job my neighbor, a woman from Taiwan named Ensue, who spoke little English, met me excitedly at my door. "You have new furniture. Inside. I let them inside," she told me.

Knowing she was mistaken, I let myself in the apartment. New furniture. She was right. There were two bed frames, two box springs, two mattresses, a Formica table, and four chairs still wrapped in brown paper.

"Who left this? This is a mistake, Ensue. I didn't buy these things. Do you know the name that was on the truck? Any papers with it? It's a mistake."

She knew it was a truck, a furniture truck that had other new stuff in it. She couldn't read the name of the company.

There were no papers. They just asked her if I was home. She told them she had the key and could let them in and that was that. "Happy?" Ensue asked me.

No. I hated dishonesty. And these things were not mine. I called Mr. Scriber to see if he knew how to go about returning these things to their rightful owners.

"They're yours," he said.

"Mine? No. No, they're not mine."

"I bought them," he said.

"You bought them?" What the hell was he trying to pull? If I was a prostitute, would I be going through this shit? I didn't think so. "What? Okay then, you need to have them come back and get them. I don't know what you're expecting in return, but I'm not dishing anything out."

"I'll be over later, Mrs. Dickerson," he said, and hung up.

I was furious. I hated men. Dammit. I liked him, and if he'd asked me out I probably would have said yes. But I was no prostitute or whore, and treating me like one wasn't going to get him anything but his ass kicked. I'd vowed when I left my husband that the next man who touched me against my will would surely die. And that went for those I disliked as well as those I liked or might like in the future.

He came over and, with his eyes on the hardwood floor, said, "I bought this for you with no strings attached. I've been working in welfare for almost ten years, and in that time I don't think I've met anyone so determined not to be on welfare a minute more than they had to. I don't know if I've seen anyone struggle so hard to explain to their children what was happening to them and yet not make it seem like being on welfare was the goal. And I've watched you treat those in your same predicament, with fewer options and less resources than you to get back on their feet, with dignity and love. I thought that somebody like this should get some help. Real help. And so I did the least that I could do. Give you and your girls something decent to sleep on and eat on. There are no strings. Really. We can just be friends."

He was true to his word. We were never close friends who talk on the phone or visit, but friends. He told me over time that he was separated from his wife. He never went into detail about why, but he did say he didn't want to be. He talked about her a lot; well, as much as a shy introvert can talk. And no matter how he was acting with her, it was clear to me that he loved her.

He didn't come over unless I phoned. I phoned mostly in emergencies. My youngest daughter had bronchitis, and late one night she had difficulty breathing. I had no ambulance money and was no longer on welfare, which meant no health care for my children. I called Hal, and he came over to take us to the hospital. I never called him Hal to his face, always Mr. Scriber, and he never asked me to call him anything else, since he called me Mrs. Dickerson. He'd listen to my progress report on my quest to get back on my feet, drop us back home, give me a quick and sometimes awkward hug and leave.

I invited him to my daughters' birthday parties that summer, and he came and brought them presents. Two heart necklaces. They called him Uncle Hal, and he referred to them as his nieces. It must have not occurred to him how strange it was for them to call him "Uncle," with me still calling him "Mister." My daughters spoke fondly of him and always asked me how he was doing. I realize now children must live surreal lives, because they never asked me why I called him Mr. Scriber. But I think he needed to keep some distance from me. I don't know for sure. I trusted him, though, and I let him call the shots for the relationship. He never once treated me with anything but respect. No passes. No pressure. Just friends. Distant friends, as my definition goes, but I've learned that each person brings their own expectations to a friendship. Sometimes these don't balance out exactly as we envision, but it does not diminish the effect.

Over time we lost touch. I later moved. Made a kazillion changes, got on my feet, stood up, walked, then strutted, and one day could even dance and shout about my successes. Fell back down a couple of times. Got back up and started dancing again.

I thought of him often over the years. Every time I'd think about calling him to thank him, something would happen and I'd be sword-fighting with life again. But it nagged me that Hal Scriber never knew what his help had meant to me and my children, who are now adults. I never paid him back for those beds, even though once I'd started working I did offer. I also wanted him to know I understood how much they had really cost him, considering what welfare workers made then and now. And in an era when I hear my own sisters and brothers talking about "welfare mothers" like that's a curse word, I wanted him to know that he made a difference in the lives of poor women. I felt lucky and blessed that I'd escaped that poverty. I had family, friends, a large support system, but somewhere there were women who might have had nothing and no one but someone like Harold Scriber. I needed him to know he made it easier for me.

I found him not too long ago via phone, working in a different office but still in the same welfare system. He told me they were phasing out his present job and long ago had phased out his position in emergency housing. I thanked him for what he'd done more than twenty years ago to save my life and my daughters' lives. He took it in modest stride, particularly since he didn't have a clue who I was. I tried jogging his memory, and even though he said he remembered I don't think he did. It meant for me that I wasn't the only woman he'd gone beyond the call of duty for and possibly risked his job. It meant that he'd broken rules, if not before me, certainly after me, in order to truly help women leave poverty. Harold Scriber understands something about poverty other people don't want to admit. It is the worst stalker a woman can have; and I wish some legislator would tackle that mother.

I suspect Harold Scriber also didn't realize he'd offered me another way to look at men through his actions. Especially Black men. Until that time, men had either been relatives, who were obligated to care, or lovers, who could leave when they got bored. He restored my faith in man and mankind at a time when I'd lost that faith. To all the Hal Scribers out there, I salute you, MY BROTHERS.

Integrated Paths

Charlayne Hunter-Gault

The year Hamilton Holmes was our high school football co-captain and I was the homecoming queen, we became a team. It was the spring of 1959, and until then, Hamp, the scholar-jock who wanted to be a doctor, and I, the aspiring journalist, had mostly gone our separate ways. But we became the team that was Georgia's entry into the civil rights revolution after we were admitted as the first Black students to the 176-year-old University of Georgia—an institution into which the governor had vowed that "no, not one" Black student would ever be allowed.

Hamp, a straight-A student, was more deeply hurt than I was by the university's year and a half of ruses to keep us out. The officials had rejected him as unqualified during the admissions procedure, and after we were admitted, they refused to let him play football. They said it was too risky. He could be killed. Deliberately. But with his old-fashioned sense of loyalty, commitment, and duty, he blocked and tackled for me, even as he ran the gauntlet of insults, including finding the air let out of his tires by some white kid who just didn't get it. When from

313

time to time I had to go to the infirmary with stomach pains of uncertain origin, the first person to appear at my bedside would be Hamp.

"You all right, Char?" he would ask. And whatever was on my mind or in my gut would recede. This must have been the manner he later brought to the bedside of his patients, after he had graduated, Phi Beta Kappa, and then become the first Black graduate of Emory University School of Medicine.

Not long before his enormously good heart failed him and he died, Hamp, a prominent orthopedic surgeon and teacher, had been asked to introduce me at a public event. I was in Atlanta for a reading of my book, *In My Place*, a memoir of our college days. At one point, I heard him say, "Of course, she's a lot nicer now than she was then." As he flashed that big face-filling grin of his, we exchanged knowing glances that took us all the way back to our intense competitions at Turner High, when they eliminated the Best All-Around Student honor because both of us insisted on having it.

Hamp had all but buried the unhappy ghosts of the past; he had even forgiven the university, becoming one of its governing officials and biggest boosters. In fact, at the foot of the blanket of flowers that adorned his coffin lay a red-and-black Georgia Bulldogs cap.

He had told me that *his* book, were he ever to write it, would probably tell our story a bit differently than mine did, and I allowed that he was probably right, especially given the importance he attached to proving to whites that he was as good as any of their best.

When I finished my reading, I assumed that Hamp was gone. As I headed for a table in the lobby, a long line of people were waiting in line for me to sign their books. At one point, I turned to a page and saw that big, round, curving signature that

I used to poke fun at in high school—unmistakably that of Hamilton Earl Holmes. I looked up, and there was Hamp working the line from the back, talking with people and signing everyone's copy of my book. Our book. About the best team I ever joined.

A Few Good Men

Orian Hyde Weeks

The real house where Flannery O'Connor's Hazel Motes died is nothing like I imagined. Gentrification has touched it by now, but in 1994, when I visited Macon, Georgia, it drooped perilously over the edge of a small cliff, leaning toward a view possibly spectacular but terminally marred by desolateness. Self-inflicted blindness spared Hazel Motes this blight; in writing *Wise Blood*, Ms. O'Connor must have suffered from this vision, which she denied her antihero. As Tom and I drive past, looping down a hill and moving farther away from downtown, we do not speak of what we surely are both thinking. Jamie, who we are going to visit, is blind. Not from stabbing his own eyes out, but from AIDS. Jamie was blind when he was brought here to die.

"In the novel he sat in the window all day, never leaving the house, staring out over the view," Tom said. "One of the best ironic endings in literature. Remember?" The exposed parts of his very white skin are slightly burned, like the skin of cooked ducks hanging in windows in Chinatown. It is July, and very hot.

"Yeah," I said. "How much farther is it?"

"Pretty close now," he says. Without missing a beat, he begins pointing out this landmark and that, where the white gentry of Macon lived. This is vintage Tom. I tune him out.

It was Tom's idea to add sightseeing to our mission. As if coming to see Jamie isn't enough. Ever since I've known him and Jamie, he has always been practical in a two-for-one way. I first met him when I was in college. He owned two houses next door to each other, until he fell into debt. He lost both.

I suppose Tom thought I would enjoy this literary diversion. After all, I had introduced him to Flannery O'Connor's work after I had been forced to read her in a lit class. Both Tom and I became addicted and read everything she wrote. That was in 1981, when, as a student at the University of Cincinnati, I rented a room in their Victorian house in the Mansion Hills section of Newport, Kentucky, on the other side of the Ohio River. Thirteen years have passed. I had not seen either Tom or Jamie in over four years, when Tom called me in New York to tell me Jamie was dying. I boarded a plane for Savannah, where Tom and Jamie had lived for the last eight years of their fifteen-year-long relationship, before Jamie's mother and grandmother took him to Macon.

Soon we turn off the main road and enter a neighborhood that can only be described as the "Negro" section of town. Poverty does not shout at passersby; it is quiet, well-behaved like Mammy in *Gone with the Wind*. An egg-shell stuccoed Baptist church with a peeling bell tower sits on a corner. Farther down the road, we pull into the driveway of a one-story brick house. An old Cadillac sits in the driveway.

Tom sighs.

. . .

Jamie is in the living room. He is waiting for us in a plastic-covered chair that swallows him up, draped in an old woman's shawl. His efficient-looking mother, Mrs. Cauls, lets us in, and she and I speak to each other, but I forget her completely, except her ammonia smell. Jamie hears me. "Hey, baby," he says.

I bend down to him, as I do to my eighty-six-year-old grandmother when I see her. In my arms he is all bones. I kiss him. I have promised myself that I will not cry in front of him. But it is hard. This is the same man in the movie *A Soldier's Story* that played the tambourine in the campfire scene before the soldiers go off to their deaths. *That* Jamie was so beautiful that the camera focused on him for a million-dollar Hollywood minute. With his Puerto Rican hair (that's what I used to call it) and square jaw, he was finer than Billy Dee Williams, by anybody's standard. Seeing him like this, it is difficult to remember what he was. In the absence of flesh, his jaw looks like a big table that his head is sitting on. I am glad that he cannot see himself.

"Hey, Poppy," he says to Tom. They kiss tenderly on the lips. Jamie's mother, who will preside over this visit, visibly cringes. She briskly walks away to the kitchen. Shortly she returns with lemonade, like any good Southern hostess, setting the tray next to a big fat Bible on the coffee table. There are Jesuses and other velvet votive paintings on the walls. And lots of acrylic crochet. Jamie always loved knitting.

"I took Orian to see Flannery O'Connor's house," Tom says.

"He sure did," I confirm. "It's so strange." I know that Jamie doesn't know who we are talking about. Not only has he never shared our interest in literature or music, but he is only functionally literate. Tom has an M.A. in German literature. I have always wondered how the two of them survived together.

"Doesn't Jamie look good?" Jamie's mother says.

We agree. "He's always beautiful," I say. "Remember that

time you guys were working on the house and you were wearing that mask and I called you Miss Darth Vader." He and Tom were painting the house, and Jamie, because of severe sinus problems, wore a napalm mask. Jamie laughs. Tom laughs, too.

"Yeah, I remember." Then he begins with the inevitable, without prompting: "I feel pretty good today, too. Some days I've got more energy than others. I just sleep a lot."

"And he's gained weight," his mother says. "He's getting better."

"Mamma cooks," Jamie says, giggling. "We had baked chicken and greens last night for dinner. I wasn't very hungry, though. This new drug takes away my appetite."

"We're gonna have to put you on a diet," Tom says.

"So how's my baby doing," Jamie says to me. "Tell me about New York and Germany."

I work for a dance company and have been traveling for years. I tell him the kind of stuff he wants to hear, about beautiful cities, fine food, and very handsome European white men. He has always had a thing for white men. As I talk I watch him. His eyes remain closed, the instinct to open and blink already dead. From what I understand of the meningitis, there is no reason his eyes should be closed. Unless he prefers his eyes closed. From the corner of my eye I see his mother. Jamie has always described her as saintly. Long before Jamie took sick, his grandmother and mother were supposed to live with him and Tom, in Savannah. Then one day his mom called and said they could not live in a house of sin. Around here, eyes should remain shut, I think. I keep talking. Telling him of my travels I feel like I'm pushing his nose in the crap of his misfortune.

Tom slips Jamie's hand into his own. Mrs. Cauls studies them for a minute, then flees the room. So do I: to the bathroom to cry.

• • •

Jamie was down on his luck when we met. I was twenty. He was thirty. It was 1980.

He'd returned from a failed relationship with a man he met over the telephone while working as a reservationist for American Airlines. Over the course of a month, the two fell in love, and Jamie packed his bags for Ann Arbor, Michigan, leaving behind the job, an apartment he shared with someone in love with him, and every friend he'd had. Four months later he was back, looking for what he'd left behind. Only there was nothing. The betrayed roommate had moved out. The airlines were laying off. His timing couldn't have been worse. He was soon desperate. I was working as a waitress in a restaurant that wouldn't hire him. I saw him a couple of weeks later, and he remembered me. He was out looking for a job. I knew then that he was gay. Not that I was even sure back then what "being" gay was. Whatever it was, as represented by him, it was okay with me. Not many women have men friends who are not pawing, or wanting to paw, them. Besides, I have never had a good relationship with a man. My father was a drunk and assaulted my mother.

Things, I learned from him, had been going sour for a long time, Patrick in Ann Arbor being only the most recent of dire events. Many of these involved Jamie being in love, and the object of his love running in the other direction.

One night, he dropped by, unexpected. He was upset. I was frantically writing a paper for my comparative literature class. There was gin in the cupboard, 7UP in the refrigerator. We made a couple of drinks. At first we laughed about how we would years from now laugh at this moment. Then sadness welled up and spilled out of him.

"I was married when I was in Cleveland," he told me. "I have a daughter. I haven't seen her since she was a baby. She's about five years old now. My ex-wife, she's suing me for child support. I owe a lot of money. I wanna pay it." He burst into tears. "I'm not allowed to see my daughter. Her mother won't let me."

He cried in my arms.

Evidently his mother and grandmother had forced him into marriage. Raised as a Jehovah's Witness, he was to have been a father and a preacher, and in that order. But he only got as far as marriage, to a handpicked woman named Kay. Within weeks of the nuptials, she was pregnant. From the beginning, the marriage was in trouble. Kay was a cross between his grandmother and mother—like a mixture of a Chihuahua and a pit bull. Being bullied, I suspect, was something he was used to. But Kay clearly was impossible: a mean-spirited, super-religious, bossing bitch. Jamie believes—though he doesn't blame anyone—that his church, led by his relatives, brainwashed him. Even knowing that he was making a mistake by getting married, he wanted to make them all happy, even at his own expense. Kay, pregnant, proved even more impossible. A dual pregnancy began, the second being the growing desire within him for something else, namely men, and to be free of Kay. The marriage, not surprisingly, ignited into flames and burned up. His mother and grandmother naturally were opposed to the dissolution and attempted to rip his ego and will to shreds, as they had done for much of his life. Something in Jamie repelled them this time. Whatever the price, he had to get away from Kay. It was a matter of life and death. Their child was his sacrifice.

Cleveland was suddenly too small. He needed to get out. The Air Force was the answer, as it is for so many young men in trouble. Being away from home—in Panama—he found freedom in discipline, and love—absolutely illegal—among men.

The object of his love was a straight man who loved him too. Though he wouldn't have sex, intimacy was very much a part of their relationship and they would cuddle. I picture a teenage boy with his father, though they were not far apart in age. In Jamie's world of good and evil, not having sex only deepened the love between them. They were more like brothers than anything else. No one could stamp such a relationship with sin. Jamie was happy.

Re-entry into the States presented him with the same ole shit. Home was Cleveland, and having been away four years, Jamie found the old wounds weren't as painful. He hoped that his absence had softened the families' anger. Back in Cleveland, he was restless. Kay wanted his money. His brother was in some legal trouble involving robbery. His mother and grandmother were on the warpath about his life of sin. Then, an Air Force friend in Texas married his high school sweetheart. As with most things, Jamie accepted this.

Things began to turn around when he got a job with the airlines as a steward. He traveled domestically a lot, moved out of Cleveland, relocating to Cincinnati. Along with distance from Cleveland, there was money and friendship with other gay men. When he met Patrick in Ann Arbor, he thought he'd found, at long last, love. Only Patrick couldn't bear such love.

And Cincinnati did not want him back. Two weeks after that visit to my house, he was thrown out of his apartment. None of his gay friends would help him. I let him move into my apartment. He was alone. I never even hesitated to offer. I couldn't bear to see such a wonderful person so down.

He stayed with me for three months. The man in Ann Arbor—Patrick—was a hairstylist. He had taught Jamie some tricks of the trade. Jamie was a natural, as he was with everything beautiful, as he was with all the things "real" men know nothing of. As shallow as it is to admit it, his looks compelled me: he was so handsome it was hard not to like him, and even harder not to care about him, and even harder still not to have a crush on him. I often called him "Mom." Not just because he was tender and loving, and loved to comb my hair almost ritualistically, but because he liked me to call him that. I'm sure at the time my own mother was on my shit-list, and I didn't mind. Sometimes, for a break from my studies, I would go out with him, usually to a gay bar. After a couple of drinks, we'd dance like twist contestants: wildly, passionately, with practiced precision. Eventually, he'd work the crowd, and I'd go home. Other times we'd curl up together and watch "I Love Lucy" reruns. He cooked all kinds of heavy, fattening food I never cared for. But he needed to take care of me. Needed to take care of someone. That is how he was.

*T*o hear Jamie tell it, he and Tom met because of me. Sometime in the fall of that same year, after the fall quarter began for me, he complained about meeting the same men over and over. I suggested that he call around and check out gay social groups. Soon after this, he told me that he was going to attend some function for white and Black men. Good, I thought, getting a little tired of his man-problems, which seemed far worse than any woman's, certainly than my own. I was focusing on school, and uniquely he satisfied my need for companionship. I was quite upset when he disappeared for two weeks. He'd become rapturously involved in a relationship with another man like Patrick, another man who couldn't bear his love. Jamie, of course, came back devastated. I felt sorry for him, but was also very frustrated. The two-day here-and-there disappearing acts were starting to get on my nerves, and at the beginning of this disappearance I said to him, over the phone, that I thought he was behaving irresponsibly. He said, "Is there something wrong with you? Do you need me?" I didn't say anything. "Because if you do," he continued, "I'll be there in a second. Otherwise, I am thirty years old."

The day of his return he sat watching TV as if nothing had happened. "All My Children" was on. I had to say something. He managed to shush me until the soap opera was over. Then he began to tell me about Patrick Number Two.

"Why do you keep doing this to yourself?" I said.

"Orie, it's not like I want to get hurt. Soon as they find out how intense I am, they just run off in the other direction. I guess gay men just don't like to be loved." Then he looked at me strangely. "He said that I wasn't Black enough for him."

"What does that mean?"

"I don't know."

Nothing could keep me agitated with him for long, and I curled up beside him and his unhappiness. I had very much missed him.

That same evening Tom showed up for a date. Half an hour or so before he was due, Jamie decided to tell me. The shock registered on my face. Reading my mind, he said, "If this doesn't work out, I give up." We both knew he wouldn't, but it sounded good anyway.

Tom was blond and skinny, with a tiny mouth that moved remarkably little when he spoke, and huge, blue, quarter-sized eyes, and that Chinatown duck tan. Jamie was finished dressing, and I suspect he wanted to make an entrance, so Tom and I, in those few awkward moments, were forced to talk to each other. He was from Kansas. He'd dropped out of a doctoral program at the university because he couldn't stand academicians or academia. He'd lived in Bolivia for seven years as a Peace Corps volunteer. He was now selling real estate in Kentucky. I told him I was an English major. Then we fell into a discussion on books. Jamie finally made his appearance, and the two went to the movies.

The next day Jamie called to say he planned to stay a couple days with Tom. After that every day there was a message. Then, three weeks later, he came by for his things. He was in the midst of packing when I got home. Tom was carrying things to the car. They both hugged me. I'd just barely passed a Western Civilization exam.

"Don't you think you're rushing this a bit?" I said, when Tom went to the car with a load.

"I'm happy. This is what I want to do."

"But three hours before Tom, you were practically living with another man."

Tom came in. He immediately came up to Jamie from behind and threw his arms around him, kissing his neck. Somehow in the gay bars such an act of intimacy seemed sex-crazed and drunken. Here, in my own apartment, it was bizarre. I was stunned.

"Orie, on Saturday, come over for dinner. We'll come get you."

"I can't," I said. "And I want you to call me so we can finish our discussion."

"Okay," he said.

He never did. And never would.

A month or so later I went to dinner at their house (one of the twin houses Tom owned). They were Mr. and Mr. Tom Williams.

Later that year I moved in too, because of horrible neighbors and because the rent was right. That's when I introduced Tom to Flannery O'Connor's work. He became involved in my education like my family never was, every day asking me precise questions about what I had read, what I had been taught, what I was thinking. Jamie fixed dinner, decorated the house, and gave small parties. Every night their bed groaned from their passion.

My own family had never been so happy. The two years I spent living with them I was content to be with them, the proud daughter of proud gay parents. Even when I moved away, I spoke to them as parents, depending upon them in a way I never would have upon my own. At first it seemed like a little joke. But when I ended up pregnant in New York my first year there, I called Jamie, not my mother. He wanted me to have the baby and give it to him and Tom.

"You know we'll be good parents," Jamie pleaded. "We can give it a home until you're ready. We took care of you, didn't we?" I hung up. He was right. I wasn't ready for any of it. Pregnancy. Birth. Motherhood.

I never told my mother about the pregnancy. I had an abortion.

*S*ix years after they met, they broke up. Tom had already lost both houses, was for all intents and purposes unemployed, and was most certainly underemployed. Jamie's life was uptempo. He'd gotten a job as front desk manager at the new Weston Hotel in downtown Cincinnati. He wanted things—a dishwasher, a pretty living room with a giant-screen color television and videos. Tom wanted to be left alone.

I was living in New York and had been for over two years, after three years of hell trying to survive in Washington. I came home for Christmas. Jamie had moved into a house in the neighborhood and was away in Cleveland for the holidays. Tom was alone. We visited briefly, talked about literature, and listened to the Schumann Piano Quintet in B-flat Major. Exactly the kind of evening that I would usually spend with Tom without Jamie. When he was present, we generally watched television.

Later that night, Jamie phoned me at my mother's house. I

hadn't spoken to him in a long time, almost a year, since about the time when they broke up. Neither of them had given any hint that there was something wrong.

Jamie said, "I guess you know about your daddy [referring to Tom] and me."

There was nothing to say, since he clearly knew that I had just come from Tom's.

"I don't know what's wrong with him. I'm tired of living like this. In the house that never gets finished. I'm not used to living like this. I want things. He's not successful. He should be successful."

Of all the things that he said, this last thing struck me the most. "Why?" I asked. "Why should he be successful?"

"Because he's white. He's smart. There ain't no excuse. He ought to be ashamed."

I also found out that Jamie had met yet another Patrick, who promised him all kinds of gifts, and in the end, ditched him. Tom, Jamie knew, loved him like nobody ever had.

After I hung up, my mother said, "I don't know why you hang out with that punk." She never liked Jamie and especially didn't like the fact that he had lived with me. My brothers had been arguing all day, and I was just sick of them, as I'd been all my life. That evening I phoned Tom back and asked if I could crash with him. He agreed, and I moved in. Jamie phoned every day. They were reconciled before I left.

*M*y husband, Jerrol, and I took a trip south one year. It must have been 1992, during Jerrol's spring break from Columbia, where he was pursuing his Ph.D. He was not keen on going to Savannah, and I was not keen on going to Atlanta, so we agreed to occupy different ends of the state. We planned to drop him off in Atlanta, for me to meet his friends, then, a week later, for him to come to Savannah to meet Jamie and Tom. I was afraid to drive from Atlanta to Savannah alone. So Jerrol came with me.

"Look, Poppy," Jamie cried, after opening the gate to the garden. They lived in a very vertical, very Louisiana-style house in a regentrifying section of town. Drug dealers ruled the block. "Our baby's home." They both rushed up to me and hugged and kissed me.

I could see Jerrol's retreat. He'd never been around gay men before, not intimately, anyway.

"And look at our son-in-law," he cried. Jamie did not wait to see if Jerrol was receptive; he grabbed him and kissed him on the cheek. He darted to me. "And he's cute."

Tom and Jerrol were more formal, which seemed to put Jerrol at ease. They immediately fell into a conversation about Savannah, the Blacks in the neighborhood, and politics.

Jamie and I walked about the garden and caught up on things. In his bedroom, he pulled out a jacket he'd made last year. Showed me part of a wedding dress he was making for one of the girls at work. Curtains for the house. He was as thin as I ever remembered seeing him. And beautiful, like marigolds are beautiful.

"You look happy, baby," he finally said.

"I am. Jerrol is a pretty good guy."

"A fine Black man, is what he is," Jamie said. "You know, if I'd ever met a man like him, I would've been happy with a Black man."

I smiled.

"Mom" and "Dad" had been living in Savannah for two years, after having lived in Atlanta for one. Jamie's job had sent him south, to open up a new restaurant for an upstart chain. Within two years, after working himself silly, he was fired. Now he was happily employed with a hotel, as a reservationist. Tom was simply following his mate. He despised Savannah, though he liked the fact that Flannery O'Connor was born there and that Conrad Aiken had grown up there. Tom even took me to see the house in which the child Aiken had witnessed his father shooting his mother to death. Still, there was just too much ignorance around for Tom's taste. And the occasional howls of "faggot" and the like bothered him. That, surprisingly, was a relatively new experience.

"Your father's still the same, but you know what, I don't care about that anymore. If I need something I get it myself. That's the way it is. He loves me, and that's enough." Jamie, for the first time since I'd known him, actually seemed happy.

Jerrol ended up spending the night. He didn't want to leave. "They're terrific," he said. "Especially Jamie. You just have to love him."

A year later Jamie was diagnosed as having AIDS.

*T*oday Porscha is eighteen years old, a freshman at Case Western Reserve. Right after his diagnosis, Jamie decided that he wanted to see his child, to bridge the gap of seventeen years since he had last seen her. She had been one year old at the time.

He flew to Cleveland and cabbed to her house, greeted his former wife, who he also hadn't seen in seventeen years. Kay was pleasant to polite, but Jamie insists that not for a second did she soften. Jamie had managed through another relative to contact his daughter, and by the time Kay found out, there wasn't anything she could do about it. She had been duped.

"Porscha is so pretty," Jamie said. We're talking on the phone. "She's just as pretty as she can be. Of course she takes after me."

He told me more. Through their secret phone calls, Jamie

had found out what her measurements were and had brought along a blouse that he'd made. It was a pale gray silk, with a long collar that could become a bow. She loved the gift, and kissed him for it. Kay stood by watching, as if she were guarding the President from assassination. Jamie was happy in a way that he had never been happy in all the years that I'd known him, and I could feel it over the phone.

I think to myself that he is tying up loose ends, that he is making peace in his life. I'm very happy for him, though I am frightened. After hearing about Jamie's diagnosis, I called every weekend. At first he cried a lot. Tom would often cry in the background. Then he stopped. Both of them were suddenly flailing about for new ways to live, new diet, meditation, and the like. But Jamie couldn't. Not wouldn't. He couldn't. I was drowning in a kind of grief, not at all understanding what was happening to my parents, though I had said good-bye to many of my artist friends. Jerrol and I weren't getting along. He'd moved to the Bay Area, where he was teaching at Berkeley. I stayed behind to give us space. I was sure then that we would divorce.

Then suddenly I stopped calling. I couldn't bear it.

*I*n the living room of the house Tom lives in there is an over-the-sofa painting of Jamie. The New Yorker in me is not impressed; there isn't vitality or energy evident. The artist was making a buck. Or maybe it is because Jamie is dying and the oils don't hide it.

It is shocking to me that Jamie does not live here, that he is dying in Macon while Tom is here in Savannah. It seems that as soon as Jamie's mother and grandmother heard about Jamie's illness, they moved in. After waiting all these years to reclaim theirs, Jamie's dying gave them just the right provocation. They immediately began to complain about how poorly Tom was taking care of Jamie, that he needed round-the-clock supervision. And he needed to eat. Except for tray-sized pancakes, Tom doesn't cook.

Tom tried to oppose them, but Jamie needed to be taken care of. He needed to be fussed over, to be prayed over, to be forgiven, and to be adored and saved by these very people who believed his relationship with Tom had earned him a reservation in hell. One evening while visiting Jamie, Tom said, he became furious. Jamie's mother was saying how nice it was that he drove all the way over to Macon to visit, that friendship was very important in the eyes of the Lord. She kept emphasizing friendship, over and over again. Tom turned to her and said, "You can believe whatever you want, but your son and I were lovers. We loved each other. We had sex together, and we lived together as a couple for fifteen years."

"You were friends," she insisted.

Jamie, Tom tells me, quietly sat there, caught between the oppositions in his life.

"Lovers," Tom said. "Lovers." Then Tom leaned passionately into Jamie and kissed him on the lips. Some spirit of his life with Tom must have taken over Jamie, and Jamie threw his arms around Tom, their mouths devouring each other's. Afterward, apparently, Jamie told Tom that his mother was quite upset, and that she wouldn't allow for that kind of show in her house again.

"*T*ears are strangers to mine eyes." I think this line as I hear their voices in the living room. A little shaken, I come out of the bathroom, where the ammonia smell is arresting, and sit between Tom and Jamie, who are talking about, of all things, a couch. An old horsehair couch that Jamie loved. He wants to speak to the person who bought it at the house sale where Tom sold off their belongings. Suddenly he grabs at his eyes with his hands, and for a second I think that he is in pain. But whatever causes the seizure-like movement, it passes. Jamie's mother is hovering.

"How's Jerrol?" Jamie asks.

"Fine," I say. I don't have the heart to tell him that we're separated.

"You hold on to that one. A good man is hard to find," he says.

Of course Tom says, "Our Orie's got lots of wise blood."

"Enough with the Flannery O'Connor connections," I say.

Jamie suddenly giggles again. At something else, having nothing to do with Flannery O'Connor allusions. It's as if he remembers something delicious, and like our little jokes, to explain it would be to ruin it. I wonder if he isn't drifting away.

It is very difficult to sit between them like this. Tom gets up and sits at Jamie's feet. Jamie's legs part wide enough to accommodate Tom. At first Jamie seems a little uneasy, but then he relaxes and his fingers immediately begin to stroke Tom's hair. I watch them—I have loved them like family, more than family—and suddenly we are transported back to Newport, Kentucky. Watching television after one of Jamie's pork roasts. Laughing at Tom's neighbor Zelpha, who has come by the house in a rush of annoyance over her troubled son. Tom refuses to help her. "She's jealous of me," Jamie says. "She just wants Tom to come over and be with her. She's in love with him. I interrupted her plans. Now he's mine."

The back door slams. His mother has left. A giggle seeps out of Jamie. He has won and, without as much as a yawn, falls asleep in Tom's arms. Tom and I smile at each other.

"He stood up to the wicked witches for you," Tom says as we head back to Savannah.

I am glad for the gift, but somehow it does not feel like what I will remember, this last time. I say nothing of this. Somehow between now and morning, when I am to leave, the right words will come to me.

A Bouquet for Arthur P.

Jennifer Jordan

Everybody remembers one teacher who was a significant force in his or her life. He or she might be some horrid creature, evil as Charles Dickens's Fagan, who excelled in browbeating and humiliation. Such a type can be a motivator for a few lucky, rebellious students, who will succeed just to prove the tormentor wrong. Usually, though, the influential teacher is a nostalgically remembered favorite, charming as Robin Williams in *Dead Poets' Society* and inspiring as Richard Dreyfuss in *Mr. Holland's Opus*. He or she earns our admiration by tapping into the potential of ostensibly mediocre students, turning them into academic or athletic stars and arming them for all the obstacles that life will present. I had a couple of teachers in my childhood who managed to discover my charms underneath a persona that was alternately shy and prickly, but I was a cocky, twenty-one-year-old graduate student who thought she knew everything about the Art of Succeeding in School when I met Dr. Arthur Paul Davis, my candidate for the world's greatest teacher.

While working on a master's degree at Howard University

in 1967, I enrolled in my first class with Dr. Davis. It was in Milton, one of those required courses in British authors. I found John Milton, though dead for several centuries, still a long-winded religious fanatic and something of a self-righteous prick. By the time I finished the class I still hated Milton, but I loved Arthur P. He used to say jokingly to whoever would listen that he had taught me everything I knew. He would be surprised to know how close to the truth that witticism was.

In my second semester in graduate school I enrolled in Dr. Davis's class in Black literature. He had already spent almost forty years teaching and writing about what his less aware colleagues at Howard University laughingly called "nigger lit." Before the early seventies, Howard was pretty indifferent to the formal study of African-American culture, so, as an undergraduate there from 1963 to 1967, I had read only Ralph Ellison's *Invisible Man* and E. Franklin Frazier's *Black Bourgeoisie*. Frederick Douglass and Richard Wright were vaguely familiar names, but I had never read the works of either. In fact, my senior year began with the student rebellion that would make it possible, even mandatory, for a Howard undergraduate to take African-American literature or history. In 1967, five Howard students had been expelled for chasing General Hershey, the old, half-blind director of the nation's draft system, off the stage of Cramton Auditorium in the middle of a speech in which, among other things, he reminded us that we had more refrigerators than the Negroes in Africa. The Howard administration also threatened to expel Robin Gregory, that year's homecoming queen, supposedly for being in cahoots with the Hershey demonstrators but mostly for having the gall to be the first homecoming queen with an Afro. By the time I showed up in Dr. Davis's class I had been to countless student demonstrations, had boycotted classes, and had discovered that natural hair was quite liberating at sweaty parties.

Arthur Davis looked like one of those high-yellow house Negroes that we nationalist types of the sixties liked to deride. He was a stout, balding gentleman who smoked a pipe—a habit he picked up in his youth, an affectation probably necessary for a twenty-two-year-old professor who looked younger than his first students at the North Carolina College for Negroes (subsequently North Carolina Central). At sixty-two, however, the pipe was a natural part of him. He was rarely without it, just as he never put a foot on campus without first donning a dark suit, white shirt, tie, and gray fedora. To see him in his shirt sleeves you had to visit him at his home. Unlike Sterling Brown, poet-scholar and Dr. Davis's more famous colleague in the English department at Howard, he never professed any particular interest in bohemian life or radical politics. He was a member in good standing of colored Washington society, showing up at all the Omega Psi Phi banquets like the dedicated "Q" he was and buying a beach house at Highland Beach like everybody else. Yet he took the student uprising with amazing equanimity.

I guess at his age he had seen a lot. His father had been born in slavery. He'd seen Marcus Garvey and his troops marching through the streets of Harlem; he'd survived World War I, the Depression, and World War II; he had seen his colleagues and friends dragged down to Joe McCarthy's hearings, where they were branded un-American Communists. Although he died a fervent believer in integration and democratic liberalism, our rebellion did not faze him. He seemed to think that such youthful explosions were part of a larger natural process. His students adored him because he seemed content to let us have our moment in history. He insisted on telling us about his and our past in great and humorous detail. Despite his disagreement with our nationalist politics, he understood very well that we were eager recipients of all the knowledge of Black literature that he had spent a lifetime gathering and that we would be the ones to carry on his work.

Being Arthur Davis's student was an experience. This was a man who had begun teaching African-American literature in 1929 at Virginia Union. He had been invited by Sterling Brown, who was at Howard, to be one of the co-editors, along with Ulysses Lee, of *Negro Caravan* (1941), an anthology of Black literature from its beginnings to 1940. Soon after the work on *Caravan* began, Davis moved to Howard University as a full professor. By 1967, when I became his student, *Caravan* had been out of print for a couple of decades, and publishers had not yet discovered that there were millions of dollars to be made by reprinting the classics of Black literature. So, when Dr. Davis instituted America's and probably the world's first graduate-level course in African-American literature at Howard in the early sixties, his students knew that they would have to sit in the Moorland Spingarn Room and read the original publications, valuable first editions of Frances Harper's *Iola Leroy* and Langston Hughes's *The Weary Blues*, which could not be checked out of Founders Library. Those long hours in that room, lined with the portraits of past Howard scholars, were the real beginnings of my intellectual life. For the first time I was not studying for a grade. I wanted to learn, and learning was a pleasure.

The formal stuff out of the books was only half the course. The other half was what Arthur Davis called his "lies," real events made magical with wit and timing and just the right phrasing. I had a refined appreciation for the artistry of his teaching style because I had grown up in a place where people didn't read a lot but knew how to cast spells with their tongues. I spent many an 85-degree night in my unair-conditioned bedroom in Phenix City, Alabama, huddling under the sheets because I had spent a couple of hours on the porch listening to Miss Jack. Miss Jack, who lived on Cemetery Hill with her gang of children and the "Daddy" of the moment, could tell some hair-straightening tales about the ghosts that turned the lights off and on in her little shotgun house. Mrs. Sara Cox, who owned the corner store, could describe to a tee the sound of the witch who scuttled across the floor just before she jumped on you and rode you in your sleep. My own mother was no slouch, turning bedtime into a theater of animal sounds and weird voices and outclassing my father, who was fired from story hour because whenever he encountered a cow on the page his *moooo*'s lacked authenticity.

Arthur Davis was in a class with the real griots. With the intellectual acumen of a Du Bois and the wit and verve of the Mrs. Coxes of the world, he would tell stories about his own life that were lessons in both the history and literature of Black people. These stories were not the result of egotism or braggadocio. They were like tiny golden threads woven through the broader fabric of his conversation. They grew out of a pride in his family and a kind of nostalgic love of the Black South that some people can never grasp. When northerners, both black and white, hear the name of my home state, Alabama, they see cotton fields bathed in the blood of lynched Black men and niggers too stupid to come in out of the hot sun. When they think of Virginia, Dr. Davis's home, they see white-columned mansions like George Washington's Mount Vernon and patrician white men who all sport the title "Colonel." The only Negroes are women with little mammy-rags around their heads and humble old Black men shuffling along with straw hats in hand. Everybody's singing "Old Black Joe."

But even in Dr. Davis's day, his hometown, Hampton, Virginia, was an odd mixture of country and cosmopolitan — a port town with a strong military presence. Both the Soldier's

Home for Union Soldiers and an artillery school for Fortress Monroe were there. In 1868 Samuel Armstrong, a former Union general with connections to the American Missionary Association, had started Hampton Institute, which offered a high school education and vocational training. According to his family history, Dr. Davis's grandfather was one of the people who invited Armstrong to found a school for Blacks in Hampton. There was only one other place a Black person could get a high-school degree, and that was in Richmond. Arthur Davis's father, Andrew, had been trained as a plasterer at Hampton and was in the second class to graduate, three years before Booker T. Washington. Arthur, born on November 21, 1904, was the last of seven children, six boys and one girl. He was fascinated by his father, whom he described as the "poorest man in Virginia and maybe in America." Light enough to pass for white on construction jobs but determined that none of his family would ever suffer any racial abuse, Andrew was, according to Dr. Davis, something of a hell-raiser, who was willing to defend himself and his children with his fists and who taught his children the value of hard work and the need for education.

Hampton was a world of daily sessions in the chapel, ringing bells, and military precision. Its faculty was all white. Three of Arthur's teachers had been men from the Ivy League, but many were New England spinsters whom Dr. Davis compared to the nuns who taught me in Alabama forty years later. One he remembered well was a Miss Twitchum, who supervised the work he had to do to pay his way through Hampton. One day he and Miss Twitchum were down on hands and knees dusting the floor moldings. Arthur felt that "the dust wasn't bothering nobody," but Miss Twitchum, in a scene straight out of Booker T. Washington's *Up from Slavery*, was determined to subdue every speck. Meanwhile, she was busy quizzing the young Arthur.

"What is the capital of Tennessee? What is the capital of

Wisconsin? Eight times two divided by four plus six? Answer, Arthur?"

The frustrated Arthur wailed, "Aw, Miss Twitchum, this ain't no classroom."

"Don't say 'ain't,' young man," replied Miss Twitchum. "All of Hampton is a classroom."

Arthur graduated from Hampton Institute as valedictorian of his class and promptly received a scholarship to Columbia University, which offered one to every valedictorian in America. To enroll in Columbia he needed a foreign language, however, so off he went to Howard University for a year. Two of his brothers had gone there before him. He found Howard very different from the paternalistic, or even maternal, world of Hampton. It was an institution where Black people were beginning to challenge all of the rules. The president was white, but during the year Arthur Davis was there, his teachers were all Black men—brilliant, highly educated, independent, and sometimes a bit eccentric. One math teacher dismissed him as a waste of time because he had graduated from "that trade school." Another professor seated his students according to his perceptions of their brilliance or lack thereof. The smart students sat up front, the less quick in the rear. Dr. Davis remembers an occasion when one of the backbenchers eagerly raised his hand to answer a question. "Look," said the professor, "one of the dummies wants to speak." Not all of his memories of Howard in the early twenties were so negative. He recalls that the women were the most beautiful he had ever seen. He also had the privilege of taking a class with Alain Locke. Locke was the first Black Rhodes scholar, editor of one of the first collections of Black drama, a collector of African art, chief publicist for the Harlem Renaissance, and an overtly gay man with a penchant for young, handsome, yellow men. Of course, when Dr. Davis was at Howard, there was yet to be a Harlem Renaissance.

That was to occur while he was at Columbia University, then an all-male institution of about two thousand well-heeled and very white prep-school boys. In Davis's day, Columbia opened its doors to fifteen Black men but treated them and the few Jews enrolled with racist disdain. Arthur Paul worked six nights a week as an elevator boy on Madison Avenue and never once doubted that he could compete with the white boys in the world of ideas. By the time he graduated Phi Beta Kappa from Columbia in 1927, he not only knew a great deal about Shakespeare and Milton but had also discovered in Black Harlem where he lived another kind of literature, that would change his life and mine.

It is a wonderful thing to have a teacher who has studied a discipline with scholarly objectivity and dedication and yet has lived so intimately with it that it is inseparable from his life. While Arthur Davis's students pondered the relationship of the literary production of the Harlem Renaissance to the African-American folk tradition, we also heard about the first time he saw Langston Hughes. Langston was wearing his sailor togs and was standing on the corner in Harlem that the Black college boys called the Campus. Langston, who had already published his famous poem, "The Negro Speaks of Rivers," in *Crisis* magazine, had enrolled at Columbia University in the fall of 1921 but had tired of the inhospitable environment and of hassles with his tyrannical father about money. The summer before Arthur matriculated at Columbia, Langston had signed on as a cook's helper on a freighter headed to Africa and tossed all of his books into the sea. Arthur Davis had seen this college dropout and sailor at the pivotal moment, when he had returned home to devote himself full-time to writing his own books. Dr. Davis's job would be to teach those books to the world.

And he was great at the job. Knowledgeable, amiable, and funny, Arthur Davis was my favorite professor. The reasons that he seemed fond of me became clear only after I had taught at Howard for years. What teacher doesn't love a student who works hard, hangs on to every word spoken, and thinks all of his or her jokes are funny? The relationship he developed with me was not unusual. His fans and disciples were legion. He taught us in the classroom and involved us in his research. As a graduate student, I was privileged to do the biographical research and some of the bibliography for his anthology *Cavalcade.* The joy with which he taught and the discipline with which he approached his research were the key to my realizing that becoming a college professor was not impossible for me. This was not an instant realization. I had gone to graduate school because I had failed in my rather unenthusiastic attempt to get a job as a high school teacher in Washington, D.C. Where I came from, Black women had two career choices—teaching elementary or high school or cleaning some white woman's house. My professors at Howard—Arthur Davis, Sterling Brown, Charlotte Watkins (one of the first Black women to get a Ph.D. at Yale)—showed me how to make a living thinking and reading and talking. Once I became an instructor at Howard, Dr. Davis recommended me for outside lectures and consultations, which convinced me to pursue a doctorate in English and American literature and to make college teaching my life's work.

Arthur P. Davis taught me other things. For instance, he wore his personal contradictions with utter grace. Such psychic balance was not easily acquired at Howard University. A perfect symbol for the tensions that existed there is a beautiful stained-glass window in Howard's Rankin Chapel. For years I thought the window pictured a brown-skinned, woolly-haired Jesus, oddly dressed as a seventeenth-century Puritan. A closer inspection reveals lettering that identifies the swarthy, curly-haired individual as simply the first of a group of Puritans "landing on Plymouth Rock." This window's foregrounding of patriotism over religion and the racial indeterminacy of the figure seem to symbolize all the tortured possibilities of assimilationism, identity, and African-American double-consciousness in Arthur Davis's generation. (According to W. E. B. Du Bois, this double-consciousness is the curse of all African-Americans, who are torn by the irreconcilable demands of being both Black and American.) But Arthur Davis was never tortured. Angst was not his thing. He took his place in the class- and color-conscious world of Washington, yet never forgot his working-class origins. He socialized with doctors and lawyers but spent hours talking, laughing, and fishing with a neighbor who made a living with his hands. He did his Ph.D. dissertation on British Isaac Watts, eighteenth-century writer of Methodist hymns while rarely attending church, and became nationally known for his work in African-American literature. He had what I considered a rather ridiculous habit of reverting to a British accent whenever he used two words in professional lectures: "class" was uttered with a broad *a* ("clahs") and "schedule" was pronounced without the *k* sound ("shedule"). At the same time he was a man of few pretensions. His modest home on Park Road was in a neighborhood that had originally housed faculty and administrators from Howard, but he stayed there long after the deans and law professors had moved on to Washington's Gold Coast or to Capitol Hill.

Arthur Davis was not an overtly religious man, but he taught me a great deal about resistance to the deadly sins of sloth, envy, lust, pride, and greed. He had learned the work ethic from a father who had to feed a houseful of children through the sweat of his brow, so he had no patience with laziness. He approached his own intellectual work with a carefulness and steadiness that produced a tremendous list of publications frequently cited by scholars today. He published his last two-volume anthology at the age of eighty-eight.

Arthur Davis also didn't have an envious bone in his body. During all of his years at Howard he had to share the stage with Sterling Brown, whose contributions to Black literature in both poetry and criticism received international acclaim. Sterling was the one with the sexy image, of the rebellious, eccentric, slightly mad artist. While the youthful Davis fashioned himself after tweedy Ivy League professors, Sterling sported black berets, refused to get a Ph.D. because he claimed there was nobody around who knew enough to test him, and hung out with blues singers. Even by the standards of the Washington bourgeoisie, Sterling was enviable. He was taller and whiter; his father was not a working-class man but a professor at Howard's school of religion. Although in his later years Arthur Davis received numerous awards and national recognition for his work in Black culture, Sterling Brown became something of a cause célèbre for the Ivy League Black professoriat who have mythicized him. Arthur Davis observed this process and never once expressed envy. Sterling Brown was his friend. And friendship to Arthur Davis meant that you celebrated the other's good fortune and tolerated the other's flaws. Friendship, above all, meant you were loyal.

Lust is a sin that frequently finds a welcome home on college campuses. If one is inclined to such folly, there are many opportunities for seductions and missteps, as when an aging professor meets an impressionable, nubile graduate student (occasionally female professors are susceptible to such temptations as well). Arthur Davis had mastered the art of being a shameless flirt while treating his female graduate students with the utmost respect. The flirting took on the guise of a kind of Victorian courtship. His eyes would twinkle when you showed up; you were made to feel that you indeed were one of the handsomest women alive. But he was always determined to be both "a scholar and a gentleman," a phrase he jokingly used to compliment both men and women who met certain high standards of performance and behavior.

The fact that he was a gentleman was reflected in the fact that his wife, Clarisse, actually seemed glad to see his female graduate students when they visited Dr. Davis at his home. Clarisse was as thin as Arthur was plump. She was a woman of cynical, intelligent wit, who let her gregarious husband do most of the talking. With the husky voice of a Lauren Bacall and an insouciant way of holding her cigarettes, she evoked the image of a hip flapper in the cabarets of the Harlem Renaissance. She struck me as a woman confident not only of the love but of the admiration of her husband. The two of them were a great match.

Arthur Davis was also a man who knew the difference between self-esteem and destructive pride. He was well aware of his own intelligence and worth. He knew how much he had contributed to saving the works of Black writers whose names most Americans had never heard. Yet he remained humble in his own way. Despite his great gift of gab and the ability to keep an audience roaring with laughter, he was a nervous wreck every time he had to give a speech. He was justly proud that the State Department frequently sent Fulbright scholars from all over the world to attend his graduate class in African-American literature. At the same time he would only half-jokingly say, "I'm just a country boy from Hampton, Virginia." Part of him would always be the Hampton boy whose daddy had worked as a skilled laborer and sometimes drank a little too much. Rather than brag about himself he loved to talk about his grandfather, a former slave who hired himself out as a boat captain and who "looked like Frederick Douglass." His motivations for talking about the past were his urge to make history live for those who came after him and his accurate understanding of how he could use the oral traditions of his people to preserve their past. He was not a name-dropper seeking to impress others.

But the same Arthur Davis was an important man who was a friend and acquaintance of some historic figures. I had known him for twenty years before I heard the story of how he had traveled to England in the thirties to do research for his doctoral dissertation. On board the ship his constant companion and daily dinner partner was none other than Ralph Bunche, winner of the Nobel Peace Prize in 1950 for his work in resolving the Arab-Israeli war of 1948–49 and undersecretary general of the United Nations from 1955 to 1971. Bunche had a grant to travel around the world. Arthur was still chuckling about how he had beaten the four-letter Bunche at a game of deck tennis. It seems the highly competitive Bunche figured that even suffering from a sprained ankle, he could trounce the unathletic Davis. He was wrong. By the end of the journey Arthur P. finally met Mrs. Bunche. She had never gotten her sea legs or sea stomach and had been holed up in the cabin with the children, unsuccessfully trying to hold down her meals. Once Davis and Bunche got to England they continued to hang out. Ralph, already skilled in the art of diplomatic negotiations, talked some African students out of their $100 tickets to see the coronation of King George VI. For six dollars apiece, he and Arthur had a curbside view of the royal procession.

Just as he was able to resist the pitfalls of false pride, Arthur Davis seemed remarkably unsusceptible to the influence of greed. He frequently said that money meant little to him. Of course, he wanted to be compensated for his work and was concerned about providing for his wife and son, Arthur Jr., but the accumulation of material wealth was not a motivating factor in his life. If it were, he would have left Howard University early in his academic career. In the sixties he resisted the overtures of a number of excellent white universities, which made lavish offers he evidently could refuse.

He laughingly told stories of the financial problems that

were incurred during the early days of teaching at Black institutions. He had high praise for James Shepherd, the first president of North Carolina College for Negroes. To supplement his faculty's meager salaries, Dr. Shepherd ran a cafeteria service and used the proceeds from football games to provide Christmas bonuses for professors who excelled in the classroom. Dr. Davis recalled that Dr. Shepherd was unusual in his concern for his teachers. One unnamed college president had forced faculty members to sign the backs of blank checks sent by the state for their salaries, then pocketed the checks and handed every teacher $125 in cash for the month. Nobody was ever sure how large the difference was between the check he'd signed and the money he had received. This man's tyranny went far beyond economic exploitation. His faculty were also forced to don waiters' attire and serve at a segregated banquet for the college's white board of trustees.

One might argue that Arthur Davis taught at Black colleges because, at the time he entered academia, Black professors weren't allowed to teach anyplace else. There is some truth to this. The brilliant W. E. B. Du Bois with his Harvard degree and German postdoctoral study took for his first job an appointment at Wilberforce, a small school run by the African Methodist Episcopal Church. He was not allowed to teach white students at the University of Pennsylvania, while he conducted the early sociological study called *The Philadelphia Negro.* But in the forties when Dr. Davis came to Howard after receiving tenure at Virginia Union, white universities had begun to hire a token Black professor or two. Arthur Davis stayed at Howard because that is where he wanted to be. He had also had opportunities to make a good living outside the academic world. While at Virginia Union he wrote frequently for *Crisis* and *Opportunity,* the magazines of the NAACP and National Urban League respectively, and had a weekly column in the Black newspaper, the Norfolk, Virginia, *Journal and Guide.* John H. Johnson of *Ebony* fame, who started his publishing company with *Negro Digest*, then a Black version of *Reader's Digest*, frequently took columns from the African-American weeklies. Because of a loophole in the copyright laws, he was able to use the material without paying for it. He so frequently used Dr. Davis's column that Dr. Davis wrote him to complain and to insist on compensation. John Johnson agreed that in all fairness Dr. Davis should be paid and promised him $15 per article, an appealing offer for a young writer who was making $50 for a whole year's worth of columns. Mr. Johnson also urged Dr. Davis to come to Chicago to join his publishing enterprise. Reminiscing about it decades later, Dr. Davis laughed, "Imagine. Instead of being a miserable English teacher on relief, I could have been a millionaire like Johnnie Johnson. All things considered, I think I made the better choice."

Like every human being, Arthur Davis had his flaws. Although a staunch believer in integration, he was never particularly comfortable around white people and felt the need to dissemble in their presence. His intense loyalty to the Black middle class made him hostile to the ideas of the cultural nationalists of the sixties, who depicted the Black bourgeoisie as assimilationists and traitors to their race. In his mind the growing Black middle class was the result of a strong work ethic and a dedication to racial uplift and progress. He was not left untouched by the negative insularity of his class and day. Like many older people, he would never use the word "Black" in place of "Negro," partly because his generation had fought for years to get rid of the previous era's use of the word "colored." Part of his reluctance about the "Black" thing was his acceptance of attitudes toward color that were important to his social group and perhaps to his family. One day when he was waxing on about how great I looked, he added, "If I had known you in my youth, I would have had to propose."

I understood that this was one of those off-hand remarks

that passed for an old man's notion of flirting. For some reason I decided to call him on it.

"I doubt that," I said with a big grin. "I would have been too black for you to marry."

Expecting him to laugh uproariously at this bit of signifying, I was taken aback when he said in all seriousness and as gently as he could, "Oh, but you are a really intelligent woman. And in those days that counted for a lot."

I had never seen any sign that he himself was guilty of any kind of color discrimination, but it saddened me to realize that our attitudes were so different about this subject that we could not even joke about it. He was assuring me that it would have been all right to be dark if I were brilliant. There was no way I could tell him that being dark was all right even if I had been one of the dumbest broads alive. Even in the pre-sixties days I had few hangups about my color. My hair had traumatized me, but I had always been quite happy with my color and complexion. Arthur P.'s remark made me realize that he was still very much a man of his times. If I had met the twenty-year-old Arthur in some smoky cabaret in Harlem during the Renaissance, the prevailing color code probably would have determined our relationship: "If you yellow, you mellow; if you brown, stick around; if you black, get back."

One of the signs of true maturity is to be able to see the hero's feet of clay and still think he is the grandest man living from the ankles up. I will always be grateful for those gifts — intellectual, spiritual, and social — that I received from Dr. Arthur Paul Davis, who died on April 21, 1996. As if responding to some epic writer in the sky, Mother Nature reflected the loss. It was a horrible spring — unseasonable cold, too much rain, azaleas refusing to bloom. Sitting in Howard University's Rankin Chapel before the memorial service, I knew I wasn't going to participate in the social ritual of viewing the body while some little old lady—the kind that made attending funerals a professional calling—commented on how natural he looked. I had already seen him as close to death as I cared to.

When someone called to tell me he was in critical condition at Washington Hospital Center, I had forced myself to go, mainly out of guilt. For over a year I had planned to visit him but could never find the right time to go. A stroke had turned him into what he had never been, even in his eighties—an old man. The last time I had seen him his memory was fading, the twinkling eyes were opaque, the deep Southern voice was halting. The real reasons I had stayed away were all selfish: too little time, too many other obligations, fear that a mentor and friend of thirty years might not remember me, and that middle-aged discomfort at seeing what time has in store for all our minds and bodies.

Still procrastinating, I had arrived at the hospital about half an hour before the end of visiting hours. When I found the room, I looked in to see a small, gaunt-faced man, who appeared to be asleep or in a coma. I thought I was in the wrong wing and moved on down the hall looking for someone who could tell me where Arthur Davis was. Less than a minute later I was standing in the same room again, trying to see Dr. Davis in the stranger in the bed. The characteristic roundness was gone. The jowls and paunch had shriveled; the friendly, bespectacled, yellow face was drawn and sallow. There was a stillness about him that was frightening. The eyes were shut and motionless. His arms lay stretched out on top of the sheets; his legs were immobile. The only movement seemed centered in his mouth, which was covered by an oxygen mask whose mechanical hisses could not compete with the loud, sucking sound that accompanied his struggle for enough air to stay alive. Each desperate gasp seemed both interminable and fleeting. It was heartbreaking to see him like that, but even as I wanted to escape out of fear that

I might have to witness his last breath, I wanted to cheer him on. He was not going to be one of those going gently into that good night. I wasn't surprised. You don't get to be ninety-one by being a quitter.

Death had to wrestle him down and strangle him in that hospital bed, but death won, of course—at least that part of the battle that involves corporeal matters. If there is any truth to the African notion of ancestral worship, Arthur Davis is never going to die. He will be kept alive by those thousands of students he taught during the sixty years spent at three historically Black colleges. He will be made immortal by all those years of writing about the literature that he loved and by those innumerable stories that made us marvel and laugh and that have to be out there reverberating somewhere in the universe.

My Handyman

Pam Ward

As soon as I pulled up in front of my house, I could see something was wrong. An official-looking dude with a clipboard was sniffing around my front gate and another one was snapping Polaroids of the house and the fence. Goose, my rottweiler, was going mad with each flash. My hairy-legged neighbor, who never came outside, was standing next to his Buick. They all turned and glared at me as I got out of my car. This did not look good.

Damn, I thought, Goose has done it again. She would break through the gate at night and wreak havoc in the neighbors' yards, leaving soup cans, chewed boxes, and orange peels scattered all over the place. That's when she wasn't chasing kids coming home after school or barking like hell at folks walking back from the store.

The last time the mailman had written me up, Goose had hidden in a bush on the side of our porch, hair spiked, eye teeth gleaming, growling and ready to bite. She had scared the mailman so bad he had dropped his whole bag when Goose chased him down the street. He was screaming, "Get back, goddammit, you crazy-ass dog." Mail blew all over the sidewalk and curb.

Goose just wouldn't let up. The mailman, a thin-ankled, orange-colored, jheri-curled dude, saw my neighbors' parked car as a refuge. He jumped as high as he could with Goose at his feet, flew off the curb, and landed right on their Buick, postal boots making huge dents in the hood. Goose had charged fast, deaf to any pleas and threats, showed her huge ugly molars, and enjoyed the spectacle she had created until she got winded. No, this definitely was not good.

"Are you Miss Ward?" the man asked, peering over thick frames.

"Who are you?" I said, not wanting to give them my name.

"Mr. Washington from the postal station downtown. We're investigating a complaint on an unrestrained dog, ma'am. It seems yours has been terrorizing this block for some time. We've taken the liberty of getting a few shots of that maniac dog and your neighbors' car, too. You'll be getting a call from the station master." He scribbled something fast, ripped it off from his pad, coughed twice, and clicked his ballpoint.

Damn. This was serious. This wouldn't disappear with a smiling apology or a quick promise that it wouldn't happen again. This wouldn't be made to go away by me waking up early to rake up the trash Goose had dragged across my neighbors' front lawn. (In the cold, I'd be down on my hands and my knees trying to clean up before they woke and caught me.)

I walked in the front door, put my purse down, and peeked through the drapes. My neighbor was nodding his head in agreement, pointing to my drooping back fence. They took shots of that, too.

I got the call the next day.

"Miss Ward?"

"Yes?"

"This is Mr. Washington again, supervisor down at the post office. Unfortunately, we're going to have to put a permanent hold on your mail service, ma'am. It seems you can't restrain that rottweiler of yours, Miss Ward. Those are vicious dogs, you know. We can by no means jeopardize the safety of our carriers, ma'am. You'll have to pick up your mail at the station downtown from now on."

"I'm awfully sorry," I said sweetly, trying to take the edge off the situation. Then I did what any self-respecting girl does when badgered by the bureaucracy. I lied.

"You know what?" I chirped. "That's my mother's dog and we're just watching her until she gets back next week from Belize. Poor dog just had major surgery, and some stitches are still in there. I think that medication makes her nervous, too. Those crazy vets just write anything down on those pill bottles. Yes, I realize she's somewhat rambunctious, but I swear she won't give you a bit of trouble again. I have a man over here right now working on the fence. Yes, I'll be happy to put that in writing."

Shit! I thought, and hung up disgusted. It wasn't my mother's dog, but it wasn't mine either! Truth was, the ol' hound belonged to my ex-husband. He'd been promising for months he'd get over here and fix my fence for me.

He had lots of advice about the whole thing, too. Told me it was a waste to pay good money for something he could do in less than a day or two. Told me Goose was a sweet dog and wouldn't harm a flea. I had to remind him about the time Goose had killed our neighbors' pet Maltese. We'd had to pry Goose's teeth loose from that little dog's neck. Cost us $1,500 in vet bills, too. I had to keep Goose tied up after that until my ex came by and chewed me out for chaining up his dog. Said it made 'em mad being roped like that. Said the neighbors had no business letting that little mutt out in the first place. What the hell was a rat-sized dog good for, anyway? Told me he'd fix the damn fence, just quit bitching about it.

I was lucky to get a bag of dog food out of him. I was only supposed to be watching Goose until he found a new place that allowed animals.

Well, it was clear now I couldn't wait for him. I was tired of putting a new battery in my watch every time my ex promised to get over here. I was sick of waiting for his good intentions to get up from the couch. I was burned out with him telling me over and over again, "I'll get there, I'll be there, I'll fix it this weekend, I told you I'd do it, so don't bug me!" Day after day turned into week after week, and the next thing I knew, six months had gone by and I ain't seen hide nor hair of him yet.

And it's not like he's the only one, either. Seems like there's a whole crop of young men out there right now who don't know squat about repairs. They've been educated right out of knowing how to be productive. The only elbow grease some of these young dudes use is to wax their new BMWs or to polish their brand-new Air Jordans. Couldn't fix an alternator or change a tire if the jack sat up and danced in the trunk. But they'll run down in droves trying to get to the repair shop if something goes wrong with their beepers or cell phones.

Since he'd moved out there were lots of odds and ends I'd learned to do myself like any sister suddenly on her own. You either pick up a pair of pliers and figure out how to change the shower head or you hire somebody else to do it. And you learn real quick when you have to dig into your wallet every time the sink faucet drips, the toilet runs all night, or the refrigerator goes on the blink. Either you learn a few basics, or those fix-it bills will bury your ass. I'd learned my way around a hardware store, and could tell the difference between a Phillips screwdriver, a monkey wrench, and a drill bit. I could change a fuse and rewire a lamp or put a new washer on the kitchen faucet with no sweat, but building a fence around the whole back yard was a bit more than I could manage. That was a bit more than I could chew for the time being.

Brothers are always scratching their heads, wondering what the sisters want. Well, here it is in a nutshell, fellas. We want someone to fix the bathroom faucet. Someone we can rely on when the ceiling leaks or the plaster cracks. Someone who'll really come when called to take care of a broken windowpane. Someone who can do more than put his feet under the table and act like he's owed a meal because he changed a lightbulb. Someone who can follow through on the promise to fix the back-yard fence.

I phoned my mother.

"You better call Mr. Rawls, honey, before somebody gets bit real bad and sues you," my mother said. "You got two girls over there you're trying to raise. You don't want to fool around and lose your house over some crazy dog mess, do you?"

Mr. Rawls had worked on the street I grew up on for as long as I can remember. He was what I called the last of the handymen. Men who could fix anything from the front curb all the way to the trash cans out back and every damn thing in between. He did yards and turned weeds into beautiful lawns, fixed faucets, drainpipes, and electrical sockets, laid down floors or nailed up some drywall, and painted the kitchen all in a day. Mr. Rawls came from that generation of men that knew everything about repairing a home. Men who never called someone else when something broke down.

"Everything can be fixed some kinda way," he'd say. "Might not be the way people think it oughta go, but I betcha I get it to work."

I remember having some plumbing work done once by a guy in a ball cap and tight-fitting Levis, with his name sewn into a label on his jacket. He scrunched his face and pointed to the spigot on my yard hose. "Who did that crap?" he asked.

"My handyman," I told him.

"Oh god, not one of those guys!"

The fact was, Mr. Rawls had done the job for me. He told

me he didn't have the long pipe it needed but he could jimmy the spigot with some smaller parts he had stashed from previous jobs.

Mr. Rawls was a husky man, built like a concrete wall. He wore huge overalls, a crisp denim shirt, and a pinstripe gray train-captain's cap. He walked slow, like old dogs do. Took laboring steps. Took his time, like most folks from the country. One of those Depression-age folks that saved everything; every liver container and worn aluminum foil, Yuban coffee cans and old tool catalogs. His truck sagged with the weight of forty years or more of doing odd jobs on various houses. He had saved every piece of extra wire or pipe he could get his hands on. He'd yank the old plumbing straight from somebody's old wall and haul it all into his van. He had stuff piled on the top and junk roped on both sides. The big stacks of torn magazines ran so high on the inside of his windshield that there was just a small place left where he could peek through and drive.

Big plastic sacks of Lord-knows-what kind of knickknacks were tucked underneath the bent windshield wipers. Rusted-out hangers held up the antenna. He had sacks made out of some little boy's denim pants. The legs were knotted and stuffed full of screws. Odds and ends hung on the edges of all six windows. Padlocks and doorknobs, light switches and wrenches were shoved in the front glove compartment. Latches and mallets, drill bits and U-joints were all mixed up in milk crates he had stashed on the floor. Whenever he parked, he placed two giant bricks underneath the back wheels so the whole thing wouldn't roll back and kill somebody.

The tires looked like they'd pop at any minute. Like the water balloons my daughters tossed against the sidewalk. Like a puppy's gut after a feeding. He had so much stuff in that truck that sometimes he'd spend more time just trying to find the right part than it took him to do the whole job. He'd finally emerge from the back of that old rattle-trap carrying just the right thing, fussing at his helpers for not putting things where they were supposed to.

"You can't show young folks nothin'," he'd say, sucking his teeth. "Fool around trying to teach 'em a thang or two, but most times I find 'em hiding 'round the back of the van. Don't care 'bout nothin' but they lunch break and they paycheck!"

I remember when he bought the van, years ago. Used to have one of those old Ford pick-ups from the fifties. Fenders all chewed up. Paint job half gone. Just a beat-up ol' dull blend of ghost blue and traces of primer. Kids on the block had robbed him so blind he stopped driving the thing. A neighborhood joke was that he still had it buried somewhere in his yard.

When Mr. Rawls bought his new truck in 1985, he got a couple of guys to go with it and got a lot more business, too. After he'd finished doing somebody's lawn on our street he would stop by our house to talk to my mother or visit a cousin up the street. He said they were the only ones who gave him the time of day some afternoons.

I'd catch him at our kitchen table holding a cup to his lips, real gentleman-like. Napkin laid neat across his lumberjack lap. Captain's cap tilted to the side. A country man at that "sweet granddaddy" age that made a woman feel safe, made her feel she could speak her mind freely. He'd be giving my mom some pointers on fixing all kinds of stuff or telling her how someone had done him wrong.

"Naw," he'd say in a real settled voice. "Never got a dime off that job. Spent over $600 in parts, too." He'd shake his head, look at his tea a long time, breathe out a long tired sigh. It wasn't like he was mad. Not like Dad got when his car wasn't ready at the shop. Not a yelling kind. It was more like disgust. It was more like Mr. Rawls had made up his mind there were some things you just couldn't win at. That's just the way it was.

Like those old southern codes about knowing your place, and what not. You'd be peeved, but you knew how to hold it in.

I called him to see if he could get over here right away.

"Mr. Rawls?"

"Well, hell-lo there, little lady," he said, sounding all happy.

"Mr. Rawls, I need to have my fence fixed right away. My dog, Goose, keeps getting out and the mailman's threatening to stop coming at all and the neighbors might try to sue and . . ."

"I 'ready know 'bout that," he cut in. It amazed me how quickly things fly through the ghetto grapevine. "Listen at this here, I'm on my way to a lady's house right now who's got water up to her elbows on the back porch. Soon as I turn that main line off and bail all that water out, I'll be over there. Got to crawl under that house and fool around and see what she got wrong down there. I don't know when I'll get there, but I'll get there, hear?"

He pulled up the next day. Parked real slow. Got out and looked at the damage.

"Looks like somebody already been working on it," he said.

The left side of the house had half a brand-new fence running the length of the yard and then abruptly stopping. My ex had built that fence when the house and our marriage was as fresh and new as the bright coat of white paint he had put on it. I used to watch him out there flailing away in the morning sun. Kids playing with the water hose, radio going full blast, his bare back and arms big from pounding. He'd come in every now and then to ramble through the junk drawer we kept in the kitchen, looking for a scraper, a spatula, or gloves to protect his hands. The only thing left in that old junk drawer now were some dead batteries, a roll of dried-up duct tape, and a few moldy pennies. I had called him up to let him know Mr. Rawls was going to be working on the fence and he didn't have to worry about it anymore.

"Oh hell, you're not letting that old fool fix it, are you? He'll have nineteen different kinds of wood hammered in, and some chair legs nailed into it, too."

"No he won't, he already left for the hardware store to pick up the cement and the two-by-fours."

Truth was, I liked having Mr. Rawls around. He was a fading relic from a bygone era of older Black men that nodded and tipped their caps when you passed, paused at the front gate and asked how were your children, told you stories about different folks they worked for or how well they remembered your grandmama from when they knew her back in Natchez, Mississippi. He had remedies for just about any old thing that might be ailin' you—distemper, how to spot if you had termites in the cellar, or how to rake the yard without hurting your back. He was honest, dependable, would always charge fair, and usually did something extra.

The last time he was here, blowing dead leaves into a pile on the lawn, I came out to chat and hand him a Coke. He stopped and cleaned his hands on his coverall before taking the glass from me and saying, "You sho' is yo' mama's chil'."

His raggedy-toothed smile made me feel good about more than just offering a cool drink on a warm day. "Most folks just want you to fix the stuff and get the heck out." He took a long swig from the can and wiped his sweaty brow with a grimy red bandanna. "You could be there all day and they barely say two words to ya. Take Miss Smith over there. I been cutting her grass for fifteen years and she never so much as said a decent hello. Just wave from the window and look away. Hand me my money through the screen door and don't never invite me in. People don't take time these days to sit on they porch and enjoy they peach trees or some plums while the sun's going down.

Naw, Los Angeles is a hurry-up town these days, didn't used to be this way. When I come up we knew just 'bout everybody on our street and the next few blocks, too. Most of 'em from down south like me and ended out here on the east side like your grandma did. Those was the days when folks stopped to speak and helped to bring in your groceries." He took out his rag and dabbed his brow again. "Now they just leap up and tear out they driveways or holla out, 'Hey ain't you done yet?' "

"How did you learn so much about fixing things, Mr. Rawls?" I asked him.

"I'd watch the men folk do stuff and I'd follow 'em all around and ax 'em 'bout it, too. If wasn't nobody 'round to ax, I'd try a way to figure it myself. Supported myself by the time I hit fourteen. Young men running around here nowadays, ain't never had nobody show 'em nothin'. Couldn't clean a drain if the snake laid right there on the floor. Folks'll spend plenty money for them big plumber outfits that charge an arm an' a leg just to drive out and look at a job. I wouldn't have none of 'em.

"I'm a do' a li'l' extra for you cuz you so sweet and you Bonnie's daughter and she helped me that time that lady say I hit her car. Drivin' one of them big Mer-say-deese numbers and what not. I didn't hit nothing!" he said, all indignant. The sun made his worn face a road map of memories.

"Wasn't even my paint on her car! But your mama, boy oh boy, now she's a sharp one. She came out with her camera and took pictures of the whole dang thang. I showed them photos to the insurance man an' ain't heard nothin' from 'em. Yes sir-ree, yo' mama'll make a nice cup of tea, let a fella sit and catch his breath for a hot minute." He drank up the rest and ducked into his truck for a good while but finally came out with a piece of screen that fit perfectly in my kitchen window. Fixed it free of charge.

Before Mr. Rawls started building the fence he took a wire

and rigged it to my sagging gate. "The onliest way to make it stay good is to get a coat hanger and wrap it up real tight like this here, see?" His big weather-beaten thumbs pulled the hanger apart and forced it through the eye hook.

"She ain't gonna get outta this side now."

We both stared down at Goose, looking innocent and dumb, nibbling on some grass by my foot.

Mr. Rawls attached the hook to a piece of wood and then nailed it to the house. He made it stand nice and straight by yanking the coat hanger through an eye screw. It wasn't the way a finished carpenter might do it but it sure worked.

"This will hold ol' Goosey-girl 'til I get through back here."

I watched him over the four days it took him to get the fence up. First he watered the ground so the soil was good and wet before digging the holes. Then he cut all six posts the same size by using a string to measure them out. He mixed the cement with an old curtain rod and then used two bricks to make sure the posts would stand straight before pouring it in. Before it dried, I went outside and wrote my daughters' names in it. The next day he tied a yellow rope from post to post so the boards would line up when he started nailing them. I watched him hammer that wood with the smooth confident moves of someone used to hard work. He was accurate and quick and got most nails in with three good whacks.

He had nails in his front teeth and in the top pocket of his overalls, and a leather belt he hooked his tools onto. The belt hung over a lumbering stomach, and someone had stamped the name "Candy" on it.

"That ought to keep that dog in and the mailmen off your back," Mr. Rawls said, laughing and scratching Goose's head as he bent down to gather his tools.

I was sorry to see him go. He showed up a few days later to pick up his flashlight that he'd left by mistake. I opened the door, and there was Mr. Rawls, all decked out in a tired brown wool suit that had seen better days, a fat ancient tie that wouldn't even get bought at a rummage sale, and a wide felt-tip daddy-mack brim hat. "I'm going to see my lady friend," he told me with a wink.

I closed the door, thinking how lucky a lady she was to have a handyman around her house. How he'd get over there and check under her sink, or maybe install a new electric socket, fit a shelf in the closet, or plane some wood at the back screen door while she fixed him his food. How she'd bring a cool drink and slowly work over his shoulders to rub the knots out and then tell him it was time for dinner. How he'd whistle softly to himself as he left at sunrise and get in his truck, tip his hat to whoever he was passing by, and tell everyone, "Mornin'."

Ready

Leslie Woodard

Last Saturday evening as I walked up Broadway, I saw three girls waiting for a bus. I recognized the long skinny legs, the big feet, the nervous pawing of the ground like race horses. They were dancers. All three were very Black and very pretty, but the tallest had a remarkable face that could have been the model for an African carving. She leaned against a big shiny car parked at the curb and stroked the chrome as if she planned to own a car like that someday. Then she seemed to forget about it and began chattering with her friends, critiquing the older dancers they'd just seen perform. In a tee shirt and blue jeans that hung loose at her waist she mimicked the placement of their feet, legs, heads, even the focus of their eyes. Her imitations were so exact that they were quickly identified and her friends laughed, but she didn't mean to be bitchy. It was just that she thought she could do everything she'd seen and wanted so desperately for someone to let her try. She was so sure she was ready. It was like looking into a mirror and seeing my younger self.

I remembered the summer I turned nineteen years old, the summer I lied and said I was eighteen because nineteen is old for a dancer. You see, dancers expect to have to retire about age thirty-five. Their backs or their knees or their tendons blow out like worn tires, or they realize that they're just plain too old for the life anymore. Some teach, passing on their legacy to a younger crop. Some marry and quit the business, and some go back to school and discover other things that make them just as happy, like writing. The point is that once you leave you really can't go back. That version of yourself is dead, relegated to a ghostly existence in videotapes and PBS specials.

There was never a time when I wasn't aware of this inevitability, so I made the most of every minute I could steal. I tossed aside a year of my age and got a scholarship. From nine in the morning until nine at night, I jumped, swayed, and stretched in the crowded studios of the Alvin Ailey American Dance Center.

In those days the school was a converted warehouse on East Fifty-ninth Street between Third and Lexington. Even before you reached the building you felt the pulse of drums and the piano music so fast and free that it seemed the fingers playing didn't need sheet music. But most of all you felt the energy, as though all the city's fireplugs were thrown open and the cool water was rushing out.

The Ailey machine consisted of three companies then, the big company you still see up on the City Center stage and two junior companies. Kelvin Rotardier directed the third. I knew who he was because all young dancers know who the directors and choreographers are. When he appeared every dancer in the room got a little bit nervous. Every waist got a little bit smaller; backs got straight and heads went up. Folks who'd been leaning on the barre suddenly stood erect and began working, showing off their high insteps and hyperextended legs. When I saw him in the doorway, I was in the middle of a Horton five-four swing, upside down with one leg overhead. I pointed my foot so hard and used so much extra energy to make the pointe that I almost knocked myself over. But dancers are like cats. They always try to look as if they meant to do everything, so I finished the sequence, walked casually to the side, and hoped no one had noticed my mistake. Especially Mr. Rotardier.

It was then that I got a good look at him. I'm not good with heights, but I believe he was at least six feet tall, maybe more. Male dancers aren't often that big, and Black men that tall tend to play basketball. He had intense dark eyes, high cheekbones like the Indians in Trinidad, where he was from, and gorgeous ocher-colored skin. A body like that you don't forget. One of the hottest men I have ever known, and I have known some hot men.

Kelvin was one of the Ailey Company's original dancers. I knew because I had seen him perform in a PBS special. He had flipped a coin in Mr. Ailey's *Masakela Language.* He had worn a Panama hat and a black silk suit, but he had moved like a polished panther and he ate up the space on that stage like it was a good meal. The music of the horn flowed through all his length of arm and leg, it poured out on the stage in torrents of exquisite, lithe choreography. Perish any preconceived notions you may have about male dancers. There wasn't an effete bone in all his body. Makes me smile and shake my head just to think about him.

But all that libido action is in retrospect; at the time it was strictly business. Kelvin had retired from performing when I actually met him and he was coaching young dancers like myself. Despite the near disaster in my five-four swing he invited me to join the workshop, or third company, as it was then known. I don't remember saying anything but "thank you" when I spoke with him. I was far too nervous.

• • •

*W*e rehearsed every evening after classes were finished in a studio with hot, overbreathed air, on a hardwood floor made shiny by gallons of sweat and smooth by thousands of bare dancing feet. Our music was an old reel-to-reel that, especially in the summer, you had to hurt in order to ensure its cooperation. Our reflections in the mirror and Kelvin himself comprised our audience.

He positioned himself at the front of the studio, and despite the very small, very hard wooden bench on which he sat, with his regal posture he looked like King Solomon holding court. He carried his back straight and his head erect and seemed quite capable of divvying up a child should it be absolutely necessary. He observed every movement, every gesture, every breath we made with judicious but unwavering exactitude.

I had never had to learn choreography before, and I found it difficult. There was much more to remember than the short series of steps we did in daily classes. Also, because I had come from a classical ballet background, I had to learn to shape the movements. Ballet dancers tend to focus on their legs and arms, modern dancers on their abdominals and backs.

Kelvin let me know in his patient but definite manner that I wasn't focusing anywhere. I would do a movement, look up at him, and wait for a verdict or some semblance of approval. He would get up, walk over, and, without a word, bend my body into the proper shape. I would do the movement again. He would watch me intensely and then say, completely without anger, "No. Not yet." Then he would get up and do the movement in front of me. It looked so different on him. I didn't know why. I knew he did, and I was frustrated. But only if I found the movement for myself would it really be mine. Kelvin understood that, even though I didn't.

One evening he brought his daughter to watch rehearsal. She wore her hair in two very long braids and had the same intense and serious expression as her father. For some reason, I wanted to dance well for her. I didn't and I felt embarrassed, even though Kelvin never said a harsh word. When we were leaving I watched him hand her her sweater and carry her bag. She was just a little girl, but he opened the door and let her pass before him. I was angry with that little girl then. I didn't know it at the time, but I was jealous. I would have given anything to have had that kind of attention from him.

By midsummer my dancing had improved. Kelvin knew it, and I knew it, too. So, I very quickly reached the point young dancers and singers and writers, perhaps all young artists, get to, where insecurity is matched only by arrogance. I thought I was a very good little dancer indeed.

One evening we were rehearsing a ballet called *Mujeres*, which called for three turns or pirouettes ending in a rather difficult finish. Turning seems to have universal appeal. There are few people who when they were children didn't run outside, spread their arms, and spin, faster and faster, until they collapsed in the grass. The sensation of a correctly executed pirouette is much the same, although without the collapse. I loved turning and wanted to sustain the feeling for as long as I could. Sometimes that meant three revolutions, sometimes four, sometimes only one.

Imagine human-sized cats betting their last can of tuna as they roll dice in an alley, and you know another side of dancers. We love risk and so do you, if you've ever gone to the ballet. It's exciting to see a performer whose work never looks safe, is always right on the edge. But great artists don't actually scare their audiences. They know exactly where that edge is, and they never topple over. I was not a great artist.

We had gone through the section four times when Kelvin rolled both his eyes and his Trinidadian accent at me and said, "Leslie, you have not done the same thing twice all night!"

I put my hands on my hips, pursed my lips, and craned my

neck in a way that would have made a rap singer jealous. How dare he not appreciate my daring. Then I announced in my most hurt and offended voice, "Well, I am trying." (Dancers are nothing if not dramatic.) "And I have a split in the bottom of my foot." (Very dramatic indeed.)

Kelvin raised an eyebrow. "If I'm in the audience and I pay my money for three turns, I expect I will see three turns. Not four and not one. Three turns every time. Accuracy makes an artist." He calmly rewound the tape. "And you gotta get used to having those splits. You're a modern dancer now."

I did the sequence again, three turns with a clean finish every time. I was determined to be accurate if only for him, but I cried that night when I got home. I liked being the little ballerina. But Kelvin was right. Whatever I was doing I had to do it well and with commitment. More and more choreography walks the line between classical and modern dance, so much so that it's difficult to know where one ends and the other begins. By morning I had stopped crying. I wrapped my feet with adhesive tape and was back in the studio again. When eventually I returned to the world of ballet, I did so with an expanded range of movement and tougher, stronger feet.

At the end of the summer we did a series of performances for Hospital Audiences Inc. that took us into the prisons and hospitals in and around New York. We rented an Avis van, packed it with our reel-to-reel, our costumes, our props, our cramped little bodies, and off we went.

The day we performed at Riker's Island it rained. This was Kelvin's baptism by fire for young dancers. He figured if you could maintain your composure in front of a crowd of rowdy lifers, you could maintain it anywhere. By the time we pulled into the parking lot everything looked gray and ominous. I saw a bird flying toward the prison and I swear to you, it looked as though it suddenly realized where it was, spun around, and went the other way. This was not a good omen.

We went through a checkpoint where guards searched our bags. Just a look at those guards was enough to scare me. They were big, hard-looking men who lovingly clutched their clubs and joyfully slammed barred doors as we moved deeper and deeper into the prison. The only book they let us bring in was the Bible.

Every sound echoed off the metallic walls, floors, and bars and chased you down the long corridors, and the whole place had that institutional smell of old vegetables or the back of a school bus. We were conducted into an enormous gym that looked like the places teenagers get brutally murdered in horror movies. A small, rickety stage huddled at one end, with a dilapidated curtain that was too chicken to come all the way down. I looked at that curtain, with safety pins trying to close the gaping moth holes, and I didn't blame it one bit.

But the guards soon had their way with it. When the poor curtain was finally down we used the stage to warm up. Kelvin had choreographed a solo called *Lady Jane,* which I was to perform for the first time.

When we worked on it, back in the studio, the choreography had seemed far from anything I could ever do. I was, as usual, frustrated and disappointed with myself, and my feet were splitting again. I thought surely Kelvin would turn off the tape and say "never mind," but he didn't. He changed the steps and fixed the music to suit me, and I tried my best to imitate his long, sweeping, and graceful movements. We spent hours on the thing, he working as hard as I, and the more we worked the more I wanted to dance it just the way he wanted it to be. As I went through the steps on that stage at Riker's Island I thought I was ready to do it.

The roar of noise as the audience arrived made me think there was going to be a riot. Kelvin had told us we would perform for the lifers since the prison officials thought they would be more sedate than men more recently off the street. As I listened to that noise, though, I thought that it didn't matter what they had done or how long they had been there because by now they were surely capable of anything. I tried to regain some semblance of concentration as I took my place to begin.

The curtain screeched up, revealing a sea of rough faces above ashy elbows leaning on the stage. This was true terror. It was as though the window shade in your bedroom had flown up and all the eyes of all the people in the next building were staring at you. I couldn't see Kelvin anywhere, but I could see that audience. I don't know how long it had been since those men had been with a woman, but they were making up for it in spades. Eyes ran up my legs, and some of them never came down. I could barely hear the music for the hollering.

The steps to the ballet abandoned me, fleeing my brain in terror. I stumbled around the stage in a stupor, doing any step I could before it hastened away. Some of them were in the ballet, some weren't. The last three steps were troupers, though, and I did them six times as the music went on and on and on. When at last it mercifully ended, the prisoners, thrilled with any form of entertainment, especially one in a transparent pastel skirt over bare legs, enthusiastically applauded my disaster.

I could only imagine what Kelvin would say. All that work and I had ruined his ballet—*his* ballet. I thought he would fire me for sure, and I thought I deserved it. After the performance was over Kelvin came backstage. He had been watching in the back with two of the guards. I tried to look as pitiful as possible so that maybe he'd kill me with a quick single thrust. No way did he plan to be so merciful. He barely looked at me when he said, "You got flustered and forgot the steps. You'll do it again this afternoon. You'll be all right."

I was actually mad for a moment. He knew what was going to happen and he should have warned me or at least tried to console poor me, preferably the way one consoles a successful friend who has had a bad day. (Did I mention that dancers are dramatic?) But that big Trinidadian Atticus Finch had said everything that needed saying. He picked up the reel-to-reel and his dog-eared canvas bag. He walked calmly through the prison looking over his shoulder now and then to see that we were all with him, and I knew it would have defeated his purpose if he had told me anything but *merde*. I made sure I sat next to him in the van on the way to the next prison.

I danced *Lady Jane* again at the Queens House of Detention and got through it. Afterward Kelvin smiled. "Well, we got a ways to go before it's art, but now, at least, you got the steps. We'll work on it. It'll be nice." He wanted nice. I wanted to quit.

During the summer a couple of friends and I had attended any performance of the big company we could get a ticket to. Young dancers tend to keep youth in their heads far longer than they can keep it in their bodies, and that lack of sophistication allows room for fantasy. We'd stand around the backstage door after the performance was over, just to watch the dancers leave. We didn't see the tired faces and exhausted bodies that disappeared into the subway. We saw only what they had been on stage, and they were magic to us. We'd dance home in our blue jeans and midriffs, unconscious of how much skin we showed. We jumped and turned the steps we had memorized all the way up Broadway. We didn't know we weren't supposed to dance on concrete. It's too hard and it gives you shin splints, but we didn't care. We sailed over the cracks in the sidewalk and the butts on the street. Restaurant and movie patrons, who are not known for their tolerance, managed to smile even when we almost ran them down, and the guys who drank beer and smoked spliffs by the park shouted, "Yeah baby, dance one for me." Every now and then someone in a foul mood would say aloud under their breath, "This is not a damn stage." But it was all the stage we had, and we didn't care how much space we took up. We wanted to show how great we were—at least in our own minds. When I got home I always wished Kelvin had been there to see us and know what fabulous talent we had to offer.

In October, the big company held open auditions. I had never auditioned for anything but schools before and had no idea how a professional audition might be conducted, but I decided to go. During all our post-performance follies I had started to think, though I never said it, that I could do what I had seen.

City Center did and still does have an old elevator with creaky iron gates. At the time I rode in it there was an old elevator operator with wrinkles in his face like an elephant's skin, very old eyes, and a very sweet smile. He looked as if he had conducted every dancer that ever rode in that elevator to audition on the sixth floor. "Break a leg," he said as I got out.

The whole sixth floor smelled of perspiration and feet and nerves. The faces were tight and eyes large. Sweat rolled over foreheads and down backs, and they hadn't even started to dance yet. Hundreds of dancers tugged at their leotards, pulled on their tights, and tried to arrange leg warmers, tee shirts, and sweat pants into the most flattering arrangements they could manage. They crowded the mirrors in the dressing rooms and the mirror on the wall before the studio. They slicked back hair, put on mascara and lipstick, and took one last look. Each hoped to see perfection but had to make the best of what there was.

I had been calm when I got off the elevator. I wasn't ready to work with the big company and didn't expect to get a job that day. I told myself I only came to see what went on and to make a good impression, but nerves and hope are infectious.

They gave everyone numbers, called the first fifty, and showed the combination—with counts and then with music. Then the first group danced alone. They moved with such determination, contracting, releasing, straining their muscles and trying to remember the steps. They poured as much emotion as they could into the choreography, and they got their legs up as high as they would go. They finished. The directors conversed, and half of the first group was asked to leave. A second group went on and followed the same pattern. I stood on the sidelines, stretching, watching, posing, evaluating, and readying myself to get on the floor. The music stopped, and half of the second group was asked to leave.

I danced in the third group. I tried to remember all the counts, to execute every step correctly, to feel my abdominals tight and my arms carried by the muscles in my back, to extend my legs more fully than I ever had before. All the while I kept one eye on the directors, trying to tell by their faces whether they had noticed me and whether they liked what they saw. The third group finished. Numbers were called, cutting out the ones dismissed. I didn't hear my number. They let me stay!

They showed the second combination. It was faster, more difficult. A boy with dreadlocks in the new first group had a big jump he couldn't quite control but that didn't stop him. Every movement he made had such guts, they let him stay. When it was my turn I tried to dance like that boy, and they let me stay, too.

I survived four cuts, and they asked me to come back for the second day of auditions. I started to think maybe, just maybe, I was ready.

I went home that night imagining how it would be to join the big company—to come into the theater and check the call board for the day's rehearsal schedule, to look for my name on the cast sheets. To perform in the hot lights where nobody could bother me, to kick and step with the sweat pouring off my body, to live from country to country, from stage to stage to stage, bowing to applauding hands I'd never have time to see again, floating offstage to my star dressing room, carried by the waves of applause and adoration. I went to bed, shut my eyes, and saw myself at the Kennedy Center, where my mother would come to see me. She'd be so proud of me. And so would Kelvin. I could tell him all about it. He'd listen to every word, the mistakes I'd almost made but hadn't, the performances that exceeded even my wildest expectations. He'd praise me for my courage and daring, admire my gutsiness, assure me that he always knew I could do it. Then he'd smile that royal smile of his and laugh.

When the auditions began the next day, there were thirty of us starting. God himself couldn't have told me I wasn't ready. One cut, two cuts, three. The boy with dreadlocks was eliminated. The fourth cut came, and we took a break for a few minutes. The director came back, and I was still there. Five cuts. The directors stopped, conversed, looked over at me, and dismissed two other dancers. Six cuts. Only ten dancers left. The directors smiled at me. We did the choreography again. The directors conversed and smiled at me again. Then they asked me to leave. In no other situation do the simple polite words "thank you" have such devastating significance.

I went home, barely containing my tears, to the Swiss Town House for Girls and politely said hello to the little Swiss ladies who ran the place. I must have looked more upset than I thought. They didn't ask how my day had been as they usually did. The little Swiss ladies with their gray curls and lace just said hello and let me go upstairs. I shut the door to my room and cried.

I had every intention of burning every leotard and every pair of tights I owned. I saw myself becoming a secretary at a loading dock of some ignominious trucking company, or worse, getting up at seven in the morning, taking the subway to a little gray desk in a dusty corner of a warehouse in Queens, pulling a calculator out of a drawer, and struggling with numbers until time to go home to my bare little furnished room. I couldn't add worth a damn, and this was the most noxious fate I could imagine at age nineteen.

I didn't answer the phone when it rang. The worst part of bad news is having to repeat it over and over to everyone you know. But one of the Swiss ladies slipped a message under my door. It was from Kelvin. "Come by school and talk."

This was the last thing I wanted. I was disappointed with myself, and I knew he must be disappointed with me, too. I walked over to school trying to imagine the disapproving look he would give me. It wasn't easy, since he'd never given me one before. I was walking up Fifty-ninth Street when an even worse thought occurred. Suppose he expressed sympathy for what I must be feeling or looked at me the way folks always look at dying people in movies. Oh, God! I couldn't stand to have anyone feel sorry for me. I saw that look on the face of every stranger I passed, but I went to see Kelvin anyway. I had too much respect for him not to.

I walked into his office, where he sat crunched behind his old wooden desk, working on some casting. His enormous hands drawfed the papers as he leafed through them. I sat down and waited. No matter what tragedy had occurred, I would never interrupt him. He didn't make me wait but a minute or two, but it was long enough to make me squirm. No good could possibly come of this conversation.

Finally he raised those intense eyes that seemed always to see more than I wanted them to and said, "So, how are you?"

"All right, I guess. Doesn't matter."

"No, it doesn't matter to the grand scheme, but it matters to you."

"Well, I didn't expect to get in anyway," I lied. "I don't dance that well."

That was his cue to contradict me. I waited, head down, gazing at a spot on the floor, massaging my calf muscles, hoping

he would reassure me that I was wrong. He didn't. I went on.
"And it probably would have been a bad thing if I'd got in. I'd
get lost in the airport. I wouldn't be able to find the theater, and
I wouldn't know anybody. And they don't have time to teach me
things. They'd yell at me, and I bet I'd be crying after every
performance." I ran out of words and finally had to look at him.
He said nothing as he leaned back in his chair.

"Well, I did worry about how you'd survive in that environment." He looked as if he knew some people who hadn't.

"How'd you know I didn't get in?"

"Somebody called me or maybe I called somebody." He
shrugged. I waited for more. "I don't remember."

"Well, it doesn't matter. I wasn't good enough anyway."

"It has nothing to do with being good enough. You aren't
ready."

"It's the same difference."

"No. It's not the same at all. Lots of people are good at lots
of things, but that doesn't make them ready. Most folks spend
all their time concentrating on whether they're good enough.
And when they think they are and they don't get what they
want, they're disappointed and mad. They run around trying to
get an opportunity someone else is ready for, and when their
opportunity comes, either they aren't prepared or they just don't
see it. Concentrate on getting yourself ready, and when your
time comes you'll know, and you'll get what you want."

I couldn't hold it any longer. "But, Kelvin, I wanted to get
in now," I wailed. "I really did. I wanted it so bad."

He leaned back in his chair and let me blubber on for a
minute. "When I was a boy back in Trinidad, all I could think
about was leaving. I wanted to travel more than anything in the
world. I used to pray every night." He clasped his hands together. " 'Please Lord, show me a way to leave Trinidad.' But
the Lord didn't answer me, at least I didn't think he did. So I

went to the priest, and I told him the Lord would not answer my prayers. That every night I asked him to show me a way to leave Trinidad, and he ignored me. I couldn't understand. I only wanted to travel so I could get a job and help my family. I only wanted to do good things.

"And the priest asks me, 'If you had a child who asked you for a sharp knife, would you give it to him?' I say, 'Of course not.' 'Why?' he asks. ' 'Cause he might cut himself.' 'But he only wants the knife to cut an orange for you.'

"I told him it didn't matter 'cause he might still hurt himself. So that priest says, 'Would you ever give him the knife?' And I say, 'Yes. When he's older and I'm sure he won't hurt himself.' 'Well then, when the Lord is sure you won't hurt yourself, he'll give you the knife. Now go home.'

"I didn't like that story, but the priest was right. If I had left then, when I was still so young, I would have gotten into trouble. But when I was ready, a way came for me to leave and everything was fine. Use your time well, so when your knife comes you're ready."

We sat quietly for a moment, while I absorbed the meaning of the story. I didn't like the message behind it any more than Kelvin did when he had first heard it as a boy, but I couldn't dispute his point. He came around the desk and gave me a pat on the shoulder before dismissing me. When I left to go to another class, I knew there was a hug in his eyes.

I have remembered that story many times, even though it didn't make me any happier than it had made Kelvin when he first heard it. It has helped me through some devastating disappointments. One of the worst was that I never did get into the big company. I can say in retrospect that it wasn't the right place for me. I was never any good at jazz. I joined a ballet company in 1980, however.

It was Dance Theatre of Harlem. I took class because the

big ballet companies don't often hold open auditions. The night before, I went through every leotard and pair of tights I owned trying to find something that would make me dance well. I finally decided on a simple black leotard and good old pink tights. As I stood before the bathroom mirror I knew Kelvin would tell me, "You can do it on your own now." But dancers are superstitious creatures, so when they asked me to take class a second day, I washed that leotard and those tights out and wore them again. When I took class that next day, the director came to watch. He wasn't going to correct me. I could either do it or I couldn't. When you audition for something you can't help but hope it will turn out well. That's the only reason you'd put yourself through such an ordeal. As I did the class, though, I managed not to think about the director and whether or not he seemed impressed, whether or not he smiled at me. I only thought about dancing well.

When class was over the director took me aside. He had me put on my pointe shoes and he pushed my legs up to see how high they would go, how flexible I was. I looked calm and serene in the mirror as he looked me over, but I was so nervous I was shaking on the inside. He had me do a double pirouette right and left, and I did it with a clean finish and it felt perfect. Then he took me to his office and asked my age. Twenty-one sounded so old that again I lied and said I was twenty. I had learned a great deal from Kelvin, but I was still myself. Losing a year or two must be standard practice in the business because they never seem to check on those things.

The first New York season I got flowers on stage. Kelvin was there at City Center. I saw him backstage after the performance, and when he smiled and said, "You look good," it was the greatest compliment I had ever had; even better than the first night of applause on that big stage. And when his daughter joined Dance Theatre of Harlem three years later, we both referred to him as "Daddy." She was always willing to share, and it's to her credit because I don't know if I would have been.

Ten years later I felt time growing short, so when the opportunity came I retired and went back to school. I ran into Kelvin on the street, and even though I wasn't in dance anymore he was still interested in how things were going. When I graduated from college, I sent him an invitation. He sent me a sweet note telling me how proud he was of me, but he would not be coming to the ceremony. He had moved on, just as I had, to a fresh crop of "babies" in the new third company. They had their first performance that day so he had to be there for them, just as he had been there for me.

So, last Saturday evening when I saw that little girl at the bus stop, I just couldn't bring myself to turn away. I watched her in her blue jeans, dancing around the sidewalk until the bus came. As it pulled off I silently wished her luck and hoped that she'd meet someone, someone like Kelvin, who would help her to know when she really was ready.

Contributors

Faith Adiele, the daughter of a Nigerian father and Scandinavian mother, grew up on a farm in the state of Washington and graduated from Harvard College in 1987. A former fellow at the McDowell Writer's Colony and the Ragdale Foundation, Ms. Adiele has had work published in *Ploughshares, Names We Call Home: Autobiography on Racial Identity, Life Notes: Personal Writings by Contemporary Black Women, Testimony: Young African-Americans on Self-Discovery and Black Identity, Miscegenation Blues,* and the forthcoming *Go Girl Guide: A Travel Guide for African American Women.* Ms. Adiele resides in Somerville, Massachusetts, and is currently the Christa McAuliffe Chair/ Visiting Professor of English at Framingham State College. She has also written for *Ms.* magazine and is working on a memoir about traveling to Africa.

Lillian G. Allen is a proud and healthy grandmother living in Pittsburgh, Pennsylvania, who has owned and operated her own beauty salon for more than sixty years. She still serves many of her older customers who are confined to nursing homes by visiting them once a week. When she is not traveling to Istanbul or Indonesia, she attends university night classes, working for her B.A. degree. This is her first published work.

DorisJean Austin was an Alabama-born, New York City–based novelist, who taught advanced fiction writing at Columbia University until her death in 1994. As a founding member of the New Renaissance Writers Guild, she taught many workshops for writers around the New York area and won the DeWitt Wallace/Reader's Digest Award for Literary Excellence in 1984. Many of her articles and reviews appeared in the *New York Times Book Review* and *Essence*. Her first novel, *After the Garden,* received the John O. Killens Award for Literary Excellence in 1988. She was also the co-editor of the anthology *Streetlights: Illuminating the Urban Black Experience.*

jonetta rose barras has written about politics, culture, and race for the past twenty years. She is associate editor of the *Washington City Paper* and writes a weekly column for the *Washington Times*. Her work has appeared in a variety of publications, including the *New Republic,* the *Times Picayune,* the *Washington Post,* and the *American Enterprise* magazine. She is also the author of two collections of poetry—*the corner is no place for hiding* and *Dawn*—and her work has been anthologized in *Sisterfire* and *In Search of Color Everywhere.* Her commentaries have been aired on National Public Radio, and she is a frequent political analyst for WHMM-TV, Howard University's public television station.

Rosemary Bray, writer and cultural critic, is a former editor of the *New York Times Book Review.* She is the author of children's biographies of Martin Luther King, Jr., and Nelson Mandela (Greenwillow Books); her political memoir, *Unafraid of the Dark,* will be published in the fall of 1997. Ms. Bray, the author of several widely published essays, is also a participant in the National Conversations Project of the National Endowment of the Humanities and appeared in the documentary "Talk to Me: Americans in Conversation" on PBS. She lives with her husband and children in northern New Jersey.

Donna Britt, a native of Gary, Indiana, joined the *Washington Post* in 1989 as a writer for the style section. After several powerful first-person pieces, including a Pulitzer-nominated essay on her older brother's death, she was granted a twice-weekly column in the paper's "Metro" section. Her column began in March 1992, and within a matter of weeks, Ms. Britt was getting sacks of mail, flowers, and hundreds of phone calls from readers who wanted to applaud her courage, conviction, and knack for addressing subjects no one else had touched. In 1994, she was honored as co-winner of the American Society of Newspaper Editors Distinguished Writing Award for commentary. After getting a master's degree in journalism from the University of Michigan in 1979, Donna Britt became a reporter and feature writer at the *Detroit Free Press.* Following a marriage, two sons and a divorce, she headed for Los Angeles, where she covered Hollywood and directed the Los Angeles bureau of *USA Today.* After three years with *USA Today,* she joined the *Post.* Ms. Britt lives in suburban Maryland with her husband, *Washington Post* national reporter Kevin Merida, and three sons.

Bebe Moore Campbell is the author of the bestselling novels *Your Blues Ain't Like Mine* and *Brothers and Sisters.* She has received a National Endowment of the Arts Literature Grant and a National Association of Negro Business and Professional Women's Literature Award and is frequently heard as a commentator on National Public Radio. She lives in Los Angeles with her husband and son.

Victoria Cliett is a Detroit native who writes creative and scholarly work. She is the Reading Programs Coordinator at Wayne State University and a doctoral student majoring in the field of rhetoric and composition. She hopes to finish her dissertation, "We Hold These Truths: Issues of (In)visibility in Rhetoric," as well as her short story collection next year. "A Macon Boy" is her first published work.

Evelyn Coleman recently sold her first mystery thriller series starring Patricia Conley, an African-American journalist, to Simon & Schuster. Coleman also writes children's books, which have received much recognition, including the Parent's Choice Honor Book for 1996 and the American Booksellers Association's Pick of the Lists for 1996. The Smithsonian named her book *White Socks Only* the Most Outstanding Children's Book Title for 1996. Coleman's adult fiction and non-fiction have appeared in magazines and newspapers. In 1989, she was the first African-American in the North Carolina Arts Council's ten-year history to win one of their $5,000 fiction fellowships.

Norma Jean Darden and her sister *Carole* are the authors of *Spoonbread and Strawberry Wine*, a best-selling cookbook, which records family recipes and several decades of stories passed down to them by the many relatives of the Darden family of North Carolina and New Jersey.

Elizabeth ("Bessie") and Sarah ("Sadie") Delany charmed the world with their best-selling book *Having Our Say: The Delany Sisters' First 100 Years*, which was developed into a Broadway play in 1995. Bessie Delany died at the age of 105 in 1996.

Marcia L. Dyson is editor-in-chief of *Voices* magazine, to be published nationally in the spring of 1997, and president of Speak Easy, Inc., a national lecture management agency.

Mali Michelle Fleming is a freelance journalist who has worked for *Essence, Newsday,* the *Baltimore Sun,* and *Hispanic* magazine. Her work has also been published in Linda Villarosa's *Body & Soul.* As a professional African dancer, she has taught and performed throughout the

East Coast and the U.S. Virgin Islands. She now resides in Brooklyn, New York.

Marita Golden is the author of three novels, *Migrations of the Heart, A Long Distance Life,* and *Do Remember Me.* She edited the essay collection *Wild Women Don't Wear No Blues* and was co-editor of *Skin Deep: Black Women and White Women Write About Race.* She teaches English at George Mason University in Virginia and lives in Maryland with her husband and son.

Carolyn Hart-Solomon is a free-lance writer/editor-for-hire and adjunct professor of women's literature at a southwestern junior college. Born in Florida and reared in New York, she is a graduate of the Warren Wilson M.F.A. program. She now lives with her husband and son in New Mexico.

Charlayne Hunter-Gault is known to millions of Americans as a national correspondent for PBS's "News Hour with Jim Lehrer." Her memoir, *In My Place,* was published in 1992. She lives with her family in New York.

Kai Jackson-Issa, Ph.D., is director of the first-year writing program and professor of writing and literature at Eugene Lang College at the New School for Social Research. Her essays, poetry, and fiction have been published in *Callaloo, Catalyst Magazine,* and *The Adoption Reader.* She lives in Brooklyn, New York, with her husband.

Jennifer Jordan was born in Fort Benning, Georgia, in 1946 and grew up in Phenix City, Alabama. She received a B.A. in English in 1967 and an M.A. in English in 1969 from Howard University and joined the English faculty there as an instructor of composition and African-American literature. In 1984 she received a Ph.D. in English and American literature from Emory University and is presently an associate professor of English at Howard. Ms. Jordan has published academic articles and essays on African-American literature in various journals and in *Race, Politics and Culture: Critical Essays on the Radicalism of the 1960s*, edited by Adolph Reed, Jr. Her creative essays and her one published short story have appeared in *Essence* and in John Henrik Clark's *A Century of the Best Black American Short Stories*.

Trinidad-born *Elizabeth Nunez* is director of the National Black Writer's Conference and chairperson of the Department of Humanities and Literature at Medgar Evers College of the City University of New York. Nunez is also the author of two novels, *When Rocks Dance* and *The Bruised Hibiscus*. She lives in Long Island with her son, Jason.

Gayle Pemberton was born in St. Paul, Minnesota. She holds a B.A. in English from the University of Michigan and a Ph.D. in English and American literature from Harvard University. She has taught at Smith College, Columbia University, Middlebury College, Reed College, and Princeton University. She is now the associate director of the African-American studies program at Wesleyan University in Middletown, Connecticut. Her essay collection, *The Hottest Water in Chicago*, was chosen for the New Jersey Humanities Book Award in 1993.

Connie Porter is author of the Addy books, a series of historical children's novels. Her first novel, *All-Bright Court*, was named as a *New York Times* Notable Book of 1991. Her essay "GirlGirlGirl" appeared in the collection *Between Friends: Writing Women Celebrate Friendship*, and a shortened version of it appeared in *Glamour*. Her book reviews have appeared in the *Boston Globe* and the *New York Times*. She was also named a regional winner in *Granta* magazine's 1996 contest for "Best American Writers Under Forty." Connie Porter is currently working on an adult novel for Houghton Mifflin, which will be published in 1998.

Contributors

Kiini Ibura Ya Salaam is a native of New Orleans and a graduate of Spelman College. As a founding member of the Red Clay Collective, she co-produces *Red Clay Magazine,* a quarterly publication of cultural criticism and artistic expression. Kiini is the author of a forthcoming collection of short stories entitled *Rebellious Energy.* She is presently working on both a book-length project and a science fiction novella, the first two parts of which have been published in the literary journal *Fertile Ground* and the erotic anthology *Dark Eros.*

Fatima Shaik is the author of a collection of novellas, *The Mayor of New Orleans: Just Talking Jazz.* Her work is included in the anthologies *African-American Fiction, Streetlights: Illuminating Tales of the Urban Black Experience,* and *Breaking Ice.* Her stories and essays have appeared in *Tribes, Callaloo, The Southern Review,* and *The Review of Contemporary Fiction.* She recently completed two children's books, *On Mardi Gras Day* and *The Jazz of Our Street.*

Brooke M. Stephens spent twenty years on Wall Street as an international banker, financial analyst, stockbroker, and investment advisor before leaving that milieu and becoming a free-lance writer and editor. She has written articles on personal money management for *Black Enterprise, Essence,* and *Ms.* and has written book reviews for the *Quarterly Black Review of Books.* She is also the author of a personal finance book, *Talking Dollars and Making Sense: A Wealth-Building Guide for African-Americans.*

Gloria Wade-Gayles is a professor of English and women's studies at Spelman College in Atlanta, Georgia. She is also the author of *No Crystal Stair: Race and Sex in Selected Black Women's Novels, 1946–1976* and the collection of poems *Anointed to Fly.*

Patrice Wagner is a teacher, writer, and activist. Her short stories have been published in *Streetlights: Illuminating the Urban Black Experience.* She was born and raised on the South Side of Chicago and holds degrees from the University of Pennsylvania and Columbia University. She lives in Harlem with her son.

Pam Ward was born and raised in Los Angeles, California. Her work has been published in numerous journals, including *Grand Passion: An Anthology of Los Angeles Writers, High Performance Magazine, The Drumming Between Us,* and *This: A Literary Journal.* She received the New Letters Literary Award from the University of Missouri and currently teaches creative writing in Manhattan Beach, where she is editing the anthology *Picasso's Mistress.* She has just completed a poetry manuscript, *Jacked Up.*

Orian Hyde Weeks is a fiction and nonfiction writer. She lives in Vienna, Austria.

Donna (Bailey) Wise is from Philadelphia, Pennsylvania, and was a foreign language major at Georgetown University in Washington, D.C., before transferring to Temple University. Donna completed the master's program in film and broadcast at Georgia State University in Atlanta, where she still resides. After twelve years at IBM Corporation, Donna began a new career which she enjoys, as an area manager for Showtime Networks. In her spare time she runs a bed-and-breakfast with her husband.

Leslie Woodard retired from the Dance Theatre of Harlem after ten years of performance and returned to school at Columbia University's School of General Studies. She graduated Phi Beta Kappa in May 1994 with a B.A. in literature/writing. She attended New York University's graduate program in creative writing and received her M.A. in May 1996. Her work has appeared in *Quarto,* the literary magazine of Columbia's undergraduate writing program, and in the Penguin anthology *Streetlights: Illuminating Tales of the Urban Black Experience.*

Permissions